Antique Kilims
of Anatolia

Antique Kilims
of Anatolia

Peter Davies

W.W. Norton & Company
New York • London

THIS BOOK IS DEDICATED TO THE THOUSANDS
AND THOUSANDS OF ANONYMOUS ANATOLIAN
WOMEN WHO HAVE LABORED AT THEIR LOOMS
OVER THE CENTURIES TO CREATE THE VISUAL
EXPRESSION OF THEIR PEOPLE.

The text of this book is composed in Perpetua, with the
display set in Perpetua and Dorchester Script
Manufacturing by Chroma Graphics
Book design by Steven Schoenfelder
Second edition production by Ken Gross

Library of Congress Cataloging-in-Publication Data

Davies, Peter, 1937 Dec. 5–
 Antique kilims of Anatolia / Peter Davies
  p.   cm.
 Updated ed. of: The tribal eye.
 Includes bibliographical references and index.
 ISBN 0-393-73047-6
 1. Kilims—Turkey. 2. Rugs, Nomadic—Turkey.
 I. Davies, Peter, 1937 Dec. 5– Tribal eye. II. Title.

NK2865.A1D38   2000
746.7'2'09561— dc21   00-041243

W. W. Norton & Company, Inc., 500 Fifth Avenue, New York, N.Y. 10110
www.wwnorton.com

W. W. Norton & Company Ltd., 10 Coptic Street, London WC1A 1PU

0 9 8 7 6 5 4 3 2 1

Contents

Forewords

I first became acquainted with Peter Davies's book on the Anatolian kilim in its 1993 incarnation, *The Tribal Eye: Antique Kilims of Anatolia*. I was fascinated by his grasp of the subject and the engaging way in which he communicated his information. Additionally, I was impressed with the ethnographic photographs of Josephine Powell, an outstanding photographer of Anatolian tribal life, as well as with the fine color plate section of superlative examples of Anatolian kilims. I was pleased to hear that he has expanded and updated its text and added additional color plates for this new hardcover edition, *Antique Kilims of Anatolia*.

This republication calls to my mind the observations I made in my review of the original in 1996 for the "Literature Report" of Pazyryk Gesellschaft, the well-known German rug society:

> There is certainly no shortage of books appearing lately on Anatolian kilims. Nevertheless, I have no reservations in recommending to readers this new book on the subject. Published in New York City in 1993, this book will have no difficulty establishing a place for itself: not only because of its plate section of 50 never-before-published kilims from American collections, elegantly presented on black backgrounds; but also for its well-written text, which despite its brevity, is amongst the best ever to be written on the subject.

There are very few books on weaving, whether carpets, kilims, or textiles, that are published in a second edition. As far as I know, Davies's book is only one of two such kilim books, the best evidence, I think, that *The Tribal Eye*, now metamorphosed into *Antique Kilims of Anatolia*, is a classic in the field of textile literature. It is a book not only for the rug enthusiast and connoisseur but also for the ethnologist. It will also serve as a rich source for designers, architects, and decorators. Indeed, it is a book for anyone with a desire to understand the kilim's ancient language of form and color. As Davies convincingly demonstrates, the Anatolian kilim is no mere decorative item but an archaic art, a nomadic and peasant mode of cultural expression in form and color.

The two new chapters in *Antique Kilims of Anatolia* deepen his investigation into the sources of Anatolian design and its evolution and reveal the ethno-aesthetics that underlie it. The special value of this second edition rests in his groundbreaking discussion of these fascinating issues. Enhancing and supporting his expanded theoretical discussion are the additional kilims depicted in the color plate section, which expand the visual record by including kilims and fragments that were produced before the nineteenth century.

Davies not only breaks new ground in his cogent discussions of the kilim but he also reveals his love for Anatolia, its people, and its exceptional kilims. This gives *Antique Kilims of Anatolia* its special character.

Dr. Michael Buddeberg

With the first edition of *The Tribal Eye: Antique Kilims of Anatolia* in 1993, Peter Davies produced a direct and to-the-point volume that skillfully downplayed the controversies of that time. One need only recall that this was a period of contention in which a variety of extravagant claims were made for flatweavings. Coming after a long period of neglect prior to the 1967 Textile Museum exhibit and catalogue, *From the Bosphorus to Samarkand*, it might seem only natural that the emergence of the kilim should be accompanied by a vigorous acclamation that, at times, overstated the case.

Among these assertions were the writings of an enthusiastic archaeologist who claimed for the modern Turkish kilim a direct descent from the Neolithic, based on drawings of paintings allegedly left on the walls of a major excavation in Central Turkey. Others began to make optimistic claims about the age of surviving kilims in a process that seemed to skip entirely past the nineteenth century, as if every piece that was clearly the product of natural dyes must at least have an eighteenth-century date. By the mid-1990s flatweavings had aggressively claimed their rightful position of parity with the pileweaving tradition, although this had been accompanied by a flurry of hype and exaggerated claims.

Into these swirling controversies the Peter Davies book appeared, and it was a great relief to this reader that it managed to avoid the partisanship and fervor of many assertions then being made about these weavings. The author seemed unflustered by all the commotion and methodically sorted through the available evidence, informing the reader how these fascinating fabrics were brought into being. He traced, in clear steps, the progression of wool from its shearing to its spinning, dyeing, and final appearance on the loom. He explored the visual language of the Anatolian kilim and what it may have meant to the weavers.

In dealing with then-current controversies about the kilim in Neolithic settlements, he simply presented the claims of several conflicting sides of the argument, pointed out their strong and weak points, and left the reader a choice of whether to believe or not to believe. It is difficult to emphasize sufficiently how valuable and level-headed this position seemed to be at the time. Here was someone simply presenting the facts as a reasonable and intelligent observer and avoiding any real partisanship. That attitude is ultimately what fueled my enthusiasm for the book. I felt then that it had a calming influence on a field that may have been overheated at the time of its publication.

This new edition builds upon the tradition of the first with very valuable additions to his earlier investigation. The last several years have seen substantial work with radiocarbon in the dating of kilims and the issues raised by this technique are now discussed. Even more important, however, is a deeper analysis of kilim design and the contributions both the local Anatolian slit-tapestry tradition and the Central Asia tradition of felt-making may have had on what eventually emerged as what we know as the Anatolian kilim.

The focus of this exploration is the Yüncü kilim, which presents a paradigm of how divergent traditions may be merged in a manner creating a fresh and vigorous new synthesis. Davies hypothesizes a fusion of the slit-tapestry tradition with the feltmaking tradition.

He plausibly assumes that feltmaking was the earlier focus of the Yüncü Yörük, who were migrants from parts of Central Asia in which felt had a far more important function than kilims. This speculation begins with his recognition that the Yüncü kilim is a "strange animal" among Anatolian kilims, and he presents a fascinating case as to why and how this difference may have arisen.

While discussions of aesthetics often offer treacherous footing for the writer, Davies also ventures into an exploration of the Ottoman Turkish concept of art and introduces terms used by the Turks to describe the creative process and its various manifestations. Thus, this edition makes a valiant effort to tell the whole story as to what kilims mean to those who live with them. *Antique Kilims of Anatolia* emerges as more than a basic introduction to the Turkish kilim and as the most convincing and profound account of what there is about these tribal weavings that has seized the imaginations of so many enthusiasts.

Murray Eiland, Jr.

Introduction

It would be no exaggeration to describe the old pastoral way of life of Anatolia as a civilization built on wool and hair. Even today herds of fat-tailed sheep and shaggy angora goats are an ever-present sight grazing on the great Anatolian plateau and on the slopes of the mountains that punctuate and surround it. Sheep appear like scattered white boulders on the immense flatness of the Konya plain; sheep and goats flow like dirty white and black rivers through the narrow gorges of the Taurus mountains; and they pick their way up the ancient worn tracks that crisscross the steep, barren hillsides on the Aegean Coast. At dusk they clog the roads, their eyes glittering like thousands of mad marbles in the glare of headlights.

Sheep milking time, Sivas Province, 1977.

The herds of sheep and goats are more of a presence in the great expanses of Anatolia than the people themselves, and they seem strangely at home in the wild countryside in a way that our ranch-raised herds never would. And well they might since they are in or near the place of their ancient origins and have been grazing the hillsides and fields of Anatolia since prehistoric times. If even now they ap-

pear somewhat wild, it is not surprising. They have never known fences or enclosures, running free as they always have in the territories of their ancestor, the *Ovis orientalis.*

While mankind transformed this wild goat-like ancestor into creatures more suitable to human needs, the domesticated herds in turn transformed man. The herds' need for year-round grazing turned man into a migrator. *Ovis orientalis* became Anatolia's domesticated sheep and segments of humanity became nomads. The needs of the

Sarıkeçeli nomads migrating to winter pasture (kışlak), **Antakya Province,** *1980.*

herds helped to form cultures with a different relationship to territory. These pastoralists evolved into tribes with their own highly organized modes of life and their strange tent architecture of woven and pressed animal fibers. The herds were the source of other life-sustaining fabrics as well: insulating felt floor coverings, felt robes and boots, woolen shawls, sweaters, and socks. And the herds provided the materials for other basic needs of daily life: storage bags, saddle bags, harnesses, pillows, rugs, and kilims. At some point in the weaving of these practical items, wool and hair also became the chief media for cultural and artistic expression as color, motifs, and design transformed weavings into a visual celebration of tribal identity and ideology.

The Anatolian fat-tailed sheep, heavy with a season's growth of wool, seems a most unlikely beginning for the Anatolian kilim with its lustrous wools, brilliantly dyed and woven into bold, geometric designs. How mankind ever learned to bring about such a transformation is almost beyond imagining. To effect such a metamorphosis required a vast amount of time, thousands of years of experiments, innovations, and discoveries. There was a gradual accretion of wool-processing lore, the invention of the technologies of the spindle, the loom, and the dye baths, and the discovery of intricate weaving techniques. Also emerging simultaneously was the "tribal eye," that is, a distinctive sense of color, geometric forms, and symmetrical designs that would make Anatolian weavings unlike any others. A tradition of great artistry evolved, which was committed to memory and sanctified by tradition.

The hand that worked the loom was the same that milked the sheep and goats, tended the new lambs when the ewes were at pasture, washed and sorted the clipped wool, combed and carded it, spun and dyed it. The hand that set up the loom and deftly wove the colored yarns into the remembered designs of the tribe was the same that processed the milk into yoghurt, butter, and cheese, prepared the grains, baked the breads, cooked the meals, tended the children, and set up, dismantled, and kept the tent in order. The intricate handiwork at the loom was only one of many domestic responsibilities, and a domestic task it was since not till recent times did tribal weavings enter the world of the marketplace.

The life of the Anatolian weaver has always had a harsh beauty to it. Given the rigors of this way of life, it is no wonder that the tribal woman has aged prematurely. Seen from one point of view it was a life of unceasing labor, as the considerable demands of wool processing and weaving were fitted into an endless daily routine that left no time for leisure. From another point of view, the tribal weaver's participation in every laborious stage of wool processing and weaving gave her a deep understanding of and almost complete control over the nature and quality of her medium. It is the kind of ideal relationship between artist and materials that is barely conceivable to artist-weavers of the West.

Certainly, the greatness of the antique kilims was not only the product of the superlative weaving and design skills of the weavers of the past but also resulted from the exquisite qualities of wool and luminous dyes they were able to work with because of their intimate involvement in the various stages of processing. This intimate relationship between the weaver and her medium was formed in the

Laying in the weft, Çanakkale Province, 1978.

earliest years of her childhood and was sustained and nurtured by the conditions of traditional life. In the past century, the industrial processes of the modern world have gradually usurped many of the traditional functions of the weaver. Today "hand made" when applied to most Anatolian weaving means that only the work at the loom has been done by hand, while all the steps leading up to it have usually been carried out in the factory. While today much of the onerous burden of processing the materials has been lifted from the shoulders of the Anatolian weaver, an important link has been broken which, despite efforts to revive old practices, will never be fully established again.

To members of a highly regimented, industrialized world, the image of a familial band of independent people roaming free with no fixed territories, living a self-sufficient life of tradition and ritual closely tied to the rhythms of the natural world, has a powerful appeal and is easy to idealize. While it is true that the role of the Anatolian tribal weaver descends from a nomadic way of life, nomadism in Anatolia has never existed in the pure form of our imaginings. Actually, it has always been in constant evolution, working out accommodation after accommodation with various forms of settled life. Even from the beginning when almost a millennium ago hundreds of thousands of Türkmen nomads, driving millions of sheep and goats, streamed onto the Anatolian plateau, they found themselves in conditions that tempted them into settled

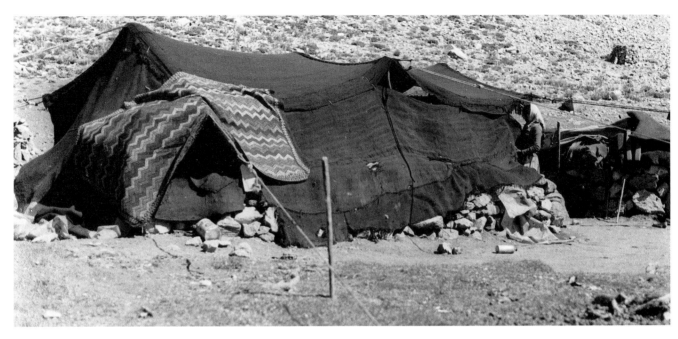

A black hair tent of the Karakoyun Yörük, summer pasture (yayla). A weaving covers the corner to shield newly made cheese, Niğde Province, 1978.

life or that significantly altered the modes of nomadic life they brought with them from the steppes of Central Asia.

Unlike the neighboring Persian territories, which have proved more conducive to traditional nomadic life, Anatolia had much rich, available land. Those nomads who resisted settled life found themselves on a great bridge-like plateau with mountain chains to the north and south. These geographical conditions enabled them to keep their herds in good pasturage year round through short migra-

tions, summering in the highlands and wintering in the lowlands. Nomadism as a result metamorphosed into transhumance, as pastoralists moved seasonally between two fixed locations. Even this mode of life has over the centuries been constantly under attack as periodic commands from the central government to "stay where you are," enforced relocations, bribes of free lands, or other inducements have reduced the role of nomadism.

As a result, nomadism and settled life in Anatolia are

A village house, Konya Province, 1976.

not mutually exclusive ways of life. There is a long continuum with transhumance at one end and fully settled life at the other, and every possible compromise in between. Nomads may tent in the summer *yayla,* the mountain pastures, and winter in adobe brick huts in *kışlak,* the winter lowlands. A seemingly settled village may divide in summer into those who go to the yayla with the animals and those who remain to carry on agriculture. Nomads may mix agriculture with their pastoral activities, settled villages may have large herds that require shepherds to take them to pasture. Tribesmen may be engaged in lumbering as a traditional way of life, while agriculturalists may also be orchardists and pastoralists. A nomadic group might choose settled life for a time, then return to nomadism. Or only a part of that group might return to the old ways. Nomads have been known to continue their migrations by hiring box cars from the state railways as transport.

While historically Anatolian weavers have lived and woven in many different forms of pastoral tribal life, there are certain conditions that appear to be necessary to a vital weaving tradition. Although settled agricultural groups have also always woven and continue to weave, nomadic groups and settled groups that continue to maintain large herds (and are hence also pastoral) have been the most active weavers. Inundated each spring with hundreds of pounds of wool, a pastoral family that does not have the competitive demands of full-time agricultural work can find the time and energy to maintain weaving as an important activity. The transition to settled life, if it means the elimination or reduction of the herds, usually leads to the decline of weaving or its relegation to a specialist group within the village.

Not only is the connection between pastoralism and tribal weaving vital, but the maintenance of a vital tribal identity is also of primary importance. Except for a few bands, tribal life in Anatolia has long since ceased to be a highly organized culture with its own internal government under an hereditary or appointed leader. The great tribal confederations of the past vanished long ago from Anatolia. Nevertheless, despite this diminution in its power, tribal identity has remained a force down to present times. In Anatolia "tribe" refers to a group, whether nomadic or settled or a combination, whose members continue to identify themselves consciously as such and who share certain cultural values, social customs, and traditions. The vitality of the tribal weaving tradition appears to be intimately connected to the potency of tribal identity. As these identities have slowly begun to metamorphose, tribal weaving, an important expression of that culture, has either fallen into abeyance or found commercial outlets in the cottage weaving industries.

It was the way of life of the tribal pastoralists of the last century and before that created the ideal conditions for the great weavings. While the disappearance of the old ways has not been without certain benefits to today's Anatolians, this transition has resulted in the loss of one of Anatolia's greatest glories, its ancient tribal weaving tradition.

The present state of this transition was captured for me several years ago while hiking on a rugged peninsula which juts out from Kaş, a tiny resort on the Aegean coast. As I returned from the tip of the peninsula, which teemed with sheep and goats belonging to the Yörük nomads who wintered there, I saw at some distance an aged Yörük woman in traditional dress standing by the roadside working with a drop spindle. Contrary to my expectations, she did not shyly vanish from the road as I approached but waited, bold as a magpie, obviously expecting an encounter. We greeted each other and she continued to spin gray goat hair yarn. I asked her when she and her clan would be moving to the yayla. She brightened considerably in anticipation, hesitated in her spinning, and replied that it would be in a few weeks. When I asked how long it would take her to get there, she replied matter-of-factly, and to my great surprise, "Two or three hours if I ride in the truck. Three or four days if I travel overland with the men and the animals." There she stood, an old Yörük woman holding a utensil unchanged since the Bronze Age, spinning goat hair, and anticipating the migration to the yayla. The chic resort village of Kaş was spread out behind her, she was conversing with an unknown male foreigner, and she undoubtedly would make the migration in a dump truck. Certainly her grandchildren will be at work someday, if they are not already, in the hotels and restaurants of Kaş.

However, it is not the present but the life her grandmother and the generations before her lived that produced the great kilim weaving tradition for which Anatolia will always be remembered. It is this ancient way of life and the kilim weaving tradition it produced that is the subject of the following chapters.

Chapter 1

From Fleece
to Yarn

In the ancient rhythm of Anatolian pastoral life one of the major beats is spring sheep-shearing time, when the shearers, usually the men of the household, clip and turn back the matted wool and then, seeming to roll the sheep out of its coat, produce the fleece, a pelt-like mass of intermeshed raw wool. Up to this time the tasks of sheep-caring are shared by both the men's and women's sides of the household, but once separated from the sheep the fleece becomes the responsibility of the women's side, which assumes the arduous domestic tasks of processing it. The fleece the women receive is a dirty, tangled mass of animal fibers, laced with burrs and twigs, which must be washed and sorted. Washing is customarily carried out in the cold, slow-moving waters of favored streams, and the vigorous use of a wooden beater is part of the process.

Sorting wool is a complicated skill which even in industrialized society is still most effectively carried out manually, since no machine yet has bested the human eye and hand in this process. Wool qualities differ greatly from breed to breed (there are at least twenty-two breeds of sheep in Anatolia), as well as from animal to animal within the same herd. The best and most copious wools come from the wethers, the castrated males, the second best from ewes, and the least valuable from intact males.[1] The first clipping of the season produces better wools than the late summer shearing. Even within the same fleece there are great variations in quality. The neck, shoulders, and back produce the finest wools, while the short, dirty wools of the tail, belly, and legs are inferior and likely to be set aside for feltmaking. Contrary to popular belief, the sheep's diet (other than extreme cases like near-starvation) and the altitudes at which they graze do not significantly influence wool qualities.[2]

The women pull the fleece apart by hand and sort it into appropriate groups depending on whether they plan to use it for knitting, for carpet or kilim weaving, or feltmaking. Further distinctions are made when they separate the wools to be used for warps, wefts, or the knotting for pile

A settled Hayta nomad woman washing wool near Kayseri, 1978.

rugs. If not sorted, the wools from the same fleece produce poor quality yarns unlikely to take dyes in a satisfactory way.[3] The involvement of the weavers at this early stage is a major factor in explaining the extraordinary qualities of the wools in antique kilims and carpets. A weaver setting aside wools for her dowry or funerary weavings would have very different criteria from those of a sorter in a spinning factory, where good, bad, and indifferent wools are homogenized to produce an adequate, but usually not exceptional, product that can achieve a certain profit.

13

A Yörük woman combing wool, Çanakkale Province, 1985.

fiber diameter of three thousandths of a millimeter.[5] We can only guess at the numerous distinctions the Anatolian weavers of the past were able to perceive when sorting their materials.

Once the raw wool has been sorted and washed, the women of the household begin the laborious process of organizing the wool fibers in preparation for spinning. There are two ways of carrying this out, each producing a kind of yarn suited for very different purposes. While the term "carding" is often used to describe both processes, there is actually a distinction between "carding" and "combing." Wools intended for kilim weaving are combed before spinning, while wools intended for knitting are carded.

In the combing process wool fibers are disentangled and organized into a roughly parallel arrangement. Using the wool comb, a device consisting of rows of evenly-spaced spikes set into a wooden block or triangle, the women pull the wool through the closely-set spikes, straightening and aligning the fibers in the process. Repetitions of this process produce the roving—a long, loose coil of porous wool. During spinning the roving is either kept under the arm, up the sleeves, or wound tightly around the wrist of the spinner. Or she may attach it to a knobbed or forked stick called the distaff, another implement descending from prehistoric times. The merits of the roving, its qualities and color, can be the subject of much discussion among the weavers. Very fine rovings, for instance, are often carefully set aside for special weaving occasions. When spun the roving becomes a hard, smooth, lustrous yarn ideally suited to the weaving of kilims and carpets.

Carding also arranges wool fibers for a particular purpose, but in this process the fibers are randomized rather than aligned. In carding the wool is worked into loose, fluffy balls as it is pulled back and forth between a pair of paddle-like wooden implements, the inner sides of which are set with rows of short spikes. Since the carded fibers lie in different directions, when spun they become a soft, fuzzy yarn called woolen that lacks the sheen of combed yarns. Compared to carded yarns, combed yarns have greater strength (for the same diameter of wool), but the fuzziness of carded yarns increases their insulating effect.[6] Woolen is thus an excellent yarn for clothing, such as sweaters and socks, and blankets.

The differences between combed and carded yarns are, however, aesthetic as well as practical. The combed wools of the kilim fabric give it a flat texture, designs that are clear and precise, and colors that are luminous and bright. The carded wools of a sweater, by contrast, give it a fuzzy texture, designs that are blurred, and colors that tend to be soft and muted. The same design if worked out first in combed yarns and then in woolen would have a very differ-

Undoubtedly, each tribal weaver developed her own criteria for the sorting process depending on her needs, and much of the decision-making was probably intuitive. However, the standard codification used in spinning factories suggests some of the considerations at work. These include:

1. The appearance and condition of the fleece and the softness or harshness of the wool when handled.
2. The length of the staple (the unstretched measurement of a fiber from tip to base).
3. The degree of luster (gloss or sheen).
4. The degree of springiness—the extent to which the wool will expand after being compressed.
5. Color—the nearness to black or white.
6. Strength of the fiber.
7. The degree of fineness—usually measured on a numerical scale.[4]

The expertise involved is demonstrated by the ability of an experienced wool sorter to distinguish differences in ent textural and visual effect.

The roving is too soft, thick, and easily broken to be directly woven into cloth, rugs, or kilims. The ancient technology of spinning is required before it can serve such purposes. Spinning, among mankind's oldest inventions, began in Paleolithic times, some fifteen thousand or possibly even twenty thousand years ago, when humans discovered that breakable, and even short fibers could be formed into supple, strong, long threads by being twisted together.[7] The wonder that this very ancient process once aroused, seeming as it does to create something from nothing, is suggested by one of mankind's most enduring myths, the Three Fates: Klōthō, the spinner, eternally sits spinning the thread of human destiny while her sisters, Lachesis (Allotment) and Atropos (the Unturnable or Inflexible), decide on its length and termination.[8] Such magical associations surrounded the processes of spinning and weaving in the distant past and have continued to do so in tribal cultures almost to present times.

Since its inception spinning has been an ever-present domestic activity, the responsibility of women throughout most of the weaving world up until the nineteenth century. Indeed, at the same time that Anatolian women were spinning the yarns for some of the older kilims featured in this book, women in Western households were similarly preparing yarns for their textiles. While the rise of industrialization in the last century ended spinning as a domestic

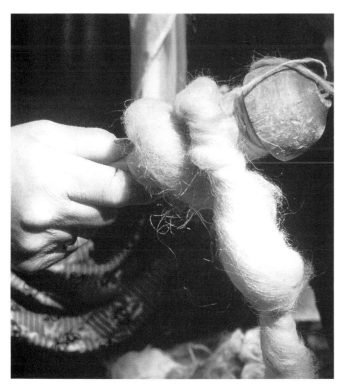

A roving on the shaft of a spindle, Malatya Province, 1978.

function in the West, Anatolian pastoral households continued to handspin most of their wools almost to the present day, using a technology little changed since the Bronze Age.

While spinning can be executed by pulling and twisting wool fibers with one's fingers—undoubtedly the way in which the process originated—this method is tediously slow and beset with problems. With this purely manual method it is difficult to prevent the finished thread from tangling and, more seriously, from untwisting, since the thread needs to remain under constant tension until the twist is permanently set. To speed up the process and avoid these problems a mechanism was needed that would produce a faster twirl and provide a convenient package to keep the spun threads tightly wound. The two earliest solutions, still practiced in some parts of the world, were to attach the beginning of the thread to a rock or a stick and to set them spinning. The next technological innovation was a combination of the two, the stick forming the shaft, and the rock the flywheel of a very ancient machine—the hand-held or drop spindle.[9] It was such a device, not the spinning wheel, that Klōthō used to spin out human destiny. And it is such a mechanism that Anatolian spinners have used since prehistoric times. Though the drop spindle has been formed of many different materials and its appearance has altered somewhat with changing fashions, it has remained unchanged in its essentials throughout Anatolian history.

The handspinning process results from the combination of three actions, one a natural one and the other two the result of the spinner's dexterity. Wool is naturally suited to spinning since a minute overlay of scales covers its fibers. The interlocking of the scales of one fiber with those of another contributes to the fusing process that makes possible the continuous thread. The spinner exploits this natural propensity for fusing by drawing out and twisting the wool fibers with the spindle. The weight of the spindle draws out the strands as they come from the roving, while the turning motion twists them into a tight, continuous thread. Actually, the root of the verb "to spin" originally had more to do with the notion of drawing out or stretching, as in "to spin a tale," than it did with rotation.[10] Once the spindle spirals to the ground, the spinner deftly scoops it up and winds the yarn onto the spindle shaft, thus turning the spindle into the storage receptacle. She then starts the process again.

Drawing from a set of whorls of different weights and diameters, the spinner can adapt the drop spindle to produce many different kinds of yarns. For instance, when spinning a long staple wool, it helps to have a heavy spindle, and for plying (that is, twisting several yarns to-

15

gether), an even heavier one, whereas a light spindle suits short fibers, and the lighter the spindle the finer the thread. A whorl with a wide diameter gives a long, slow spin, while the same weight whorl with a smaller diameter gives a faster spin. Small diameter whorls are best for tightly spun threads with more twist per unit, while wider whorls produce threads with fewer twists.[11] Using this compendium of knowledge and technique, the drop spinner has an incredible amount of flexibility in producing yarns suitable for particular purposes, whether it be kilim or carpet production, knitting socks or sweaters, or weaving a tent. In kilim weaving, for instance, yarns for wefts must be thin and loosely spun for flexibility while warps should be thicker and more tightly spun for strength. Now that spinning is largely done in factories, by standardized industrial processes, the weaver in Anatolia has lost much of the control she once had to shape her own materials.

While the spinner has many choices as to which whorl to place on the shaft, the location of the whorl along the shaft, whether it be high, middle, or low, seems to have been culturally determined in prehistoric times. Anatolia along with Europe is a low whorl spinning region, while Egypt and the Middle East are high whorl. The location of the whorl seems to have been determined by the kinds of fibers historically spun in a given region, the flax spinning region of Egypt employing the high, the flax and wool spinning regions of Europe and the Near East the low.[12]

The location of the whorl on the spindle apparently determines whether the threads are spun in a clockwise or counterclockwise direction. High whorl spinners typically begin the process by rolling the spindle down the thigh before letting it descend to the ground, the spindle turning counterclockwise to create what has become known as S-spun yarn (c). In low whorl regions like Anatolia the spinner typically begins by dangling the spindle before her and giving it a twist with finger and thumb as one would start a top, setting it spinning in a clockwise direction that produces a Z-spin (d). For purposes

A wool fiber magnified two thousand times.

of study, spins have been designated as S and Z twists depending on whether the trend in the spiral or twisted element conforms when held in a vertical position to the slant of the central portions of the letters S or Z. Probably the different twists reflect the typical manner a right-handed person (and ninety percent of all populations are right handed) would have handled the thigh rolling and finger-twirled movements.[13]

While in spinning wool there seem to be no advantages to one twist over the other, the different twists do have a value to scholarship since a structural analysis of the yarns of woven pieces can help to determine questions of provenance. The wools used in Anatolian kilims are generally Z-spun. If, for instance, a kilim appears to be Anatolian but its wools are discovered to be S-spun, one would have to conclude that either it was not woven in Anatolia despite its appearance or that it had been woven by a group that had migrated into Anatolia from an S-spinning region to the east. There is also the remote possibility of a recalcitrant left-handed spinner!

Once the yarn has been spun it is suitable for some, but not all, weaving purposes. At this stage it is still a single ply yarn and would be suitable for most kilim wefts. (However many kilim wefts are two- or three-ply yarns.) Kilim warps

c.   d.

typically consist of two strands of yarn twisted together, that is, two-ply yarns. Usually on the same drop spindle and using a special winding apparatus, the paired yarns are twisted in the opposite direction from which they were originally spun. Thus the Anatolian plying would be an S-twist. The technical identification for a typical Anatolian warp would be Z2s, that is two Z-spun yarns plied in an S-spin.

Why Anatolia continued to use the drop spindle while

a.   b.

Europe very quickly shifted to the spinning wheel—one of the greatest innovations in spinning technology since the Bronze Age—after it was introduced from China in the fourteenth century is largely explained by the advantages of the drop spindle to the tribal way of life. The flexibility of the drop spindle gives it decided advantages, particularly in the greater control over the kinds of yarns produced, something the spinning wheel, which while faster, cannot equal.[14] However, it was probably the very portable nature of the drop spindle, which meant that it could be carried about and used virtually anywhere, that explains why it remained the predominant method in Anatolia. Even more portable than knitting, spinning can be carried on while the spinner is engaged in a multitude of other activities, including shepherding animals, minding children, tending the oven, walking, riding on donkeys or camels, and sitting with friends in the sun. Given the huge volume of wool a pastoral household had to process and the demanding circumstances of the weavers' lives, spinning could not be limited to a fixed period of time in a set place, but was of necessity often performed on the move or simultaneously with other activities or in the spare moments in between. The superiority of the drop spindle in certain circumstances is evidenced by its continuous use in Europe and Latin America well into the present century by women shepherding flocks. The other obvious advantage of the drop spindle over the spinning wheel for a people who are either nomadic or were very recently so is the need for simple, portable household effects. The ideal fit of this ancient mechanism to their traditional way of life, rather than a refusal of the weavers to adjust to new ways, explains the survival of the drop spindle in Anatolian tribal life.

While handspinning had until recently almost disappeared in Anatolia, the revival of interest in the old methods of weaving, fostered by a renascent cottage weaving industry, has created a new demand for handspun wools. While mechanized spinning has brought speed and uniformity in production, other important qualities that only handspun yarns can create have been lost. The interesting irregularities of handspun yarns, it is more and more realized, produce a rich and varied texture as well as beautiful subtleties in the dyeing process. It is not only that the great kilims of the past were handwoven that gives them their beauty and character, but that the wonderful yarns used were hand-sorted, combed, and spun.

While it is certainly possible to perceive the beauty of Anatolian kilims without an awareness of the many laborious processes by which they were created, this awareness immeasurably increases our appreciation of them. The way in which we value and enjoy an object of beauty is certainly affected by factors other than the intrinsic merits of the object itself. In fact, our appreciation of a beautiful artefact cannot be separated from our estimate of its material worth, its rarity and preciousness, and its cost in labor, skill, and sacrifice.[15] It is not only the time at the loom which is a factor in this appreciation but all of the knowledge, expertise, and toil involved in the processing of the weaving materials. In a sense, the mechanization of these processes not only changes the character of the object but is also a factor in changing the way we value it. Further, an awareness of the way of life of the Anatolian women who created these artifacts, together with a sense of their labors, gives us something akin to a personal connection with the anonymous, almost alien, creators and thus deepens our experience of the kilims.

Drop-spinning with spindles made of wooden crosspieces, Uşak Province, 1978.

Chapter 2

Dyeing:
The Lost Process

The ancient yarn processing methods and implements described thus far continue to be used down to the present by scattered nomadic and settled weaving groups throughout the more remote parts of Anatolia. In contrast, when we turn to the next stage of the process, the dyeing of yarns, the story is quite different. Indeed, in little more than a century the ancient Anatolian tradition of natural dyeing seems to have almost completely vanished.

The recent renewal of interest in traditional dyeing sponsored by government and commercial agencies has led to over eight years of intensive and still ongoing research. Since these old techniques were transmitted orally through the centuries, they could only be pieced together through interviews with the few aged survivors who remembered some of the processes, by analyzing old weaving fibers, and through botanical studies cataloguing the locally available dyestuffs.

However, the picture is far from complete, since it is easier to reconstruct what the dyestuffs were than it is to discover the exact recipes and methods traditionally used. It is one thing to understand the basic chemistry involved but quite another to replicate the wide experience and well-developed instinct for color reactions that once must have existed in the minds and eyes of the Anatolian dyers of the past.

This great dislocation in the dyeing tradition has been a fateful one. While weaving techniques and wool qualities have remained very high down to the present, the dyed yarns produced as the shift took place from natural to synthetic dyes have been an unmitigated disaster, particularly for the kilim, since one of its greatest glories has always been its brilliant use of color.

Since prehistoric man first discovered how to attach color to plant and animal fibers, weavers the world over were restricted to dyes made from natural dyestuffs, such as leaves, roots, bark, galls, nutshells, onion skins, and insects. This ancient tradition began to come to an end in the early years of the Industrial Revolution when textile manufacturers needed easily produced dyes that could create the uniform colors required for mass-produced textiles. Beginning in 1856 and continuing to the 1950s, a series of synthetic dyes were derived from coal-tar substances, a byproduct of the generation of coal gas for heating and metallurgic coke-making. A precursor of these synthetics, and the earliest to become commercially viable, was aniline (from the Arab word for indigo *anil*), a name which came to describe all subsequent coal-derived dyes; however, synthetic is a more accurate term. For synthetic dyes to have an effect on Near Eastern weaving, inexpensive versions first needed to be developed that could be used effectively on wool and in rudimentary working conditions. Between 1875 and World War I, "the early synthetic period," such dyes were distributed worldwide and quickly overwhelmed the natural dyeing traditions.[1] By the 1880s, for instance, in the western regions of Anatolia, particularly in the orbit of commercial centers like Smyrna (now Izmir), it would have been virtually impossible to find new rugs and carpets that did not contain at least some synthetically dyed yarns.[2] While the infiltration of synthetics into the more remote areas of Anatolia was slower, by around World War I the indigenous dyeing traditions had been almost entirely overwhelmed. When one compares the cultural resistance in Anatolia to changes in such basic technologies as spinning and loom design with the alacrity with which tribal weavers were won over to the new synthetic dyes, the contrast is extraordinary.

Not only has it been difficult to reconstruct how natural dyes were formulated and used prior to the triumph of synthetics, it is even difficult to determine the degree to which dyeing was the province of the weaving household versus that of the professional dyer. It could be that the dyeing of yarns was one of the stages of the process not entirely carried out by the relatively self-sufficient Anatolian weaver.

It is well-documented that dyeing was practiced in the Near East as an hereditary male craft, and still exists as such in some places today;[3] however, little is known of this craft tradition in Anatolia. The complicated nature of some of the dyeing processes and the considerable time commitment required suggest that some dyeing might have been carried out by specialists rather than the weavers themselves. Dyeing with indigo is one such process. Since the processes of indigo dyeing were complex and the dyestuff could not be gathered locally (and therefore had to be bartered for or purchased), it is probable that Anatolian tribal weavers were dependent for blue yarns on a professional indigo dyer who traveled from village to village on horseback or had dye houses in the towns.[4] *Indigofera tinctoria,* the plant from which most indigo dyestuffs were derived, requires a subtropical climate and was, until replaced by synthetic indigo, largely imported from India and eastern Iran in the form of blue cakes. The use of indigo dye in the Near East has been traced as far back as 2500 B.C. in Egypt. Surviving records substantiate that indigo was historically an important commodity on the ancient trade routes of the Near East.

Anatolian weavers could have and probably did also gather a local plant, woad *(Isatis tinctoria),* which along with fifty or so other plants produces indican, the source of the blue colorant. However, nothing surpasses indigo, particularly for dark blues. The indigo plant contains thirty times the concentration of indican that woad does, so it is not surprising that indigo was favored in Anatolia even though not locally produced.[5]

The dyeing process begins when the blue cakes—indigo in its insoluble form—are set to ferment for several weeks in a vat alkanised with urine, a cheap and readily available source of ammonia. Next, the liquid in the dye vat is heated to boiling and the wool dipped into the dyebath. Instead of being left in the dyebath to soak until the requisite shade is achieved, as is true with most dye processes, the wool is very quickly drawn out of the dyebath, emerging a yellowish hue—indigo in its soluble form. Then, seemingly miraculously but actually through exposure to the air, the yellow soluble form oxidizes spontaneously into blue—the insoluble form. The wonder this process excited is evidenced by the folk expression "working miracles and dyeing blue." The desired intensity of blue is achieved through repeated immersions, a time-consuming process that probably explains why dark blue yarns were highly prized and more expensive.

Rather than permeating the wool fibers as most dyes do, indigo actually coats the yarns and ultimately serves as a protective covering on the fibers, making them more durable. This is undoubtedly one of the reasons for the traditional blue of laborers' work clothes, denim being the most obvious example. Further, its preservative qualities may have also contributed to the association of indigo blue in Near Eastern folk traditions with talismanic powers and practices having to do with death and mourning.[6] Unfortunately, little evidence survives as to what special significance indigo might have had for the Anatolian weaving populations. That indigo dyed yarns are found in the vast majority of kilims despite the fact that the dyestuff was not locally available and the process not within the skills of the ordinary weaver suggests that there was a special significance to the color. Next to red, blue is the most commonly used color in the tribal palette and was probably the second color to establish itself widely throughout weaving regions in prehistoric times.

Red is by far the dominant color in Anatolian kilims and the most popular color in most weaving regions from earliest times.[7] The abundant sources of red to brown dyestuffs is certainly an important factor in the prevalence of red.[8] But cultural factors also seem to be involved, for red was the traditional color of both the Byzantines and the Türkmen tribes who supplanted them.

In Anatolia red dyestuff was easily produced from a plant that could be gathered or cultivated locally. *Rubia tinctorum,* the madder plant, is gathered for its roots, which are dried and ground into powder. Instead of containing one dyestuff as indigo does, madder contains up to nineteen different dyestuffs and is, depending upon how it is processed, capable of producing a remarkable range of colors. Four variables—the mordant (an additive that fixes the dye to the fiber), the quantity of madder in the dye bath, the acidity or alkalinity of the water, and the temperature to which it is heated—all help to control the colors produced, which include shades of pink, rose, apricot, scarlet, numerous brown-reds, purple, and brown-purple.[9] Although dyeing with madder is simpler than with indigo, it is still quite complicated and requires a considerable amount of time, lore, and skill to arrive at the desired effects. However, dyeing with madder certainly could have been carried out domestically.

Using only six materials—oak galls, a yellow dyestuff

found in a great variety of plants, of which weld [*Reseda luteola*] is one of the best, alum, iron sulphate, madder root, and indigo—a palette of between six to thirteen colors can be created.[10] There is nothing to be gained from listing all of the dyestuffs available to tribal weavers, since each group would have gathered a slightly different selection depending on its locale, the time of year, and the regions through which it passed on its migratory routes.

With the exceptions of blue and green, both dependent on indigo, most of the typical colors found in the tribal palette are not difficult for the nonspecialist to produce, and the dyestuffs required are easily found in most regions. Consequently, despite the fact that there are some experts who feel that only in exceptional cases did weaving households do their own dyeing,[11] it seems more likely that Anatolian weaving households, particularly those in the more remote regions, usually did much of their own dyeing but probably turned to professional dyers for difficult processes, in particular, indigo dyeing. The introduction of synthetic dyes unquestionably enabled the domestic dyer to take over more of the processes, and this undoubtedly undermined and supplanted whatever may have existed in the way of professional dyer crafts in Anatolia.

As for the dyeing process itself, wool is an ideal reactive substance since its fibers naturally contain certain mordants, chemical substances that fix the dye to the wool. Compared to fibers such as cotton and flax, wool readily takes dyes. Nevertheless, most natural dyes do not take readily to wool or remain fast unless a supplementary mordant is used. Mordant dyes, such as madder, are so-called because they require the addition of the metallic mordants—iron, alum, or tin—to act as the link between the fiber and the dye. The use of certain mordants on the same dye may darken, brighten, or drastically alter a color. Iron mordants make a color more somber, tin and chrome mordants cause a color to brighten, and copper makes it greener. The final stage in the dyeing process is often the use of a developer, a chemical solution into which the yarns are dipped in order to alter or enhance the color and to fix the dye again. For example, wool that has been dyed in madder with alum mordant takes on a richer, deeper red when dunked into ammonia water.[12] While mordants are necessary to certain dyeing processes, the use of mordants such as iron pyrite can ultimately contribute to the degradation of yarns over time.

Anatolian tribal weavers may have fermented their yarns before dyeing, but this practice is still being studied. We know that this was one of the first steps in indigo dyeing. In the yarn-fermenting process, hanks of wool are soaked for a period ranging from three to ten months, usually in a solution of wheat bran, sour dough, and mordant

salts. The effect is to create in the wool the ideal environment for dyeing, in particular the right degree of acidity which increases color fastness to light and washing and produces more evenly dyed yarns. Examinations by electron microscopes of fibers taken from antique textiles woven in Anatolia suggest that fermentation was practiced in the past.[13] However, the length of time required for the process together with the unevenness of tribal dyed yarns suggest that yarn fermentation was more a function of the professional dyers working for court or commercial ateliers.

Certainly one of the greatest difficulties in using natural dyestuffs in the rudimentary conditions of rural Anatolia was achieving precisely the desired colors or shades, particularly when attempting to dye large batches a uniform shade, or, even harder, when mixing up a dye lot to match an earlier dye batch. The frequent mismatching of colors evident in the two- or three-panel kilims attests to these difficulties. Even though time-tested formulas and practices were followed, there were many variables to deal with. These include the hardness or softness of the water, the quantity of the dyestuffs dropped into the dye bath, the time of year the plant materials were gathered (for example, leaves from the same plant call for different quantities depending on whether they were freshly gathered or dried), the length of soaking (usually the longer soaked, the darker the colors become), whether the wools were summer- or winter-sheared, the amount of lanolin content in the wools, and the varying thickness and irregularities in the yarn resulting from the handspinning of yarns.[14]

In contrast to the yarns used by urban and court weaving workshops, which were dyed by professional craftsmen, tribal yarns are, despite the beautiful palettes produced, very unevenly dyed. Achieving uniform perfection in dyeing was probably never a possibility in the tribal weaving tradition given the part-time nature of the task and the rudimentary working conditions. Nor does such uniformity seem to have achieved a high place in the aesthetic values of Anatolian weavers. The lack of uniformity in tribal yarns was always regarded as a serious flaw by practitioners and connoisseurs of court weaving and still is by most commercial weaving ateliers. Even before the introduction of synthetic dyes, high levels of uniformity were achieved in these traditions. Yet it should be remembered that what may be viewed as a defect in one context or place or time may be seen in others as a decided virtue. For instance, in Britain late-Victorian mill owners and managers tended to look back with condescension on the period before the 1860s, when they were dependent on natural dyestuffs and restricted to a limited range of colors of often unpredictable hues. Now in the final decade of the

Dyeing wool red (with synthetic dyes), Niğde Province, 1978.

twentieth century a sizeable proportion of the consuming public is rejecting the standardization and uniformity of mass-produced factory textiles in favor of the handspun, natural dyed look. Certainly the present appeal of antique Anatolian kilims is in part because they are clearly made by a series of hand processes that have produced textures and colors unfamiliar and exotic to modern eyes and tastes.

When the unevenly dyed yarns of the typical Anatolian dye lot are woven into a tribal kilim or rug, the Anatolians admiringly use the term *abrash* to describe the visual effect. Literally translated as dappled, mottled, or speckled, abrash in weaving refers to the subtle gradations of shades within the same color areas. An accident of the spinning and dyeing processes, and therefore technically a defect, abrash produces color nuances that are highly prized and that can be manipulated for artistic purposes.

Abrash gives a liveliness, depth, and subtlety to tribal kilims. It takes simple palettes of five or six basic colors and multiplies the colors through hundreds of shadings. The slit-weave tapestry technique, which is effected by juxtaposing blocks of colored areas, becomes flat and uniform without the softening variations of abrash. The illusion of depth produced by the subtle shadings of abrash is not unlike what a painter does in shading the skies of a landscape. In a sense, abrash in kilim weaving creates an effect similar to the feathering of color possible in the pointillist-like technique of the knotted pile rug.

Abrash may be evident in the yarns at the completion of the dye process or it may appear later as the result of

Hanks of natural dyed wool drying, Çanakkale Province, 1985.

exposure to light and use, which over time cause the dyes to mellow and fade. With indigo-dyed wool, for example, much of the abrash seen in older pieces results from wear as the indigo coating is rubbed off the fibers, a phenomenon we are familiar with in blue jeans. The abrash that occurs after the weaving process is, of course, accidental, but these subtle alterations nevertheless can contribute markedly to the visual beauty of old kilims.

Abrash resulting from wools that were uneven in color before the weaving process is also largely of an accidental nature, since the weavers on the whole probably used the yarns at random. Some scholars would argue that all abrash is unintentional, either the result of weavers using yarns as they come or of changes in the dyes after use and aging;[15] however, from observing thousands and thousands of kilims over the past thirty years, I feel that there is frequent evidence of a conscious, contrived use of abrash for artistic purposes. In such instances, the weaver seems to have "painted" with the subtle gradations of color. In large areas of negative space, as in the typical Obruk *mihrab* (prayer arch) for example, there is often a subtle shading achieved by alternating narrow bands of light and dark shades in a systematic manner. Or a plain area may be relieved by a shaded patch of irregular size whose form and placement suggest that it was consciously arranged to achieve an artistic effect. Further, there are kilims in which the colors reach their most intense shade at the top of the mihrab, precisely where the focal point should be. The manipulation of abrash can control the eye of the viewer, as a spotlight would, thus defining the focal point. While abrash must have begun as an accident arising from the combined processes of hand combing, hand spinning, and natural dyeing, it has apparently evolved over time, particularly in the hands of creative weavers, into one of the distinctive visual attributes of tribal weaving. With the mechanization of yarn processing and the triumph of synthetic dyeing, abrash has tended to vanish in contemporary weavings and with it all the beauty and visual interest it once provided.

The convenience of commercial synthetic dyes reduced the labor involved in gathering, processing, and using natural dyestuffs and in a sense gave weaver-dyers more control over the final product. These factors explain their rapid acceptance by groups not known for abandoning traditional practices without compelling reasons. The result, however, was not only the loss of abrash. The new dyes also led to the total disruption of the beautiful tribal palettes that had evolved over the centuries and to the destruction of the natural color sense of the eye of Anatolia.

The traditional Anatolian palettes were, it would seem, contained within and controlled by the natural world itself

as, down to the mid-nineteenth century, weavers worked within the confines of a very limited palette producing still unsurpassed effects of color. The Anatolian kilim tradition demonstrates that there is a kind of mastery that can be achieved working over long periods of time with limited materials. The antique kilims are proof that the eye of Anatolia, so long as it was not affected by the influences of modern factory production, had achieved a color sense that was uncannily perfect.

The decline in the tribal palette was a gradual one and took place at different rates throughout Anatolia. Synthetic dyes seem to have been first used in a sparing way, for minor colors and highlights, probably because they were novelties and had to be purchased. Undoubtedly, the deep

Abrash: "Contrived" abrash in the "striping" of the border of an Aydın kilim (left). "Contrived" abrash shading in the half-hexagon of a Rashwan kilim (center). "Random" abrash in the border of a West Anatolian kilim (right).

respect for traditional designs was also an inhibiting factor in the use of new colors. The tribal weaver learned the motif and the weaving technique as a single entity—and undoubtedly the palette itself originally was a part of that organic whole.

The truth seems to be, sad to say, that despite all the weight of custom and tradition and the obvious worth of all that had been achieved, the Anatolian eye grew to prefer these synthetic colors. For instance, the resistance that initially greeted recent attempts to revive the use of natural dyed wools in Anatolian cottage weaving projects was not only directed at the increased time and labor involved but also stemmed from the women's attraction to the hot pinks, julep oranges, electric purples, and other vivid colors popularized by synthetic dyes. Even in the older, naturally dyed kilims, it is evident that tribal weavers in their exuberant celebration of color had always favored the clearest and brightest hues they could achieve, and exploited to the fullest the color potential of the natural palette. Synthetic dyes simply provided a new, if often unfortunate, avenue for their love of dazzling color. What has happened in the last century is comparable to taking a precocious child who has been creating striking pictures working from an old box of crayons with twelve colors and suddenly turning over to him a new box with sixty different colors. The innate preference for bright, vivid primary colors on the part of children has been scientifically established, and it would appear that tribal cultures around the world, as well as many of our best Western artists and designers, have retained these natural inclinations.[16]

The tendency in weaving discussions has been to overstate the case against synthetic dyes, which obviously have worked well in industrial situations and gained worldwide acceptance. It is undeniable that good and bad quality synthetic dyes were available over the past one hundred years and that it has always been possible to replicate, if not duplicate, the natural palette with the better synthetics. This is proved by numerous instances in which only chemical analysis can distinguish between yarns that were naturally or synthetically dyed. With the better synthetics, if they are properly mixed, it is possible to fool the human eye.

While better synthetic dyes certainly existed, unfortunately the tribal weaver usually did not choose or have access to them. Instead of the natural world, which the tribal weaver originally knew and understood, it was more likely the small village grocer's shop, with its haphazard stock of synthetic dyes, predominantly of the cheaper variety, that became the new source for dyestuffs. Further, the dyeing directions often proved to be unintelligible or misunderstood because of illegible labels, illiteracy, and an unfamiliarity with industrial products.[17] Given the circumstances, it is no wonder that the synthetics, which worked very well in industrial situations, often resulted in ugly, muddy, poorly fixed colors, and very inharmonious effects in ethnic weaving contexts.

However, the differences in the effects created by natural and synthetic dyes are not simply the result of the misuse of the latter. Chemists using scanning electron microscopes have identified some of the different effects of natural and synthetic dyes on wool fibers. When synthetic dyes are used, there is apparently a stronger penetration in the cell interstices and the base material of the wool fiber. Conversely, when natural dyes are used, the wool fiber re-

tains more of its original whiteness and the intensity of the hue is softened. The effect of natural dyes is generally perceived as soft and muted, almost introverted in character. They seem to draw one into them. The effect of synthetic dyes, particularly the inexpensive kinds used in rural situations, is by comparison usually harsh, loud, and aggressively extroverted in character. These impressions proceed in part from microscopic differences in the way the dyes permeate wool fibers.

Not only do natural and synthetic dyes take differently to wool, but there are also important differences in the way natural and synthetic dyes are perceived by the human eye and brain. A dye, whether synthetic or natural, absorbs certain light wavelengths and reflects others; its hue depends on which wavelengths are reflected. One dye, for instance, may reflect primarily long wavelengths (hence appearing as red), while another may reflect middle wavelengths (appearing as greenish-yellow) and another short wavelengths (appearing as blue). Or the dye may reflect a mixture of different wavelengths producing secondary and tertiary colors. Synthetic and natural dyes differ in the mixture of wavelengths they reflect. Natural dyes, particularly a dyestuff like madder, tend to reflect a greater mix of wavelengths than do synthetics, which are distilled and therefore more precise or pure. In other words, natural dyes rarely appear to be a single hue. Instead of a true primary red, for instance, the greater likelihood is that a natural red will appear as reddish-yellow or reddish-blue. The hues of anilines by contrast are pure reds, blues, and yellows. The broadness or narrowness of the range of wavelengths reflected by dyes is an important factor in how readily different hues harmonize.[16] If, for instance, three strands of wool are each synthetically dyed red, blue, and yellow and placed side-by-side, the effect of the combination will be disharmonious. Whereas, if three strands dyed with indigo blue, madder red, and onion yellow are similarly placed the effect will be quite harmonious.[18] It is precisely because natural dyes are impure, that is, give off a broad range of wavelengths, that harmonious combinations are possible. In a sense, in a kilim design effected by wools dyed with natural dyes it is the "overlapping" of the hues that makes for color harmony.

With the gradual shift from natural to synthetic dyes, it would seem that tribal weavers, without realizing it, not only changed the source of their dyestuffs but also left behind an ancient weaving tradition in which it had been virtually impossible to create grossly disharmonious color combinations. Apparently the natural dyes and the ways they interact obviated the need for weavers to have conscious theories of color, thus enabling even the average weaver to reach high artistic levels. It is quite possible that

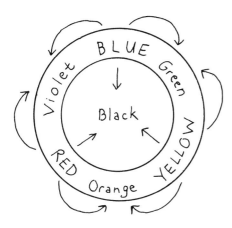

one of the factors in accelerating the breakdown of the traditional palettes was that color combinations which had worked beautifully in natural dyes ceased to do so once synthetics replaced them. Apparently once these traditional palettes began to break down the weaver/dyers of Anatolia gradually lost their way.

It could be argued, however, that synthetic dyes might have been and still may be used in such a way as to replicate the hues of natural dyes. Technically, with synthetic dyes any hue created by natural dyes can be replicated by mixtures of the three synthetic primaries: red, yellow, and blue. Mixing these colors in pairs results in the secondary colors: violet (blue and red), orange (yellow and red), and green (blue and yellow). Mixing the three primary colors produces black. Black mixed in different proportions with the primary and secondary colors produces the tertiary colors such as red-brown, or yellowish-brown.[19] While replicating the mixture of light wavelengths characteristic of natural dyes by mixing the synthetic dyes was always a possibility, the bulk of the weaving produced in Anatolia since the introduction of aniline dyes demonstrates that this was not the usual practice. Instead the synthetic dyes seem to have been used for the most part as they came from the factory packets rather than by mixing them in order to replicate the hues of natural dyes. Instead of the Anatolian weavers adjusting the new synthetics to replicate the effects created by natural dyes, they seem to have experienced a conversion, as did ethnic weavers worldwide, to the new standards of the industrial world. While it is true that the new synthetics led them to use some new colors outside the traditional palette, creating the illusion that synthetics increased color possibilities, in fact the opposite seems to have been the case.

As the weavers of Anatolia were drawn without preparation into the uncharted new world of synthetic dyes, they were never able to master this new science of dyes and produce weavings that equalled the high standards of the past. Their experience demonstrates that the desire for standardization and uniformity central to industrial production inevitably leads to reduction and simplification. While a standardized red dye which can be produced in consistent, uniform batches is regarded as a sign of quality in industrial processes, such a monotonous red is perceived as a diminution of the kinds of color effects prized by those involved in artistic endeavors. When the Anatolian weaver rejected madder, with its nineteen different dyestuffs and extraordinary range of color potentialities, for a packet of synthetic primary red she left behind an ancient tradition and a distinctive color sense and began to enter the new aesthetic of the modern industrialized world. Ironically, now we of the industrialized world are attracted to the antique kilims of Anatolia because to our eyes the kilims contain a palette very different from the industrial palette we have been conditioned to as modern consumers.

Not only are the immediate effects of natural and synthetic dyeing different, but the long term effects are different as well. It is unquestionable that antique kilims with naturally dyed yarns have aged better than the more contemporary, synthetically dyed kilims. The colors produced by natural dyes such as indigo and madder, if correctly processed, remain true and fast, as long as the weavings are not exposed to excessive sunlight or damp. Natural yellows, however, are an exception and do not tend to stay true. There is a prevailing misconception that natural dyestuffs will always age better than synthetic dyes which are generally believed to fade or run. The fact is that in tribal weaving the cheap synthetic dyes typically used, together with imperfectly understood methods, produced yarns that often did not remain true. In some cases registers changed completely, destroying the original color compositions and harmonies.

There is now an admirable and evidently very successful movement afoot in Anatolia to reinstitute the old natural dyeing tradition. These efforts are chiefly aimed at the cottage weaving industry and commercial productions such as the DOBAG and Kavacık projects. This return to natural dyeing, and even in some cases to hand-combed and hand-spun yarns, bodes well for the renaissance of the rug and carpet industries of Anatolia and even for the emergence of a new cottage weaving industry producing decorative kilims largely for export. However, the tribal weaving tradition, which produced kilims that were an expression of its culture and intended for use within the tribe, seems to have been so completely overwhelmed and become so marginal that such a revival is unlikely to affect the scattered groups that continue the old ways. Rather than experience a renaissance, the ancient tribal tradition almost certainly will continue to wind down to a point at which it will disappear.

Chapter 3

The Loom

While Anatolian weavers in the last hundred years have shown little hesitancy in abandoning natural for synthetic dyes, they have shown an amazing conservatism in remaining faithful to a form of loom that has not changed in any significant way for thousands of years. The *istar,* as the loom is called in Anatolia, evolved, as did the drop spindle, into its optimum form in prehistoric times and has required little in the way of refinement since. Consisting as it does of several logs, a few poles, some ropes, and string, it seems a strangely minimal artifact for a culture in which weaving has been a central and constant activity over the millennia.

Even before the loom, in early Neolithic times, certain processes existed for combining fibers into textiles. These included such ancient methods as looping, coiling, twining, and braiding. The textiles formed using such methods, however, were primitive and painstakingly slow to produce. Basketry and feltmaking are also assumed to predate the loom weaving of textiles. That neither of these crafts required highly processed materials like wool yarns and flaxen threads was probably a factor in their early emergence. In feltmaking, unspun wool is put through a process involving pressure, heat, and moisture, which causes the wool fibers to interlock and fuse, creating large panels of fabric without the technology of the spindle and the loom. Basketry likewise does not require a loom since the stiffness of its materials enables the emerging basket to keep its form without a supporting frame.

Wool yarns, however, are limp and crimpy. They require a framing device to provide the stiffness and tautness the fibers lack. The loom's function is not only to keep the fibers under tension but also to keep them spaced evenly in parallel lines, as warps, facilitating the insertion of the wefts. The tension stretches out and straightens the crimpy yarns, keeping the warps spaced and preventing the scales of the wool fibers from snagging. The maintenance of the optimum tension during weaving is a primary concern of the weaver since the failure to do so results in a sleazy fabric.

Anatolian weavers in prehistoric times used a simple warp-weighted loom. This was certainly the established loom technology in central and western Anatolia by the fourth millennium B.C., while there is evidence that suggests its use as early as the sixth millennium B.C.[1] This primitive device consisted of a horizontal beam suspended at head height from which the warp threads hung down to the floor. Attached to the ends of the warps were individual weights that pulled the yarns taut and kept them aligned. Anatolia shared this loom form, as it did much of its weaving technology, with the European weaving regions, but it bordered on regions to the east and south where the horizontal ground loom was the dominant weaving technology.[2] At some point in time not yet determined the horizontal ground loom and its vertical variation displaced the warp-weighted loom in Anatolia.

In its most basic form the istar consists of two small logs—the length varying considerably from place to place—which are placed on the ground the requisite distance apart (depending on the desired length for the weaving) and held in position by stakes. The warps are run back and forth between these two beams, and are either tied at each end to the loom or looped completely around the beams. While the two-beam version has sufficed, particularly for nomadic groups, the loom has also been elaborated upon through the addition of side

a.   *Bahşiş Yörük women preparing a goat hair warped ground loom, Niğde Province, 1978.*

beams, thus creating a complete frame. If space is a problem, as, for instance, when the loom is placed inside a tent or cottage, the frame can be set on end in an upright position, creating a vertical loom. As a general rule, though certainly not a hard and fast one, nomadic groups tend to work on the horizontal ground loom while settled groups use the vertical loom.

The setting up and warping of the loom are one and the same process. This function is carried out by the weaver or weavers and other family members or friends, usually in close proximity to or inside the tent or cottage. Warping is an important skill, and the quality of the weaving produced is to a great degree dependent upon the kind of warping job done. Certainly the advantages of such a loom to tribal weavers included its simplicity and the availability of its materials, the portability of its components, and the ease of its assemblage and dismantling. And while we as moderns might assume the opposite, it is possible to achieve highly sophisticated results using a simple mechanism. The high artistry of Anatolian kilims certainly is a testament to that.

The partially assembled warped loom illustrated above undoubtedly resembles the original loom as it emerged in prehistoric times. The earliest weavers, virtually without tools or any form of mechanization, manually raised and lowered each warp to admit the passage of the weft, a tedious process that was not much of an improvement in speed on pre-loom weaving techniques. Over time, such instruments as the weaver's sword, a wooden instrument used to beat the weft into place, and the beater, a comb-like instrument that both compacts the weft and helps to space the warps, evolved into the traditional shapes still in use today.

Once the loom had been invented to produce the requisite tension on the warp, the next major problem the weaver faced was to find a means of facilitating the introduction of the weft into the warp.[3] Before other solutions were found the primitive method undoubtedly was to darn the thread in by running the leading end under the first thread, over the second, under the third, and so forth one thread at a time, back and forth across the width of the loom.

The first step in facilitating the introduction of the weft was the discovery that a rod, called a shed bar, could be inserted into the warp threads in such a way that every second thread passes over the rod while the threads in between pass under. By simple adjustments of this bar the two groups of warps can be separated by one motion into a passageway, or the shed, through which the weft can be passed all at once, speeding up the process considerably. While the invention of this shed, called the natural shed, solved the problem of facilitating the entry of the first weft thread, the return row of that thread still had to be darned in, otherwise the second row of weft thread would have had the effect of negating the first.

To solve this problem required the invention of a device that would produce a second shed, the countershed. Such a solution was effected over time providing the warps in the second group with individual holders, called heddles, in the form of string loops, which in turn are attached to a bar running above and perpendicular to the warp. When the heddle bar is raised, it pulls up only those threads looped by the heddles and does not interfere with those warps controlled by the shed bar. The opening and closing of the sheds by adjusting these poles—a process called mechanical shedding—introduced a primitive level of mechanization into the weaving process, facilitating different kinds of weaving techniques and increasing the volume of weaving possible.[4] The shed and heddle bar mechanism seems to have existed in the Middle East and Egypt from at least the fourth millennium B.C.[5]

It is essentially at this stage of the evolution of the loom that Anatolian tribal weaving technology has remained fixed. And even this stage of the technology is not fully used by weavers working in the slit-weave tapestry technique typical of the kilim. Only in the striped plain weave skirt ends and areas of simple kilim patterning with broad (weft-wise) areas of color does mechanical shedding have a function. In the rest of the complex kilim designs found in the majority of recent kilims woven in the slit-weave tapestry technique, the weavers do not use the mechanical shedding. Instead they strum the warps with their fingers, and when using the alternate set of warps (one shed is automatically open) in a small area, they hand pick the sheds with their fingers or sometimes with a small stick.[6] The level of loom technology adequate for slit-weave tapestry is actually a very basic one; even mechanical shedding is a level of technology beyond its needs.[7]

The modifications that have been made to the loom in Anatolia have little to do with the basic weaving process. Instead changes have been made that allow the weaver to remain stationary while the section of the weaving to be worked on is moved to her. On the traditional horizontal loom, the weaver moves forward over the loom, sitting on the completed portion of fabric (under which a board or rock has been inserted), undoubtedly providing additional tension as she works. However, with the vertical loom the weaver needs to follow the area to be worked on up the loom, necessitating a system which raises the seating benches as needed. One innovation that enables the weaver to stay at ground level is the "roller beam" loom, which has rotating beams at top and bottom that allow the weaving to be cranked around the bottom beam, bringing the area to be woven to the weaver's level.

In contrast to the conservative Anatolian weavers who had very different objectives in their weaving, European weavers by the Middle Ages worked at more complicated looms equipped with foot peddles to control the shedding devices. Mechanization proceeded apace with shuttles to move the weft back and forth. With the invention of the flying shuttle in 1732 and the introduction of power looms in the 1860s, handweaving as a major means of production was largely displaced in the West. While handweaving continued as an art and a craft, the West satisfied its practical needs for textiles with mass-produced, mechanically woven fabrics. The mechanical nature of the weaving process in the West made huge volumes of textiles available for the first time to a large public. Along with these obvious advantages, however, there was also a breakdown in the special prestige and significance textiles once had, particularly in their ancient role as a major form of human expression. Only when textiles are relatively rare and the product of

Laying in the discontinuous wefts, Uşak Province, 1979. *Compacting the weft with a wooden beater, Uşak Province, 1979.*

arduous hand processes do they maintain their ancient place in the hierarchy of expressive forms.[8] Thus it is obvious that the aims of tribal weaving, in which weaving is an act of social obligation and cultural expression, have little in common with those of an industrial culture. With its suitability as a medium for human expression and its simplicity and portability, the istar was ideal for a self-sufficient tribal people.

Rather than compare the Anatolian weaving tradition with the industrial weaving of the West, it would be more apt to compare the tribal weavers of Anatolia with Western artist weavers, who also generally work on hand looms and seek out handwoven, natural dyed yarns. The human need for self-expression has little to do with speed and efficiency. It should be remembered that each step toward the mechanization of the loom (including in some cases the ancient development of the shedding device) actually limits the freedom of the weaver and reduces her control over the design. The closer the weaver is to her medium—that is, the more manual the process—the less she is separated from the weaving by mechanical counterparts of her actions and, hence, the greater the capability for human expression.[9] As we have seen, the mechanical shedding devices, even though available on the Anatolian loom, are used only in a very limited way in kilim weaving.

The chief aim of mechanizing weaving has been to speed up the process and achieve greater uniformity, thus reducing the cost and increasing profits. In tribal societies, kilims were primarily woven not for commerce but for home use and, as we shall see in chapter seven, were intended to serve as an important form of cultural expression, often associated with particular ritual stages of life. The apparent benefits of mechanization were therefore largely irrelevant. Since there was no real separation in tribal culture between what we would consider utilitarian and aesthetic objects, and all woven items were embellished with meaningful motifs and designs, a hand loom like the istar proved to be the correct vehicle because it allowed for artistic and cultural expression.

Chapter 4

The Weave

Reduced to its essentials, all weaving consists of the interlacing of warps and wefts, creating a basic grid. An Anatolian weaver, working on the same simple loom using different adjustments of these two structural elements—the warp and the weft—and by adding certain supplementary wefts, has been able to produce a variety of weaving techniques: the tapestry weave of the kilim, the supplementary weft weave of the *cicim*, and the knotted pile technique of the rug or carpet, to name a few. Anatolian tribal weaving has always been carried out by individual weavers or a family group who have mastered a range of weaving skills and memorized a small repertoire of designs and motifs to go with them, not by specialist weavers working in organized groups.

Tapestry weave, practiced in the Near East at least as far back as the early to mid second millennium B.C.,[1] seems to have been a major technique throughout much of Anatolian weaving history. Indeed, the terms kilim and tapestry weave are practically synonymous. Whereas in the West kilims are thought of primarily as floor coverings, in Anatolian tribal life kilims have always served a wide variety of functions: as wall hangings, dust covers for luggage piles and loaded camels, divan and cushion covers, wrappings for packing household items, cloths for use under drying grain and over bread dough, saddle bags, cargo bags, and saddle rugs, and, in the more distant past, clothing. It is the weaving technique, not its function or even appearance, that makes an artifact a kilim. In fact, many of the items just listed can also be executed in other weaving techniques and would then be described as *cicim, zili, soumak,* or *halı* (knotted pile). In addition to the structural element, "kilim" also has geographical and cultural components, since

the term (and its variants such as *gelim, chelim,* or *kilimi*) is commonly used to describe tapestry woven artifacts produced by tribal pastoralists in largely Muslim regions spanning from southeastern Europe to Central Asia and including North Africa.

While tapestry weave is a very ancient technique, it was certainly not the first to evolve; plain weave, for one, predated it. Tapestry weave is actually a simple variant of plain weave, a technique generally accepted as the basis for a wide variety of warp/weft interlacing techniques. In plain weave (a) the warp and weft are equally balanced and, therefore, equally visible. In tapestry weave (b) the warps are more widely spaced and thicker and the

a.

b.

wefts so dense and tightly packed that they completely cover the warp threads. This "off balance"—the weft predominating over the warp—creates what is called a weft-faced fabric. In weft-faced fabrics like kilims the warps are evident only indirectly through the bubbly effect they give the wefts and as extensions beyond the borders of the woven surface in the form of fringes or braided ends. Significantly, the weft functions both as one of the major structural elements and as the carrier of the design.

One of the reasons for the evolution of the weft-faced fabric undoubtedly was that while plain weave was faster to produce and used less yarn, it failed to capitalize fully on one of the primary advantages of wool, its insulating qualities. To maximize this feature a sufficient number of yarns need to be compacted into a given space—hence the tight packing of the wefts over the surface of the warps. Further, the desire to transfer to woven fabrics the kinds of images depicted in earlier forms of visual expression—for example, cave and wall paintings, felt coverings, and basketry—must also have been a factor. While plaid and other simple patterns like checks are possible in plain weave by varying the colors used in the warps and wefts, it is not possible to create the geometric or pictorial motifs typical of kilims.

Shifting to the weft-faced technique alone, however, was not sufficient to enable weavers to produce designs composed of geometric or pictorial motifs. At most, in such a technique different colored yarns could be combined in alternating bands of colors creating striped designs. Striped designs—actually a very ancient solution to effecting polychromatic designs—still survive in kilims, and in particular as the backings of storage bags and saddlebags, and for drop cloths of a very practical nature.

One early solution for taking the design possibilities of plain and weft-faced weaves beyond the simple check or stripe was the innovation of the supplementary or extra-weft technique (c). This technique, which has produced another large body of flatweavings with its own design tradition (commonly called *cicim* in many parts of Anatolia), consists of a ground weave composed of warps and wefts (either in plain or tapestry weave) onto which supplementary wefts are superimposed to create the design. To those not familiar with weaving techniques, the effect of supplementary weft weaves is not unlike that of embroidery. While the kilim was to evolve from yet another solution to effecting designs other than the check or stripe, the extra-weft technique has also commonly been used in combination with kilims as tiny floats, that is, extra-weft motifs superimposed or floated on the

c.

d.   e.

surface of the kilim usually serving to fill in areas of negative space. A more extensive use of extra-wefting appears in the kilims of a number of localized traditions, in particular the Malatya banded kilims (see plates 6 and 7), which are decorated with large bands of extra-wefting.

It is out of another design solution—the discovery of the discontinuous weft and hence the slit-weave tapestry technique—that the Anatolian kilim was to emerge. Plain weave, with its wefts running from one side of the weaving to the other, that is, from selvedge to selvedge, depends on a continuous weft (d). In contrast, the weft of the tapestry weave is discontinuous (e), in the sense that it travels back and forth only within its specific color areas or surfaces. Rather than running the weft from selvedge to selvedge, the tapestry weaver uses her tiny bobbins of dyed yarns to one by one fill in the desired color areas.

The discontinuous weft technique transforms the weaving process from a steady, even progression of a line of weaving into an uneven growth of

different patches of color. With the continuous weft technique, the weft zigzags across the entire width of the weaving, an action a mechanical shuttle could replicate, while the discontinuous technique can only be effected efficiently by dexterous fingers. The use of the discontinuous weft in the tapestry weave certainly explains why both Anatolian weavers and artist-weavers of the West have not moved on to more mechanically advanced looms.

The adoption of the discontinuous weft, however, presented the first innovators with important structural complications. One of the first of these was how to deal with the discontinuous wefts at their turning point—where they must reverse and go back over the color field under construction. Over time a number of solutions emerged; one was to turn the weft back on its own warp field, that is, on the last warp in its color field. When the wefts of each color field are repeatedly run back and forth within their own set of warps, and not interlocked with the warps or wefts of laterally adjoining color fields, a slit forms between these fields.

Hence, the first solution to working with discontinuous wefts led to the slit-weave technique, the subdivision of tapestry weave that the vast majority of surviving Anatolian kilims employ. While slit-weave tapestry was a solution that facilitated the creation of motifs by using discontinuous wefts, this technique was not without structural problems of its own. The chief one was that a slit, if it was not to jeopardize the structural integrity of the fabric, could only be of a very limited length. At the heart of the problem is that the same discontinuous wefts used to create the design are also one of the two components of the structure of the fabric itself. Therefore, whatever is done to construct a weaving design must also simultaneously contribute toward making a sound fabric. The necessity for achieving a balance between using enough slitting to create motifs and limiting the length and frequency of slitting in order to maintain structural integrity has had a profound influence on the character of kilim motifs and designs. The distinctive character of the imagery thus produced is a major factor in differentiating the look of kilims from that of other flatweaves and from knotted pile rugs and carpets.

An obvious example of the need for slitting and the need to control it is the rendering of vertical lines in the side borders of kilims. Given the Anatolian weaver's penchant for framing her main field with a series of borders, the problem of executing lines running the length of the kilim is one frequently encountered. If the weaver were to attempt the vertical lines using the slit-weave technique with no modifications, an impossibly long slit threatening the integrity of the fabric would be the result. However, the denticulated border (f), in which a straight line is interrupted every half inch or so by tooth-like protuberances into the lateral fields, is a technical solution to the problem that has also become a very characteristic decorative element. There are many elaborations of this technique (g), ranging from simple one-sided denticulations to very elaborate stalactite-like repetitions on a line (h).

There is a marked tendency in kilim design to avoid vertical lines altogether in favor of the diagonal line, that is diagonal in reference to the ninety-degree angle created by the intersecting warps and wefts. This bias towards the diagonal has led to an abundance of such motifs as the triangle and its agglutinates, the diamond and the hexagon (which appear more often than the motifs of the square, the rectangle, and the pentagon). The diagonal line gives the illusion of a straight line (whereas actually it is more in the nature of a stepped or serrated line), effectively dividing the abutting color fields while eliminating the need for additional slits. The horizontal lines of the triangle and the hexagon, of course, create no problem since these are lines that run parallel to the weft.

As complex as Anatolian kilims appear to be, and as varied as the designs are from region to region and tribe to tribe, the repertoire of designs is actually formed of very simple geometric motifs, a great many derived from the basic unit of the triangle. While square and rectangular motifs and designs feature heavily in Anatolian kilims, their inclusion is possible only if a solution such as denticulation is used on the sides of the motifs (which run parallel to the warps). The denticulated rectangle or box design (j) is yet another example of the weaving medium shaping design.

There were also other design solutions available to Anatolian weavers. A number of interlocking and dove-tailing techniques evolved in the ancient Near and Middle East (probably, although this has not been established, after the slit-weave technique), which did away with the slit and the structural and design problems it created. In the shared warp, or dove-tailing solution (k), for instance, the wefts from laterally adjoining color fields share the warp that forms the boundary between them. And in the double interlocking-weft technique (l), the wefts from laterally adjoining fields interlock with each other between the warp fields of their respective color areas.

While there are subtle differences in their appearance, both solutions avoid the use of the slit and give the weaver greater flexibility in the creation of motifs and designs. However, these solutions to structural and design problems result in certain losses in the ability to draw designs. The

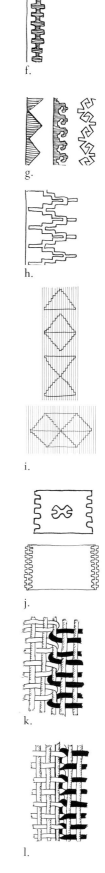

f.

g.

h.

i.

j.

k.

l.

33

Weaving a storage sack (alaçuval) on a ground loom, Maraş Province, 1977.

clarity of line, the hard-edged precise drawing, the sharp contrasts between color fields that can be achieved in slit-weave tapestry are to a degree sacrificed. The lines produced in the dove-tailing and interlocking techniques are, by contrast, blurred and fuzzy. Despite the considerable limitations imposed by the slit-weave tapestry technique, there seem to be inherent in it decided aesthetic compensations. The visibility of the slits helps to intensify the colors and heighten the contrasts, giving an extra drama and shimmering dynamism to the motifs and designs. Indeed, at some point in the evolution of the kilim, slitting in some cases becomes not just a structural solution but also an important design element that is used even in instances that do not structurally require it. On the human level, that is, from the weaver's point of view, slit-weave tapestry is faster, more enjoyable, and allows for much greater spontaneity than other tapestry-weaving techniques.[2] It should never be forgotten that the weaving occasion, both because of the creative nature of the activity itself and the lively social occasion that has often grown up around it, has probably always been one of the happiest activities of the Anatolian woman. What the weaver herself would have found most enjoyable should obviously not be discounted in explaining how a weaving tradition came into being.

While shared warp and interlocking techniques are not unknown to Anatolia and the surrounding regions, it is indisputable that the vast majority of Anatolian kilims are woven in the slit-weave tapestry technique. For example, just to the east of Anatolia, in the Zagros Mountains, tribal groups such as the Lurs and the Bakhtiari favor weaves with interlocking techniques. The more the Anatolian tribal weaving tradition is studied, the more ancient it seems and the more remarkable its character becomes. Not only has the Anatolian weaver over the millennia faithfully explored the design possibilities of slit-weave tapestry, but she has also remained loyal to the original four square character of weaving. Given the very rectangular orientation of weaving, resulting from the ninety-degree interlacing of warps and wefts, the weaver is naturally inclined to work with straight lines rather than curves, with geometric forms rather than naturalistic vegetation or anthropomorphic forms, with abstraction rather than representation. It is significant that the circle—the ultimate curvilinear shape and one of mankind's most ancient motifs—is absent from kilim imagery. Rather it is the hexagon that is the natural image of the Anatolian kilim.

Historically, when weavers have confronted the problem of creating designs in a medium that inherently is filled with restraints, they have had two major paths to choose from. One is to accept the natural limitations of weaving and to evolve a system of imagery and design that is essentially rectilinear, geometric, and nonrepresentational. The alternative is to work against the natural limitations inherent in weaving and to evolve remedial techniques that give the weaver the flexibility to render motifs and designs that are curvilinear and naturalistic. Within the Turkish tradition, the tribal weavers of Anatolia have tended to choose the first, while weavers in ateliers of the Ottoman court favored the latter.

In reference to this great divide, it has been convincingly argued that the greatest heights in the medium of weaving have been reached when the orthogonal character of weaving has been accepted. The more clearly this original structure is preserved, or even exploited, in the design, the stronger the weaving ultimately will be in the unique characteristics that set it apart from all other visual art forms.[3] Apart from a few localized exceptions, Anatolian weavers in the distant past chose to exploit to the fullest the four-square char-

acter of weaving and to ignore weaving techniques, in particular the eccentric weft, that would have enabled them to explore entirely different design possibilities. Even when they assimilated into their designs motifs originally of a very curvilinear character, such as the Ottoman floral motifs of the carnation and the tulip, the Anatolian weavers tended to stylize and geometricize them, absorbing them into the basic orthogonal technique, rather than adjusting their technique to the eccentric weft in order to render them in a curvilinear fashion.

The technique of eccentric wefts (n), that is wefts that deviate from the horizontal, is created on the standard weaving grid of warps and wefts. Instead of running the weft back and forth in straight, horizontal lines, the weaver forces the wefts into the curving configurations required by the design, packing them tightly enough to cover the warps and creating a weft-faced fabric capable of a whole new repertoire of designs. Such an innovation has formed the basis for major weaving traditions. European weavers who pursued the possibilities of eccentric wefts have produced throughout the Medieval, Renaissance, and Baroque periods a major tapestry weaving tradition that is representational and curvilinear in character.

However, while recognizing the heights of artistry reached by the European tapestry tradition, particularly in such masterpieces as the Unicorn Tapestries, weaving purists have persuasively argued that weavers in this tradition, instead of exploring the unique potentialities of weaving as an artistic medium, have transformed it into a secondary art whose chief aim has been to translate into woven terms the visual creations of another very different art, painting. This subservient role of weaving in the West as the handmaiden of painting, it has been argued, has led to the relegation of textile art to the place of a minor or decorative art.[4] Certainly it is true that our appreciation of European tapestries is based to a large degree on admiration for the weavers' *tour de force* achievement in making a weaving look as much like a painting as possible. In contrast, the Anatolian kilim has no reference to any other art outside of itself, and thus has preserved a kind of potency rarely possible in the European tradition. A kilim is not the working out of a cartoon based on another visual art form but is a self-sufficient form of artistic expression, a world unto itself.

While certainly unaware of the European tapes-

m.

n.

o.

p.

try tradition, Anatolian weavers were not entirely unfamiliar with the Ottoman court and urban kilims that also exploited the eccentric weft to produce the graceful floral designs so central to its tradition. And to the west of Anatolia in the Balkans and to the east in the Senneh region of Kurdistan, weaving traditions employing the eccentric weft have predominated. Even within Anatolia itself, in localized tribal regions, there have apparently always been small pockets of weavers, the weavers of the *parmaklı* kilims being one, who used eccentric wefts. And even within Anatolian kilims that are primarily orthogonal in character small areas of eccentric wefting can be found. However, Anatolian weavers as a whole have shown a deep and lasting cultural preference for the orthogonal character of weaving.

Whatever their reasons for largely ignoring the possibilities of eccentric wefting, Anatolian weavers have consistently demonstrated that when limitations are approached inventively they can spur the imagination not only to make the best of them but to triumph over them. Anatolian weavers, many hundreds of years before Abstract Expressionist painters, were intensively exploring the design possibilities of a flattened plane or space and demonstrating the visual boldness of strong, simple geometric shapes and the drama of juxtaposing hard-edged, highly differentiated colored forms.

It was not simply the limitations of the tapestry-weave technique that restricted Anatolian weavers to designs of a stylized, geometric, non-representational character. Even with the other, more flexible weaving techniques available to them such as the knotted-pile technique, Anatolian weavers in their traditional design still tended to avoid the curvilinear and the representational.

The common misperception is that the knotted-pile technique is a different and quite separate weaving tradition. However, like the flatweaving techniques thus far examined, it is just one more variation on the warp, weft, extra-weft combinations that underlie all weaving. The basic warp/weft combination in this technique is supplemented with what is more accurately described as weft pile-wrapping, not knotting. Pieces of yarn are wrapped around a pair of warps, also encircling one of the wefts, and locked into place as the wefts are compacted. The cut ends of the extra wefts stand upright to create (as pile) the designed sur-

face of the weaving. Though an accepted term (and the one, therefore, used here), the "knotted technique" is a misnomer, since while wrapping and intertwining of the warps and wefts take place there is no complete knot involved. In the Near East there are two common ways of "knotting," the asymmetrical knot (o) (also called the Persian or Senneh Knot) and the symmetrical (Turkish or Giordes Knot) (p). The use of these two different knots has tended to be a regionally determined factor. Anatolia inclines to the symmetrical and Persian weaving areas to the asymmetrical. The asymmetrical knot is more suited to fine, detailed work of a curvilinear character, while the symmetrical knot is reputed to produce a more durable fabric.

The knotted-pile weaving technique is one in which the structural and design elements are in a sense separate, allowing increased flexibility in the kinds of designs that can be created. The possibilities for true curvilinear design are greater, particularly if very small knots are used, than in the eccentric wefting of tapestry weaves, which cannot quite achieve the same gracefulness. Since in the knotted technique each weft wrap can be a different color almost complete freedom is allowed in the distribution of color, and no structural considerations need be taken into account. In a sense the weaver is working out a design in a pointillist technique. The creation of motifs and designs through these myriad color dots allows for a more illusionistic rendering and far more subtle blendings of color and form. There is a tendency toward the feathering of colors rather than the abrupt juxtaposing of solid blocks of color, and toward more complicated curvilinear designs.

The design possibilities inherent in the knotted-pile weaving tradition have been thoroughly exploited in works inspired by the court and commercial traditions. While rural Anatolian carpet weavers have been strongly influenced by these traditions since the sixteenth century, tribal and village rugs have nevertheless perpetuated down to the present an indigenous tradition that has tended toward the angular and the geometric rather than the curvilinear and the floral.

For Westerners the greatest obstacle to appreciating kilims is the preconception formed as the result of our almost exclusive experience with knotted pile rugs and carpets. Our tendency is to see flatweaving as a minority tradition within a larger and older tradition dominated by the pile carpet and rug. In fact, chronologically the knotted pile weaving technique is considered to be a later development and was never the dominant technique in the Near East. Throughout the more than five-thousand-year history of woven textiles in the Near East, in both urban and rural traditions, it has been the flatweaving tradition that has predominated.[5] The West's ethnocentric obsession with the pile rug or carpet is largely a factor of the tendency to regard weavings as floor coverings. Another factor is an accident of history, Europe having been since Medieval times the recipient primarily of knotted pile rather than flatwoven textiles. The theory that the West has favored, particularly since the late nineteenth century, Near Eastern knotted pile because its durability as a floor covering made it more suitable for household uses has some plausibility; however, the huge production of Aubussons and needlepoints—flatweavings in the Western tradition—suggests that this may not be the complete answer.

A more likely explanation is that since kilims were such an integral part of tribal culture they did not ordinarily end up on the commercial market and therefore did not find their way in any numbers to the West. It is only in the last twenty-five years or so, at the time when traditional Anatolian culture has virtually disintegrated, that the weavings have been given up for commercial sale and become known in the West.

The kilims that have survived are chiefly from the last hundred years or so. The dearth of historical information on the Anatolian kilim combined with the fact that the only extant examples are of a relatively recent date have led to much speculation on how old the Anatolian kilim tradition is. Presently, older extant pieces are being subjected to intense scrutiny in an attempt to establish a timeline for them.

Until recently the conventional methodology in dating kilims has largely relied on the following: educated guesses by experts; the presence of an early synthetic dye, indigosulphuric acid, which came into use in 1780; the use of certain aniline dyes introduced after the middle of the nineteenth century; the occasional kilim with interwoven dates (largely from the nineteenth century); and the depiction of kilims in a few late nineteenth- and early twentieth-century Orientalist paintings by artists such as Cezanne and Matisse.

Generally it is understood that carbon-14 tests are too imprecise for dating artifacts made after A.D. 1200, and prove to be practically worthless for items made after A.D. 1650. Thus, Anatolian kilims, which largely survive from the nineteenth century, with a tiny minority possibly from the two centuries before, have been outside the ken of this scientific approach. Recently, advances made in carbon-14 dating methodologies may have made this scientific approach a more useful tool in determining when the oldest surviving kilims were produced.[6] This new approach is the AMS (Accelerator Mass Spectrometry) method, an improved carbon-14 dating method for detecting very low concentrations of carbon-14 in organic materials.

The AMS method was first applied, as an experiment, to a group of Anatolian kilims gathered for an exhibition and symposium in 1997. Fifty kilims, believed by their owners to have been woven before the 1800s, were subjected to AMS carbon-dating tests. The experiment produced interesting, but still not uncontroversial, results.[7] While fairly consistent and relatively convincing results were achieved in this 1997 test with the six flatweavings that appear to have been produced between the fifteenth and sixteenth centuries, the tests of the remaining kilims nearer to us in time seem much more unpredictable in giving "single value results" in age ranges. Indeed in some cases, two, three, or even four, different age ranges resulted.[8]

It would appear that for the period from which most kilims survive—the nineteenth century and the few centuries before—the age range achieved by carbon dating is still too wide. In order to increase usefulness the precision in using carbon-14 still needs to be considerably enhanced. A careful reading of the individual dating results of the fifty kilims demonstrates that with the exception of the handful of oldest kilims the process in its present form is, unfortunately, not very helpful.[9]

Thus, we still lack a methodology for accurately dating most of the surviving kilims. And while it is certain that the kilim has a very ancient history in Anatolia, establishing exactly how old the tradition is with the fragmentary evidence we have is impossible.

Chapter 5

The Visual Language of the Anatolian Kilim

No kilim weaving region in the world comes close to rivaling Anatolia in the remarkable diversity of its design tradition. While it once seemed that the many tribal, ethnic, and regional weaving groups of Anatolia speak a veritable Babel of visual languages, it is becoming more and more apparent that beneath all the many regional and tribal dialects is a common tongue. If a representative group of Anatolian kilims is compared with a group from another weaving region, such as the Persian, Caucasian, or Balkan, the very distinctive character of Anatolian visual expression is readily apparent. While the recognition that such a visual language is at work in kilim design has rapidly gained credence in recent years, we are still only at the beginning in deciphering how such a language is structured and how it functions. A definitive understanding of this language remains a distant and possibly unattainable goal.

As we have seen in the previous chapters, the visual language of the Anatolian kilim has been significantly shaped by a combination of the orthogonal character of weaving together with the structural imperatives of the slit-weave tapestry technique. Since Anatolian weavers chose to accept these limitations—rather than circumvent them by exploring alternative techniques such as eccentric wefting—these structural imperatives have profoundly shaped the character of the kilim. Consequently, the Anatolian kilim is characteristically rectilinear rather than curvilinear, abstract rather than representational, and predominantly geometric in character.

Beneath the welter of hexagons, ram's horns, rhomboids, squares, triangles, rectangles, and sigmas, a kind of visual grammar seems to operate with recognizable rules that shape the kilim lexicon. For instance, the Anatolian slit-weave tapestry technique

has established a rectilinear character that virtually precludes circular, oval, or arabesque forms. Even in its natural métier of rectilinear forms, the slit-weave tapestry technique—as we have established in the previous chapter—favors those forms with a predominance of diagonal lines and an absence of lateral sides. The predominance of such motifs (in particular, the triangle and hexagon) together with the prevalence of denticulation establishes a distinctive form of kilim expression—an overall visual style. As in any language, it is possible to trace large segments of the vocabulary back to a common root. The triangle, as we have seen, is one such major root. In its many different combinations it is the basic building block of so many kilim motifs: the reciprocating triangle, the rhomboid, the hexagon, and various kinds of stars, to name a few.

However, more than technical imperatives have pushed the kilim lexicon in the direction of the abstract. Even that part of the visual lexicon not controlled or influenced by these imperatives also tends to be abstract and nonrepresentational in character. Undoubtedly, there is a predisposition in the Anatolian tribal culture against including a representational vocabulary in its design lexicon. In contrast, the weaving populations in neighboring Azerbaijan characteristically embellish their weavings with pictorial motifs of humans, animals, birds, and strange beasts. The Anatolian bias against such representation seems to be an age-old, indigenous one. Long before the Türkmen introduced Islam, with its rigid strictures against the depiction of human and animal forms, Anatolia in Byzantine times was torn by violent upheavals, caused by iconoclastic reactions against representation in religious artifacts. Thus, while Anatolia has a long history of creating images, stretching back beyond Neolithic times, it has also for at least the past few thousand years been a region that has had a deep and enduring bias against the realistic depiction of those images. Out of such an opposition has emerged a very powerful abstract form of visual expression.

While the tendency towards abstraction and geometry has possibly been more extreme in Anatolian tribal culture, it is certainly not unique to this region. Surrounded by a natural world in which order and regularity are rare exceptions, cultures the world over have always derived great pleasure in exercising a sense of order by making and contemplating simple configurations regardless of their reference to the natural world. As a rule this man-made world of design is composed of simple geometric forms. Since such forms are rare in nature, one wonders why they should occur so frequently in man-made order.[1] Because we now take pure geometric forms for granted, it is all too easy for us to forget what alien constructions triangles, hexagons, rhomboids, and squares must have been to eyes accustomed only to a world of natural, chiefly irregular forms. It is even, for instance, difficult for us to realize how strange and abstract the straight line actually is. Undoubtedly, it is precisely because geometric forms are so rare in nature that the human mind has chosen to include these manifestations of regularity in its constructs.[2] In creating kilim designs of ordered geometric forms the Anatolian weavers are responding to the chaos of the natural world in the same way that other weaving cultures have done all over the world. The Anatolian eye only differs from that of its neighbors in systematically eschewing most of (but not all) the geometric forms found in flowers, leaves, insects, and crystals of the natural world and focusing almost exclusively on invented forms.

Despite these considerable constraints, a few borrowed, vaguely representational forms did find their way into the Anatolian lexicon. They are conspicuous when they do appear and often suggest, as we shall explore at a later point in this discussion, a foreign, imported vocabulary. Even these uncharacteristic borrowings seem to succumb over time to the geometry of the tribal language and pass through stages of increasing stylization until they, too, vanish into the realm of abstraction. Certainly one of the likeliest ways of misinterpreting the language of the Anatolian kilim is to focus too heavily, as much recent scholarship has, on the few elements that seem to be representational. As members of a culture in which art has been, at least until this century, predominantly representational, Westerners tend to seek out recognizable forms almost in spite of themselves. Thus among all the abstract geometry of the kilims, any image, no matter how minor or atypical, suggesting a human, animal, or bird form, tends to call forth an inordinate amount of interest, seeming as it does to give a glimpse into an otherwise closed world. However, being distracted by such minor images and failing to deal with the lexicon as a whole can only lead to interpretations that are hopelessly distorted if not irrelevant.

Symmetries

Another valuable method for identifying and defining the Anatolian visual language, an approach still very much in its infancy, is to focus on the characteristic symmetries common to both its motifs and overall design.[3] It is becoming more and more apparent that at the root of Anatolian kilim design is an identifiable vocabulary of certain kinds of symmetries. Symmetry, it is now generally recognized, is not simply a characteristic of certain kinds of design but is a basic cognitive tool that the human mind uses for processing information.[4] While all cultures seem to depend in this way on symmetries, each particular cultural group chooses from a wide range of possible symmetries a small number which then underlie its particular way of processing and remembering information and through which it expresses its design. These symmetries are unconsciously absorbed as each culture inculcates its members with specific preferences.[5] For instance, American school children, it has been established, prefer double mirror symmetries at age six, shift to bilateral symmetries at age seven, and then favor horizontal symmetries at age eleven.[6] Unfortunately we have no such evidence for Anatolia. However, it is apparent that young Anatolian girls working at the loom, ostensibly to memorize and learn to weave the traditional motifs and designs of the tribe, are also unconsciously absorbing much deeper and more basic lessons—the preferred symmetries of the tribal group. Thus it appears that the conservative loyalties of tribal weavers to their design tradition are much deeper and more complicated than was once assumed.

Anatolian weavers descend from a tribal culture that apparently settled far back in its past on mirror symmetry as its preferred mode of constructing motifs and designs. In their kilims asymmetrical motifs are employed infrequently, and as a result stand out conspicuously in the design when they are used, and are believed to be foreign borrowings. Mirror symmetry is characterized by motifs that contain a mirror reflection of the size, shape, and relative position of parts that are on opposite sides of an invisible dividing line or axis. The human form, to take an obvious example, is, when arranged frontally and at rest, an image with a bilateral mirror symmetry. On the other hand, the reflection of a château in its ornamental pool lends itself to a form of horizontal mirror symmetry. These two mirror symmetries are present in the form of the square, which combines bilateral and horizontal symmetry. The geometric forms typical of kilim design to a large degree contain these mirror symmetries. The equilateral triangle has, of course, bilateral symmetry but in its reciprocating ⋈ or rhomboid ◇ forms it becomes simultaneously bilaterally and horizontally symmetrical.

While examples of rotational symmetry in kilim imagery are also plentiful, they are likely to be mirror symmetries as well. For example, the cross, which exhibits both mirror and rotational symmetry, is a more characteristic Anatolian motif than the swastika, which has only rotational symmetry. Also there are less obvious kinds of symmetries that are not mirror symmetries (in popular usage a plane figure is considered symmetrical only if it admits reflection). These non-reflecting types are translation (h) and glide (i) symmetries and are more likely to be found in kilim border and banded designs.[7]

While the Anatolian lexicon consists predominantly of bilateral, horizontal, and bilateral/horizontal symmetries, the weavers' preference seems to be strongly for the double form, which predominates in most kilim design. For example, those images that appear to have originally entered the Anatolian kilim lexicon as bilateral symmetries, as for example the elibelinde (an anthropomorphic, usually female, form with the arm position of hands on hips) and the niche, seem in many cases to have passed through an evolutionary process leading to the favored double symmetry. The first stage in this evolution appears to be the repetition of the bilateral motif in a water reflection type of arrangement in which the mirrored images are still separate (j, l). This is followed by what seems to be a later stage in which the two bilateral mirror images fuse into one, creating the double symmetry (k, m°). This preference for double symmetry seems so strong that even in instances where such combinations are illogical, as in fusing two human forms to each other upside down (either head-to-head or sharing the same head or feet-to-feet), it still triumphs.

While in some instances the cultural predilection for certain symmetries does manage to adapt the human form to the kilim lexicon, its more characteristic effect is to exclude the human form, particularly in its naturalistic poses. For instance, unless the human form is posed in a rigid, frontal position—arms at rest or hands on hips, or arms extended out, up, or forward—it does not lend itself to the required bilateral symmetry. In fact, the human form in profile or in realistic poses or motions does not conform to any of the preferred mirror symmetries. Such constraints would presumably also operate on the representation of any bird, animal, insect, or plant form. Thus even in the rare instances when Anatolian visual expression verges on the realistic—and imitates human, animal, or vegetative forms, the imperatives of the favored symmetries translate these into stylized abstractions.

The preference for mirror symmetries, in particular double symmetries, not only shapes the individual motifs of the kilim lexicon but also acts as a kind of grammar ordering the overall layout of the design. The mirror image quality of many kilim designs is highlighted by the two panel weaving format. In such a format, the two halves of the kilim have been woven as mirror images of each other and are then sewn together to form the whole (plates 14, 15, 20, 21, 25). Often the major motifs centered in the design are themselves divided in this format, further highlighting the mirror imaging (plates 18, 19, 39, 42, 45). The major exception to this general pattern of overall double symmetry is the prayer kilim (plates 58–73), together with its multiple form, the saf (plates 56, 57), which is uncharacteristically bilaterally symmetrical (r, s). Perhaps the functional requirements that made the kilim conform to the proportions of the human body at prayer and include a directional motif in its design have prevented what appears to be a cultural preference for overall double symmetry. Or perhaps the association of the prayer kilim with the sacred world dictates that it violate the norms of everyday design and thereby partake of the power of other worlds. Significantly, when the niche is used in kilims that have no obvious sacred function the impulse for double symmetry does seem to triumph (t, u). There is decidedly a formal compulsion at work in Anatolian kilims which is powered by favored mirror symmetries and which is not evident in other flatweaving traditions such as those of North Africa—in Tunisian kilims, for instance.

These Anatolian preferences for mirror symme-

a.
b.
c.
d.
e.
f.
g.
h.
i.
j.
l.
k.
m.
n.
o.

41

p.

q.

r.

s.

t.

u.

v.

w.

tries are not, however, the entire message. A type of subtext also seems to be at work. A closer examination of a seemingly symmetrical kilim or motif or design usually reveals that within the apparent symmetries there are a host of asymmetries created by random insertions, idiosyncratic variations, and color changes. While these variations seem to work against the established symmetries, they actually create an interesting tension between the culturally established lexicon and grammar and what might be described as an improvised subtext created by the weavers themselves. What is suggested is a dialectic between authority and freedom. This dialogue between the rigidly defined statements of the cultural tradition and the idiosyncratic voices of the individual weavers certainly provides a primary appeal of the Anatolian kilim. The most obvious example of this subtext is the cluster of filler motifs scattered in the negative spaces surrounding the major motifs. The kilim pictured in plate 19 is an excellent example of this dialectic. More subtle examples are the tiny variations and color changes within a single seemingly symmetrical motif. It is, perhaps, the point at which the individual subtext begins to overwhelm and obscure the symmetries of the main text that we may say that decadence in kilim design begins. The clutter and incoherence of so many modern Anatolian kilims, particularly those woven since World War I, is a prime example of such decadence. The disintegration of tribal culture during this period has seemingly reduced the potency of the main text allowing the subtexts of the individual weavers to overwhelm it.

It is the redundant property of mirror symmetries that make them so useful in aiding a culture in recalling and reproducing its patterns. The composition of a given symmetry facilitates memorization and reproduction in that only one fraction of the total image contains the information necessary for the completion of the rest. The remainder of the symmetry is, in that sense, redundant.[8] In bilateral mirror symmetry, for instance, half the motif contains the information for the other half, while in bilateral/horizontal symmetry one fourth of the motif encodes the information to complete the whole. Once the Anatolian weaver has committed to memory the design and the mechanics for the weaving of a fourth of a hexagon, she is able to repeat the rest by imitation. Thus, while the Anatolian design lexicon might at first glance seem elaborate and complex, it takes on a greater simplicity once its redundant properties are made apparent.

Expanding the Kilim Lexicon

The visual lexicon of the kilim is expanded through a process of elaboration or simplification by presenting the same motifs in different sizes, and by presenting the geometric forms in varying degrees of distortion and regularity.

One form of elaboration and simplification in kilim motifs begins with a common root upon which all of the variations are worked. Adding to or subtracting from this root can create a large vocabulary. The shared major element makes the vocabulary easy to recall and reconstruct. It is difficult in retrospect, lacking as we do an historical chronology of kilim design, to say in which direction the process originally flowed—from simple to complex or the reverse or back and forth. But to turn to an example, there is a motif in plate 19 that through a series of variations passes into the following forms: ⊷ to ⊷ to ⊷ to ⊷ or ⊷ to ⊷ . The process also seems capable of being reversed to ⊷ or to ⊷ or even to ⌂ . All of this "word-play" goes on among and upon the double symmetries of the dominant motifs, the main text of the piece.

This "word-play," a kind of improvisation that forms a subtext, seems to be the expression of the individual voice of the weaver who while apparently accepting and duplicating the culturally determined main text supplies her own personal levels of meaning. It is these variations that in part prevent the expression of the main text from degenerating into lifeless repetition. The liveliness of this subtext is indicative of a vital weaving tradition since it gives evidence of a mind still actively engaged in invention. The degree to which the subtext elaborates on and plays off the main text—but does not overwhelm or obscure it—suggests that the weaver still understands what is primary in the message and what is subordinate. Once that understanding is lost, as we have already seen with symmetries, decadence sets in because the message of the main text becomes garbled and confused.

In another process, one of elaboration, hexagonally shaped medallions take on an amazing variety of complicated forms. In this process the genesis of the motif is as a simple, basic motif; this motif then passes through intervening compositions, and is finally circumscribed by the outlines of a hexagonal frame.[9] Generally, three major stages can be seen; however, stages may be skipped or occur in different orders.

One such hexagonal motif seems to begin with a vertical line with arrowhead shapes at top and bottom (x). This simple form is then set within a hooked diamond- or lantern-shaped form composed of six triangles extending horizontally to balance the verticality of the internal motif. When that form is boxed inside a hexagon, the intervening composition is established. Then the hexagonal form is boxed inside a larger hexagon enclosing a ring of minor motifs, which hook outward.[10]

Once this elaborate motif has evolved, its vocabulary can further expand through the many decorative variations that can be worked out within its silhouette; for example, the repetition of different colored hexagons within each other (y), or through embellishments added to the silhouette in the form of ram's horns or hooks (z). Or a kind of compound vocabulary can be erected through stacking the hexagons into column-like structures (aa–cc).

Another example of typical kilim design elaboration is a rhomboid medallion. This motif seems to have evolved from a simple cruciform motif (dd), which is then inscribed in a diamond decorated with hooks along its outside edges, which is then placed inside another diamond, and then another, all similarly hooked and repeating and radiating outwards (see plate 34).[11]

The kilim vocabulary can also expand by variations in the size and regularity of the same basic motif within a kilim design. Using the characteristic Anatolian economy of means, the weaver renders a hexagonal motif as a dominant motif and also repeats it in miniature with intermediate renditions in between. Likewise, the weaver depicts the hexagon in its regular form but then, within the same kilim, may also present it in a distorted or irregular (and hence asymmetrical) form. Through repetitions of the same motifs in different sizes and degrees of regularity within the same design, as opposed to forming a design composed of a repertoire of very different motifs, the weaver achieves a highly unified effect.

Thus, with an economy of means but endless inventiveness, the Anatolian weaver has apparently explored almost every conceivable avenue of geometric expression over the centuries thereby creating a rich lexicon of visual effects.

Reciprocality

Another kind of subtext, this one producing a poetic kind of ambiguity, seeming as it does to question the viewer's perception of reality, is a design form called reciprocality. Ordinarily a motif is seen in the context of its background, that is, the standard figure/ground relationship. The Anatolian weaver's view of such a relationship is typically more complex, the tendency being to obliterate the distinction between figure and ground, creating a design field with motifs of equal or fluctuating weight, in which what is dominant (figure) and what is recessive (ground) remains unresolved (ee–ii). For example, this motif ✕ if left on a plain ground has the standard figure/ground relationship, but if several of these motifs are juxtaposed ✕✕✕, then what would be ordinarily the ground appearing between the two becomes another motif ⬙, a reciprocal one (ee). Which of the two images is dominant and which recessive is dependent on adjustments in the viewer's perception. Such figure/ground illusions occur when what would seem to be spaces between motifs actually become complementary motifs. (See plates 19, 24, 30, 39, and 53 for kilims that use this form of reciprocality heavily.) There are a number of other categories of reciprocality. In kilims woven by the Yüncü Yörük weavers, for example (plates 2, 4, 5, 6, 7, and 8), an overall reciprocality (jj) plays a major role in the visual language, since the design as a whole can be given totally different readings because of the equal value given to what would ordinarily be described as figure and ground. This form of reciprocal design undoubtedly descends from the felting tradition (See Kirghiz felt, p. 84). Yet another kind of reciprocality commonly found at the color junction between field and border depends upon a constantly shifting visual balance (kk).

The ambiguities engendered by these different forms of reciprocality create an interesting dynamic. It is the unresolved nature of this unending dialectic that in part explains the power of kilim imagery continually to delight and intrigue. The dynamics of this unresolvable conflict prevent the viewer from ever arriving at a definitive concept of the kilim. Once there is a breakdown in the reciprocality—as often occurs in contempo-

x.

y.

z.

aa.

bb.

cc.

dd.

ee.

ff.

gg.

hh.

ii.

jj.

kk.

rary kilims—this dynamic is lost and the intricate patterns collapse into a confused muddle. A high degree of understanding and superior weaving skills are necessary to maintain the tricky balance required in effecting reciprocal designs.

As with so much of the visual vocabulary of the kilim, the very nature of reciprocality facilitates the memorization and execution of what seem to be very complex designs. For instance, if the weaver has learned a ⋋ and then copies another and juxtaposes it ⋊⋋⋊, then she simultaneously produces ⬦. The advantage to the weaver is that the information for the whole series of variations is encoded in a small fraction of the whole.

Structural Principles

ll.

We now turn from the lexicon to the larger grammar, that is, the layout or structural principle[12] of the kilim design. The underlying structure of the vast majority of kilims seems to have descended from the most ancient design tradition of all, the stripe (ll). Believed historically to be the weaver's first solution to polychrome design, the simple striped design dates back to the beginnings of weaving. What may be the first recorded evidence of it in the Near East dates from the fourth millennium B.C.[13]

mm.

While the necessary body of weavings does not survive to document the evolution of kilim design, it seems self-evident that over time striping became increasingly complex as bands of different widths were combined into patterns (mm). Eventually small motifs were introduced into those bands, and at some point bands were widened to include even larger and more complicated sets of motifs (nn). Thus bands evolved to provide the formal structure so characteristic of many Anatolian kilim designs. Even after bands ceased to appear in certain designs, the principle of order encoded by the ancient banded format continued to serve as an invisible superstructure, creating the orderly rows of patterns so typical of Anatolian kilim design (oo) (plates 14–25). Thus, the overall layout of a variety of Anatolian kilims is ordered not only by the preference for double symmetry but also by a banded format descended from the primitive stripe.

nn.

A second major format for overall design, totally different in concept, is one in which the entire surface of the kilim is treated as a single undivided unit or canvas which is usually framed

oo.

pp.

qq.

by a border (pp). The most obvious example is the large white background kilim typical of the Aydınlı tribes, and the Türkmen tribes of the Konya region in central Anatolia (see plates 39 to 46). In these designs a centered row of hexagonal medallions embellished with ram's horns is framed by an elaborate border with banded skirts at each end. This distinctive configuration is commonly believed to be a late development and its origins, which have not been satisfactorily explained to date, may, as we shall see in chapter 9, descend from Türkmen influences.

While these two major principles of organization together with the preference for double mirror symmetry do not explain all of the structural principles of Anatolian kilims,[14] they certainly account for the vast majority and demonstrate that far from being random in nature the visual language of the kilim is based on a highly ordered grammatical system.

Foreign Borrowings

It would be difficult to discover a language that has not borrowed from other languages—and so it is with the kilim. Given the highly defined, distinctive character of Anatolian kilim design, it is easy to single out those parts of the lexicon that are not native to it. One significant borrowing of vocabulary took place after the sixteenth century, when decorative motifs from Ottoman art, with its distinctive court design tradition, began to find their way into tribal weaving. Ottoman art, though highly stylized, is a more representational art, which, with its subject matter of flowers, leaves, tendrils, and palmettes, speaks a very different visual language. These pretty Ottoman curvilinear motifs (qq) are decidedly not at home among the more austere abstract shapes, geometrics, and symmetries of tribal art. Significantly, the refined court lexicon seems to have made its greatest inroads into a group of prayer designs generally regarded as a late development in kilim design and one that probably originally had commercial origins. However, once this foreign vocabulary was introduced, it apparently began to metamorphose into the established character of Anatolian style (rr). Had the Anatolian weavers adopted the technique of eccentric wefting, the assimilation of Ottoman motifs into the kilim tradition could have been effected in such a way as to preserve their original character. However, Anatolia's predisposition for the four-square character of weaving and slit-weave tapestry, its apparent bias against representation, and its preferences for mirror symmetries has metamorphosed the Ottoman motifs into an Anatolian idiom (rr–tt). It is a tribute to the strength and vitality of the tribal weaving tradition that when it did absorb these alien motifs from its ruling class it did so only on its own stylistic terms. The visual language of the tribe, while it was not immune to outright borrowings, was like any living language able to make the foreign borrowings its own. In contrast, in this century the tribal kilim is under repeated attack from so many different directions that it seems transformed by its borrowings instead of transforming them.

Thus, we are beginning to understand, at least in its rough outlines, the way in which the visual language of Anatolia is organized. However, a cautionary note is certainly in order. We should not assume that we always perceive kilims in the way the weavers originally did. In important respects, the eye of the West and the tribal eye could conceivably register the same reality in very different ways. Obviously, Westerners see kilims as unique folk artefacts through eyes that have been trained in the methodologies of art appreciation suitable to enjoying Western painting.

The eye of the West has been formed by a wide exposure to numerous national and ethnic traditions while the tribal weaver, until recent times, had little experience with any visual expression outside her own. It could very well be that since the tribal weaver only experienced a small repertoire of designs that she characteristically saw each kilim by way of the minor variations that distinguished it from all others. For the tribal eye, therefore, the kilim as a whole could function as the given, while only the variations and idiosyncrasies in the design may receive conscious attention and serve as a focal point for experiencing the kilim.[15] Further, something as simple as the fact that we have grown up with the printed page and are thus culturally predisposed to seeing white as background and dark colors as foreground could also seriously skew our reading of a kilim. Indeed, an incident recorded by a nineteenth-century English traveler in Turkmenistan suggests that at that time the visual bias of the Türkmen was 180 degrees out of sync with that of Europeans.[16] Apparently, when the Türkmen were given a copy of the *Illustrated London News*, they puzzled over a

linograph depicting a British general being crowned by young women with garlands of mistletoe. Finally, they were heard to cry: "Baluk! Baluk!"—the word for fish. The only form the tribesmen could make out in the picture, presumably because they were reversing positive and negative, was a form they recognized as a fish. Are we similarly misreading Anatolian kilims? While we have no proof that the Anatolian eye similarly reversed positive and negative, we can conclude the awareness of such different ways of seeing should temper our interpretation of kilims.

This aside, the recognition that Anatolian weavers have created a common visual language with an identifiable vocabulary, structure, and character promises to be a valuable approach to the study of the kilim. In attempting to decipher the way in which the language of the kilim works, we may eventually begin to discover what kilims actually mean—that is, exactly what the Anatolian weaver expressed through the kilim and how her culture experienced and interpreted it. Apparently, an examination of the kilim artefact in isolation can take us only so far, revealing how the language works but not what it says or does. If the key to the meaning of the language is to be found, we must first reconstruct the eye and the mentality of the weaver and place the kilim in the context of the Anatolian culture that created it.

rr.

ss.

tt.

Chapter 6

The Tribal Weaver

While magnificent kilims survive from Anatolia's great weaving past, there are, as is true of folk weavings the world over, no weavers' names to attach to them. Always anonymous, despite their considerable accomplishments, the tribal weavers of the past remain a mystery, for they and their people, the nomadic and settled pastoralists of Anatolia, until recent times have lived outside of recorded history. Their old way of life has almost entirely passed away, in some cases so completely that we are left only to conjecture how and why certain things were done. In particular, nomadic life has nearly vanished in Anatolia, and the tiny clans that still survive are only pale shadows of the flourishing tribal cultures that once existed. The settled pastoral villagers—many of whose ancestors were nomads in the not-too-distant past—are rapidly losing the old tribal identities under the irresistible onslaught of the modern world.

The small pockets of nomadic and settled survivors who still maintain the old ways seem to have one thing in common: While they cling to many of the outward forms, they regrettably seem to have forgotten the inner content. Even those who stubbornly continue to resist the pressures for settlement and assimilation into the emerging Turkish nation recognize that the end of their way of being is only a matter of time. As an aged Sarakeçeli tribesman once eloquently put it: "the ever-narrowing paths of daily struggle to survive have left us with no choice. Like the Arabs, we are left with no pastures, no autumnal home." Using the ancient expression, "autumnal home," he refers longingly to a place of rest, of contemplation, and of peaceful death.[1]

Fieldworkers in kilim studies who have interviewed individual Anatolian weavers inevitably re-

port that the weavers can tell little about the meanings and the original purposes of the kilims they continue to weave, often in debased and misunderstood forms. And even they see the end in sight as the younger girls of the tribe refuse to learn to weave, insisting that "the fashion has changed." The general feeling in kilim scholarship is that unfortunately we have waited too long; the way of life we are belatedly attempting to reconstruct has already evaporated, leaving little record of itself. Ironically, it is the weavings themselves that are the enduring record, but without a knowledge of the world out of which they have come we find them virtually indecipherable.

This being said, the effort to understand the Anatolian tribal weaver goes on and, despite the dearth of evidence, some faint outlines do emerge which give us some valuable insights, particularly when comparisons are made with the artist-weaver tradition in the West.

Invariably Western artist-weavers, when confronted with the great Anatolian kilims of the past, are awed and baffled by the high artistic and technical levels reached by these tribal mothers, daughters, and wives who throughout their lives never left the confines of their tribal world. Artist-weavers in the West who have passed through training programs and spent years as professional weavers find it astonishing that "amateur," part-time weavers, fitting this activity in among a host of other demanding domestic and animal husbandry responsibilities, including even the processing of their own weaving materials, reached levels of performance to which professional weavers in the West can only aspire. How, it is asked, could an illiterate, seemingly untrained tribal weaver who lacked even a consciousness of art or craft as we

47

Villagers communally engaged in weaving tasks. In the foreground one woman weaves a band on a card loom; in the rear women are spinning or twining. To the left a woman weaves a storage sack on a ground loom, Elazığ Province, 1980.

would understand them achieve what she did?

Certainly one reason for the artistic achievements of the Anatolian weaver was the particular conditions of tribal life. In this world, weaving was an activity that was carried on around the children as a normal part of domestic routine. When the loom was set up it was always in close proximity to, if not inside, the tent or cottage. Further, before the days of formal schooling children shared in most adult activities, weaving being one domestic pastime among others. In a culture in which children expected to learn everything from the family, a young girl was drawn into weaving at her mother's side from her earliest years. In fact, giving tiny toy looms and colored yarns to a little girl is still not uncommon in weaving households. The dividing line between playing at weaving and actually weaving in such a situation would be an ambiguous one, since once the child achieves the necessary manual dexterity, often by the age of four, she is ready to join the older women at the loom.[2] It would seem that learning to weave in childhood, as in learning a musical instrument or ballet, gives a head start that no amount of hard work in adulthood can surpass.

The climate for learning a traditional craft in a tribal household has always been in many respects ideal, since from a Western point of view, societal roles and activities were and still are in many places in Anatolia rigidly predetermined. In this culture the collective good, not individual freedom, is of primary value. In marked contrast to the individualism of the West, the desire has always been to be like everyone else, to have no differences, to be a part of the whole.[3] For a young girl, learning to weave has been regarded as part of the process of entering into the collective

life of the tribe and the motifs and designs she learns to weave are part of the process also. The important role of the kilim in the dowry, and thus in the marriage, was also a powerful motivation in the learning process. Tribal weaving in Anatolia has traditionally been more of a social duty[4] than an economic necessity and therefore has always been anticipated with pleasure.

Perhaps one of the most powerfully conservative factors, and one that differentiates the Anatolian weaver most from the artist-weavers of the Western tradition, is the manner in which tribal weavers have always learned to weave. Rather than going through a series of preliminary stages to learn technique, the tribal weaver simultaneously learns the motif and the technique, the two become inseparable in her mind. In contrast, novice Western weavers move systematically through a series of weaving exercises, beginning with simple techniques before moving to the more complex. When the necessary level of expertise is reached, the artist-weavers have the skills to produce designs as they choose. Just as in the folk music tradition the singer learns through imitation both the song and the mode of singing it, so the Anatolian weaver learned the motifs of her tribe together with the weaving technique required to execute it.[5] Instead of mastering a variety of techniques and developing a mentality intent on exploring all of the possibilities in weaving, the Anatolian weaver has always learned a small body of sanctioned designs and techniques (more accurately a design/technique) which she will rework together with other weavers of her family for the rest of her life.

Weaving is only an intermittent activity for Anatolian weavers. In some tribal groups it may take place during little more than four or five weeks in the summer campgrounds, which means that the Anatolian weaver does not have the leisure to sit at the loom exploring its possibilities. The notion of introducing new designs, therefore, probably would not even occur to the weaver. Such a self-enclosed world of perpetuated design was even more common in the past, since weavers then very likely only saw their own clan's weaving, all sharing in the same images, palettes, and designs. Not until the introduction of commercial mass-produced textiles for clothing in the second half of the nineteenth century would tribal weavers have seen design traditions outside their own.

Even today, in the declining days of the tradition, the few areas that have preserved tribal ways and continue to weave reveal a kind of immunity to outside design. The attitudes expressed by these small pockets of population suggest what it must have been like in the distant past. For instance, in central Anatolia the *yerli,* villagers who consider themselves part of the indigenous population of Anatolia and different from the neighboring Türkmen and Yörük tribes, will not buy kilims from other nearby tribes because "they do not weave our kilims and in our village we like to be like each other without any differences between us." Similarly, in the Tekke Province of southwest Anatolia, the response to the same question was that they had no desire to own kilims different from those of their tribe.[6]

Some Anatolians go further, revealing that not only do they not want such alien kilims but they do not like them largely because they are different from their own.[7] There appear to be only two instances in which tribal weavers in Anatolia normally would have rejected their tradition of weaving for another. First, a woman marrying into another tribe has usually been expected to take on the identity of her husband's family, leaving behind her own weaving tradition. Just as she would have altered her dress, manners, and customs to assimilate into her new group, so she would have had to abandon the weaving tradition of her mother and learn that of her husband's family. In the past, when there were larger tribal groups and confederations, the absorption of a smaller, weaker group into a larger one was apparently accompanied by a wholesale shift on the part of the absorbed weavers to the tradition of the dominant group.[8] Apart from these instances, the idea of an Anatolian weaver rejecting her tradition in favor of another, or substituting an original creation of her own for one of her tribe's has until recently been inconceivable. The degree to which kilims are tied into and help define tribal identity is readily apparent from such attitudes. Tribal weavers, therefore, would hardly see kilims from alien traditions as objects to be imitated, since their visual tastes were usually almost exclusively restricted to those of their own tradition.

While the world of the tribal weaver, restricted as it was to the immediate family group, seems to have been very narrow, it was not as limited as it would first appear. She collaborated not only with the living members of her family but also in very real ways with her ancestors. The relationship of the Anatolian weaver to her family tradition is one very important way that her experience differs from that of the artist-weavers of the West. Like her forebears, when an Anatolian weaver begins to weave she does not, nor could she, nor has she ever wanted to approach the process as a Western artist-weaver would, that is in attempting to create an original work. Artist-weavers in Western culture are expected to begin with a "blank page," to do something original. To duplicate another's work would be considered unoriginal, if not an act of plagiarism.

By Western standards, therefore, the individual Anatolian weaver has never been a creative artist but rather an interpretive artist, a brilliant transmitter and interpreter of the creations of her own cultural group. To choose not to use her people's symbols, images, palettes, and techniques would have amounted to an act of betrayal, an act of incomprehensible individuality that threatened the group identity.[9] Just as she would have accepted the uniform of tribal dress and jewelry, and her roles as daughter, wife, and mother, so she would have accepted the weaving tradition of her family and clan, dedicating the weaving intervals of her life to reworking the handful of traditional motifs and the small repertoire of designs she had received from her ancestors and contemporaries. The oral tradition preserved by the older women, combined with the surviving examples of weavings displayed in the tent or cottage, were the ways by which the traditional techniques and designs were transmitted to her, becoming over time part of her memory. She in turn, at least until recently, has been expected to do likewise with her children.

While not a culture that welcomed individual creativity, the tribal tradition through centuries of refinement and development collectively created designs of great beauty and sophistication. The weavers in such a collective tradition have a far greater chance of reaching exceptional heights, building as they do on the distilled best works of hundreds, if not thousands, of their predecessors. In contrast, Western artist-weavers must in a sense begin each work anew. Thus great creative works are not only the product of individual effort but, as the Medieval cathedrals of Europe also demonstrate, can also be the product of a highly traditional society working collectively over the ages. Malraux has captured this distinction in the opposition he sets up between "art by destination" and "art by metamorphosis," that is, art produced by the individual artist versus art produced by an ethnic tradition, or art as a personal expression versus art as collective expression.[10] True, we might use the terms art versus folk art or art versus decorative art; however, implicit in these very ethnocentric categories is a decided bias against non-Western traditions, relegating ethnic art to a separate and usually lower category.

Having emphasized the very conservative nature of the Anatolian weaving tradition, it is necessary to strike a balance by also pointing out that the Anatolian weaver was certainly not an automaton turning out mechanical imitations of older kilims. Even though individuality in the Western sense was never encouraged in tribal life, there still were inevitable human differences. And even though change came very slowly in such a culture, still it invariably came. Further, the tradition undoubtedly produced a kind of "sense of ownership," since over time the weaver would have assimilated and internalized her tradition to such a degree, the traditional designs becoming so much a part of her, that she would have felt comfortable introducing variations and minor innovations to the traditional design. She apparently could do so as long as she maintained and did not displace the accepted forms. As limiting as this tribal tradition may seem, there would appear to be considerably more freedom in the Anatolian tribal weaver's involvement in the tribal weaving process than there is in today's cottage weaving industry in which weavers sit copying designs elaborately worked out for them on graph paper. In the past, in the court tradition, weavers similarly followed elaborate designs created for them by the court designers. These have always been the only alternatives open to an Anatolian weaver: to be the interpreter of her tradition and thus to embody the roles of designer and weaver, or to serve as the weaver of designs given to her by others.

Interviews with tribal weavers indicate they have traditionally had greater latitude in the introduction and rendering of the small motifs used to fill negative space in the main field, and in the choice of the border motifs. But, these changes could not be made at the cost of displacing the major motifs, which were protected by tradition.[11] However, the slightly differing filters of individual personalities, the differences in levels of expertise, and changes in the conditions of the tribal group itself would inevitably have influenced the character of the designs as well. For instance, on the larger single panel kilims, which are usually created by two weavers working side by side, marked differences appear in the rendering of what should be mirror images because of such variables as the weavers' different sensitivities to color, facility at design, weaving skills, and temperament. Thus tradition, no matter how faithfully adhered to, still takes on individual colorizations and undergoes a continuous slow evolution. People, no matter how much their individuality is monitored, still are not machines, and societies no matter how conservative still undergo constant change.

The tribal weaving tradition differs in other important ways. Memory, rather than invention or creation, seems to play the supreme role.[12] The memorization of a kilim design, as well as the mechanics of how the design is to be executed, is a feat comparable to a conductor's or singer's memorizing an entire musical score. One positive side to an illiterate culture is the heightened capacity for memorization or at least a heightened capacity for memorizing different kinds of things, even on the part of the average mind. The degree to which we in the developed world have lost this ability is easily demonstrated if one looks at a kilim for a period of time and then attempts to draw and color it exactly from memory. This task is further compounded in weaving a copy by having to memorize exactly how to weave each motif: How many lines of given colored yarns run back and forth between how many warps,

and so forth. Even copying an old design with the original kilim as a model, a typical practice in the learning stages, is a virtuoso accomplishment. That using older kilims as models was a common practice is corroborated by fieldwork. When a Yörük woman was asked, as she wove a new kilim based on one she had woven in her youth, why the newer one was so simplified, she replied that the old design "takes too much time."[13] This anecdote demonstrates how as a "modern" conception of the value of time develops, and the importance of the kilim as an artifact diminishes, the tribal memory begins to dim. Whoever in the future uses the simplified kilim as a model has thereby lost part of the memory of the tribe.

It has been argued that the tribal weaver's dependence on memory explains the distinctive visual character of the kilim, whose design tradition appears to rely on the repetition and variation of relatively simple motifs, the dramatic use of color, and the exploration of the visual possibilities of space and proportion. In contrast the court and commercial workshops have always relied on more elaborate, complicated designs. Dependence on memory, it is argued, would necessitate that in order for a cross-section of the population to weave, the design tradition would need to be accessible and within the memorizing capacity of the average weaver. Therefore, it is argued, a weaver learned a fairly large number of small, simple motifs and created designs in a variety of combinations and colors. Small motifs obviously are easier to remember than large, complex ones.[14]

That the character of kilim design can be attributed to the need to keep motifs simple so that they could be retained in even the average mind is, however, called into question by remarkable feats of memorization on the part of Anatolian weavers still practicing today. For instance, in the Kavacık Project, a workshop near Istanbul composed of weavers who have recently migrated from Anatolia, weavers apparently are able to work completely from memory after weaving the same complicated rug three times from designs worked out for them on graph paper.[15] Of course, it could be counter-argued that these are cottage weavers working year-round on the same designs, whereas the tribal weavers tend only to weave in widely spaced intervals and thus have lengthy periods when elaborate details could fade from memory. However, the tribal weavers, as we have seen, began to absorb their motifs, designs, and techniques from their earliest years, and repeated the same same repertoire of designs throughout their lives. Further, there were always older weavers and weavings to turn to for guidance and to jog the memory.

Kilim designs when compared with those of the court or commercial carpet traditions are relatively less complex; however, most kilim designs can hardly be described as simple. Certainly other factors help to explain how the Anatolian weaver could have committed kilim designs to memory or passed them on orally. As we have seen in the discussion of symmetries in chapter five, the kind of redundancy that is a feature of mirror symmetries is one factor that facilitates the memorization of designs. Further, the way in which typical kilim motifs, even those that might appear complex, can be reduced to a single building-block element is another. Through ingenious combinations, which must have evolved over the centuries, simple building-block elements are fitted together to create larger motifs, which in turn are arranged into larger designs. For example, it is the simple triangle that is at the bottom of so much kilim imagery. If we begin with the triangle, not only a basic geometric form but also an age-old symbol filled with universal meaning, and add a second one, a reciprocating triangle turned on its apex ▽ , and pass a line through it ⧖ , we arrive at an extremely common kilim motif, one that has a vague anthropomorphic character. Placing a pair of these reciprocating triangles side by side ⧖⧖ we give birth to ⬡ in the reciprocal space between them. Next, if we take three reciprocating triangle combinations ⧖ ⧖ ⧖ , remove one, separate the triangles, reverse them, and place them centered above and below the remaining pair ⧖⧖ we arrive at an elongated six-pointed star. If we repeat the same process, this time not reversing the divided reciprocating triangle motif, we arrive at ⧖⧖ , creating yet another variation.

Returning to two simple triangles, if we superimpose the two triangles, reversing one of them, we create another common six-pointed star motif ✡ . Running the triangles on a horizontal line and reversing every other one, we arrive at a border motif △▽△▽ . If the triangle is repeated vertically ⧗ we have a side border motif.

Returning to the reciprocating triangle ⧖ , if we reverse the triangles, having them touch base to base, we create a diamond or rhombus ◇ , another important kilim motif. Or, taking six triangles and arranging them so ⬡ we arrive at yet another major motif, the hexagon.

Turning to less obviously geometric motifs, if we take two triangles and separate them by placing one above the other, one with the apex reversed, and connect them with a wavy line ⧘ we end up with a sigma motif; if it is doubled, one being reversed, we end up with ⧘⧘ , or turning the motif inside out ⧘⧘ , and so on.

These puzzle-like arrangements of simple geometric elements are an excellent mnemonic tool for committing to memory both the motif itself and the mechanics of its construction. The scale of the motif, its completeness or incompleteness, its color, its combination with other mo-

tifs—all of these variations create a huge range of design possibilities. Another avenue for understanding the mental process at work in memorizing weaving designs is suggested by psychological literature on the development of expertise which has described a process called "chunking." By this theory, extensive experience within a given domain changes the size of functional units for the observer—that is, so long as the material is structured and not random. For example, memorizing a patch of starry sky would be a formidable, if not impossible task, but "chunking" the area into constellations changes the nature of the task. The memory load remains about the same but because the units are larger, that is, "chunked," the task is feasible. The Anatolian weaver, engaged as she was from early childhood in her weaving designs, was able to absorb fully the grammar and elements of her designs and, undoubtedly, engaged in her own process of "chunking."[16]

While this discussion is certainly not meant to explain how the Anatolian weaver's mind consciously works, it does help to suggest what may be underlying the process. Describing the design process in such a mechanistic manner, however, risks giving the impression that Anatolian weavers traditionally have worked out puzzle-like arrangements of empty geometric forms devoid of meaning. The potency and longevity of this design tradition tend to belie such a conclusion. The geometric motifs characteristic of kilims, in particular the triangle, the rhombus, and the hexagon (if it is seen as a weaving approximation of the circle), have appeared in textile, pottery, basketry, jewelry, sculptural, and mural designs since ancient times and some motifs were already invested with religious meaning in Neolithic times. Whether or not these motifs, together with much of their symbolic content, have descended directly from ancient times (either from indigenous Neolithic sources or from Central Asian and Far Eastern traditions) is the focus of much kilim scholarship at present. Conceivably many of the motifs used by Anatolia's weavers could have such ancient origins. It is also conceivable that the Anatolian weavers working over the centuries within the imperatives of their culture and the weaving technique discovered many of these motifs anew. Pre-Columbian weavers, it should be recalled, developed a weaving vocabulary with many similar geometric motifs in the New World, completely isolated from the weaving traditions of Europe and Asia.

Our fascination with these theories of origins is chiefly an outgrowth of our interest in the central question: What meaning or symbolical significance did the Anatolian weavers perceive in their kilims? As the following chapters will demonstrate, we are only beginning to arrive at answers to this question.

Chapter 7

The Meaning of the Kilim

The recognition that there is a visual language at work in the Anatolian kilim together with a growing understanding of how it functions appear to move us closer to discovering the key to its meaning; however, it is becoming more and more evident that the meaning of the kilim cannot be understood apart from a deep knowledge of the Anatolian culture that produced it. Wrestling with the question of meaning cannot be avoided since the Anatolian kilim, with its abstract geometry, enigmatic archaic motifs, and few references to reality, has a peculiar power—its imagery arouses intense curiosity and begs for interpretation. The kilim's geometric forms seem invested with what E.H. Gombrich describes as "symbolic potential."[1]

However, some scholars, biased heavily in favor of fine art and high culture, argue that rugs and kilims are "folk art" and, therefore, have no meaning. Instead, it is reasoned that the understanding and appreciation of a folk weaving depend on its qualities of color, line, and intended function and not on interpreting symbolic content which, if expressed at all, was borrowed and hence foreign to the weavers and not understood by them. In such a view, motifs and designs are either the product of weavers improvising within the technical demands of their craft or borrowings from superior cultures, not an invented visual language rich in symbolism.[2] As we have seen in chapter four, technical constraints have unquestionably been an important factor in shaping the visual vocabulary of the kilim. It is difficult, however, to accept this as the entire explanation since a large part of the kilim lexicon obviously derives from other sources.

At present we are undergoing a great sea change in our understanding of history. Many traditional historians who once dismissed folk cultures as passive and unconscious entities are today taking their lead from anthropologists and focusing on what they call the "history of mentalities." In such studies rural people and their cultures are no longer dismissed as primitive or folk. Instead there is a growing awareness that they have always been engaged in constructing mental or cultural systems of their own, systems that were often different or even at odds with those of literate societies. Until recently, these cultural systems have tended to remain unknown since they perpetuated themselves only orally and have never been regarded seriously enough by the dominant society for inclusion in its cultural studies and histories.

Our ignorance about Anatolian tribal culture is a prime example. Given the West's long fascination with the weavings and way of life of Anatolia, it is surprising how little is actually known about its tribal peoples. One of the unfortunate results of this ignorance is that the possibility of the weaver or her culture playing a creative role in the invention of motifs and designs has never been seriously considered. The weavers are portrayed either as mindless automatons who happen on motifs by interacting with the imperatives of weaving techniques or as mere conduits channeling visual forms borrowed from ancient or foreign sources. There is a reluctance even to consider the possibility that the culture of the weaver might have created a visual language of its own to express its mentality— that is, its own ideas, values, and identity. While the tribal weaver herself may not have functioned primarily as a conscious, creative artist in the Western sense, this is not to say that her tribal culture over time could not have performed comparable creative functions.

Also the possibility that the motifs and designs

of the Anatolian kilim served a purely decorative function, divorced from meaning, is unlikely given the ancient history of weaving as a primary vehicle for human expression. In fact, decorative textiles without meaning are actually more a feature of modern life with its mass-produced textiles than of the rural handweaving traditions. Weaving, we need to be reminded, is, with cave paintings, one of mankind's earliest transmitters of meaning, predating written language in the Near East by at least three or four millennia.[3] Anatolian tribal culture has perpetuated this ancient primacy of weaving as a potent form of cultural expression almost down to the present day. Indeed, it would seem that when meaning must be conveyed by visual forms rather than written language, weaving attains a power it rarely achieves in literate cultures.[4] It would be reasonable to assume that Anatolia, like pre-Columbian Peru, which also produced a highly developed textile culture but no written language, evolved weaving forms that served as repositories for its cultural, religious, and artistic expression.

On a more subjective level, it is legitimate to ask why, if tribal weavings are mere exercises in color, line, and form, do they inspire such intense curiosity? Why, when contemporary kilims are compared with the masterpieces of the past, is there always a tremendous sense of loss in expressive power? What is this "something" which has been lost? In considering such issues it is important to distinguish between visual forms that have symbolic potential and those that do not. For instance, such ancient motifs as the cross, the crescent moon, the lotus, and the winged sun disk of Egypt, and even that tool of modern psychology, the Rorschach blot, suggest hidden meanings because of their provocative forms. Thus they have symbolic potential. Similarly so do many of the hexagonal medallions, hooked rhomboids, and rams' horns of the Anatolian kilim. Not all visual forms, however, have this symbolic potential, and, undoubtedly, neither do all motifs found in kilims.

In visual art and decoration there is a valuable distinction to be made between the "sign," a motif that carries symbolic meaning, and "design," a use of ornament for purely decorative purposes which may involve a form of expression but not necessarily the communication of meaning.[5] When, for example, we sit facing a living room wall we may be vaguely aware of the "design" of the wallpaper, which may express a mood or a degree of formality, but when we focus on the painting hanging on that wall we consciously look for the "sign," the communication of the meaning or the vision. This distinction, while it can be used to differentiate between decorative and art forms, can also be applied to elements within the same artifact as, for instance, the "sign" of the painting being surrounded by the "design" of its frame. Or, to turn to the kilim, possibly we could describe the "sign" of the main field and the "design" of its border. Rather than close the door completely to the possibility that much kilim imagery may function as a sign, it makes more sense at present to leave such questions open and to continue to examine the evidence accordingly.

However, any investigation into the motif as sign needs to be tempered by the realization that while we can set up useful comparisons between spoken or written language and visual language, in reality they do not function identically. We know the function of language must always be communication but we can never be sure that certain visual forms were necessarily intended to communicate meaning.[6] There is always the danger that in our enthusiastic search for meaning we refuse to accept the possibility of the autonomy of decorative design.[7] From the recognition that visual motifs can express symbolic meaning it is easy to slip into the temptation of concluding that all visual forms were originally conceived as symbols and that their meanings have been lost over time. Certainly there is no spell more potent than that cast by mysterious symbols that seem to stand for forgotten meanings and there is no greater temptation than believing in any visible token that seems to lead us back to our primeval origins.[8] The vagaries of much recent kilim scholarship attest to this.

If our interpretations of kilims are not to degenerate into a kind of subjective fantasy that may reveal more about us than the artifacts we are studying, we must take as our starting point the weaving culture itself. Obviously questioning and observing the weavers who appear to perpetuate the old traditions is a logical starting place; however, the kilims we are interested in understanding were for the most part woven over a century or more ago, and we cannot be certain, given the great changes that have taken place in Anatolian life, that the mentality of the present day weavers resembles that of the weavers of the past. Yet since we have little evidence of what the weaving culture was like during its creative period, we are forced to depend primarily on the accounts and practices of contemporary weavers.

When confronted with questions pertaining to the meaning of kilim motifs and designs, today's weavers invariably reply: "They were handed down to us from our family. They bring us luck,"[9] or "How should I know? It's our tradition. It's the way we do it. We learned it from our mothers and grandmothers,"[10] or "That's how they were always woven."[11] Even though their responses sometimes indicate a vague awareness of the significance and importance of the motifs and designs, they are hard put to discuss specific meanings.

To serve their purposes at the loom, the weavers have customarily relied on a language of convenience to describe the motifs: the "comb" (a), the "wolf's mouth" (b), the "trousseau chest" (c), "running water" (d), the "burdock" (e), the "amulet" (f), the "eye" (g), the "hook" (h), the "scorpion" (i), and so forth. These names appear to have little to do with what the motifs may have signified to the weavers of the past. Further, researchers interviewing weavers today seem to hit a blank when they pose questions that are essentially about aesthetic, cultural, and historical matters to minds that have no conscious conception of art, craft, and history as we know them. It is not just that the weavers do not have the answers but often that they cannot even comprehend the questions. To Westerners the contemporary nomadic and village mind seems strangely incurious and closed to matters that intensely engage our own. In places where there is still a potent tradition, as was true until recently with the Yüncü Yörük tribe near Balıkesir in northwestern Anatolia, fieldworkers' questions have frequently been met with suspicion and possibly outright evasion.[12] Presumably if the tribal tradition is to preserve its potency, its secrets must be kept.

Occasionally a glimmer of what might be seen as older significances seems to appear as, for instance, when weavers north of Antalya use the term *gökkol* instead of *koç boynuzu* for the ram's horn motif. The use of the evocative gökkol, which translates roughly as "light blue arms," or "celestial arms," or "arms of the sky," seems to suggest older religious meanings.[13]

More than any other motif the *elibelinde,* an anthropomorphic form used throughout Anatolian weaving regions, has been analyzed for esoteric

meanings. In fact, there is probably no Near Eastern weaving motif at present that seems more invested with symbolic potential. While most of today's weavers seem oblivious to any significance beyond its literal meaning, "hands on hips" (that is, a human form, almost always female in that pose), there have been a few isolated instances in which weavers seem to recognize something more. The weavers of the village of Yeşilova, formerly Acemköy, are reputed to associate the elibelinde with childbirth and fertility.[14] In a similar vein a weaver in Sivrihisar when questioned about the four rhombs descending from the base of an elibelinde motif she had woven (o) replied that they represented her children.[15] As we shall see in the next chapter, proponents of the Goddess theory, which sees the origins of Anatolian kilim imagery in a Neolithic cult devoted to a Goddess of Fertility, regard the elibelinde as a kind of fossil of ancient religious practices. However, it is also conceivable that the elibelinde is simply the weaver herself or a generalized symbol for woman and that fertility enters the picture only insofar as she has fulfilled or hopes to fulfill one of her primary functions as a tribal woman, the bearing of children.

The present-day weavers' inability to contribute to our understanding of the kilim may be in part because they no longer live in a vital weaving tradition and in part because when the tradition was still vital its individual members may never have been able to articulate their cultural beliefs clearly. Typical responses such as "It is not our place to understand such things" as opposed to more straightforward responses such as "I don't know," or "There is no meaning," tantalizingly suggest either a polite avoidance of disclosing sensitive information or, more likely, a vague awareness that there was some higher significance to the designs, meanings that were known at one time to some members of the tribe. Perhaps it has been a mistake to focus the fieldwork so exclusively on the weavers themselves, tending to leave out the men of the tribe, particularly those in positions of leadership who, while they never wove kilims themselves, lived in spaces defined by them. It is conceivable that in the past when there were large tribal confederations with a recognized leadership and members with specialized functions that there were tribal elders or religious leaders who understood the significance of the visual language of the kilim. Possibly not only were they able to interpret

a.

b.

c.

d.

e.

f.

g.

h.

i.

j.   k.   l.

m.

n.

o.

the weavings but actually once monitored the form the weavings took. In all societies, including our own, the real understanding of religious concepts and symbols has always been in the care of a small group or caste dedicated to preserving and promulgating the tradition for the larger culture. Possibly the understanding of the tribal symbolism was the province of a shaman-type member of the tribe or the itinerant Sufi monks who once traveled among the nomadic populations.

It has been established that during the Selçuk Period (the European Middle Ages) in the Konya region, the traditional center of mystical orders, dervish brotherhoods were encouraged by the government to work as missionaries converting the nomads and convincing them to settle. A credible argument has been made for strong Sufi influences on the design of a type of *cicim* woven in Keçimüh-sine, a village near Konya. In this cicim the imagery seems to have been used to teach certain religious concepts and obligations. The present weavers of Keçimühsine, however, have no notion of such symbolic meanings.[16] Possibly the oral tradition that preserved the meaning of the weaving tradition disappeared as the tribal orders collapsed into today's less structured village groupings.

Another explanation for the meager results of fieldwork is the methodology itself. Though there are certainly many instances of solid, objective fieldwork that follow a sound methodology, the most common practice is for ethnographic fieldworkers to arrive in villages or camps for short visits, clipboard in hand, in order to pose direct questions and to observe some activities at the loom. In contrast, the more indirect methods of anthropology, in which fieldworkers join the cultural group for extended periods and, working indirectly, tease out meanings from the activities and artifacts, seem a more productive approach. Furthermore, it is likely that the data elicited would be more trustworthy, tending to be less biased by the preconceptions of the interviewer.

An example of such an indirect approach is fieldwork conducted in Susanoğlu, a Yörük village in Içel Province, on the south coast of Turkey.[17] As part of a larger field group, an American woman gained the friendship of the women of the village and convinced some of them to help her learn to weave a rug incorporating their traditional designs. In the summer-long process she produced a flatwoven rug, but more importantly she gained valuable

insights into the weaving activity itself and what it meant to its participants. For example, during the warping process she encountered one custom that suggests the original ritual character of weaving. Once the loom beams were staked into the ground and warping was ready to begin, an old rug was spread on the ground near the first stake and the oldest woman of the village was asked to take her seat there and preside over the warping. The villagers explained that this practice was a tradition and that it brought "good luck." This custom was apparently never violated. Beyond this information little else about this practice was elicited.[18] However, in many other cultures outside of Anatolia, weavings are believed to possess powers of creation and fertility because the weaver fashions a unified solid object from seemingly insubstantial materials. The weaver's role at the loom is seen as being not unlike the procreative function itself, a function for which women were held in awe by ancient civilizations.[19] The possibility that the elderly woman presiding over the loom is a vestige of such ritual associations, however, remains to be proved. It is also conceivable that it is her image that the elibelinde captures.

This same fieldwork also provides an interesting insight into weaving as a social obligation, and, in particular, demonstrates how weavers encode meaning into visual expression. One morning in Susanoğlu a girl and her mother set themselves up at a loom outdoors to weave a dowry rug. They became the center of a lively social occasion as other women of the clan gathered to observe and participate. Besides the mother and daughter, other women took their turns at the loom. Of course, they continued to weave the traditional design, but they also encoded into it their own personal signs. An orange square added to a design that did not call for it represented one woman, and an enlarged square represented another. These were the "signatures" of the weavers, which were intended to function as simple mnemonic devices, evoking in the memory of the bride the weaving occasion and especially those who participated in it. As the weavers themselves explained, they inserted their signs so that they would be remembered.[20]

This dowry custom suggests that some of the variations in the minor motifs of a kilim are expressions of personal histories. Among illiterate and protoliterate cultures, it is not unusual for a clan or social group to record the most important events

Anatolian Turkey (Asia Minor). The location of tribal weaving groups in Anatolia is too complex to capture in a single map. The tribal areas indicated here are only approximations of larger tribal groups. Other yörük tribal groups are indicated by ::: and the major Kurdish populations by xˣxˣx. The yerli of the "Phrygian Highlands" are in a mountainous region bounded by the cities of Eskişehir, Kütahya, Afyon, and Bursa.

of a period in a series of images more mnemonic than explicit in order to perpetuate the fame and history of the clan.[21] In the past, when tribal confederations had distinct identities, governing structures, and histories of their own, kilims may have encoded more important events than dowry preparation. Such histories, of course, do not survive since the mnemonic devices have no meanings in themselves but exist only to trigger memories in the minds of an individual or a group. Undoubtedly hundreds of thousands of such meanings have vanished over the centuries, while possibly some of the visual forms so created have been perpetuated by tradition.

In contrast to the ephemeral nature of mnemonic devices, the amulets (muska) (p) and talismans to ward off the evil eye (nazarlık) (q) have ancient, fixed meanings which are still largely understood. Among the tribal weavers they have a special reality that sets them apart from symbols as we understand them. They reflect the degree to which Near and Middle Eastern weaving groups have always been preoccupied with appeasing spirits, in particular the evil eye, and avoiding sickness and death.[22] Given these preoccupations, it is not surprising that talismans and amulets figure heavily in kilim decoration, especially considering the role weavings have played in defining the sitting, work-

ing, and sleeping spaces of the tribal household. Nazarlık can be actual objects, such as blue beads, tufts of mohair wool, scraps of calico, or cowrie shells, attached to or woven into the kilim. Or they might be in the form of motifs woven into the kilim such as the ağhrepli, the scorpion (r), and the çapraz, an s-shaped motifs, to name a few. The weaver and her culture perceive these not as symbols but as the thing itself. They are believed to give off a field of force able to interact with and overcome unseen evil forces, thereby protecting the weaver's household. Even color, as was noted in chapter two, could perform such a role. The three blue bands of the traditional funerary kilim is one example. Also there is a belief in many weaving cultures—but one that remains to be corroborated in Anatolia—that a blue thread or stripe must begin the work on the loom.[23] The alternating red and blue stripes that frequently decorate the plain weave skirts of Anatolian kilims may have had their origins in such a belief. These nazarlık, together with the vague notion among today's weavers that kilims "bring them luck," may be the last vestiges of a vanished system of beliefs.

Symbol

Most current discussions on the meaning of kilims focus on what kilim scholars and connoisseurs

p.

q.

r.

s.

perceive as motifs with ancient symbolic meanings. However, discussions of this subject have frequently been hindered by questionable methodologies and confused terminology. A symbol, whether it be an act, a sound, or an object, stands for or suggests something else by reason of relationship, association, convention, or accidental resemblance. Unlike a talisman or an amulet, a symbol is not perceived as real in itself. Possessing a cultural significance, it has the capacity to provoke a response and to open a way to an understanding of a hidden reality.

Symbols function in a number of different ways. A symbol can be used consciously to stand for something else, as the crown represents the legitimacy of the monarch, the flag the nation-state, and the gavel the authority of the judge. It is this type of symbolism that most people who seek meaning in the kilim expect to find. However, such conscious symbolism may belong more to the province of "art by destination," that is, the expression of an individual artist who is for the most part consciously employing (along with personal symbols) the accepted symbols of his culture. In contrast, the symbols of tribal culture are the expression of the collective whole, not necessarily the individual weaver. The symbols of such a tradition are possibly of the less conscious sort, at least for the majority of the weavers. For instance, motifs or objects may be used unconsciously to express symbolic purposes, the meanings of which the user is able to articulate only upon reflection. In our culture clothing functions in this way: The choices we make in style, color, palette, and quality make symbolic statements about our status, values, and achievements. While we are usually not fully conscious of these symbolic statements, we can interpret them if need be.

Another category of symbols is a wholly unconscious type, containing meanings that the maker or user could never articulate, meanings produced by the culture itself. For instance, anthropologists have analyzed the structure of ritual performances, myths, taboos, and other sets of complex symbols as a means of categorizing the reality of a cultural group and resolving inherently contradictory principles of social organization at work. It is likely that the symbolic visual language of the kilim has always operated for the individual weaver at the vaguely conscious or unconscious end of the spectrum. Therefore, the methodology of the anthropologist

rather than that of the ethnographer or art historian is probably more suited to discovering the key to the kilim's language.

Symbols are often regarded as examples of universal archetypes, and indeed some experiences are so universal as to produce broad similarities across cultures. However, most modern anthropologists will not credit any understanding of symbolism that does not grow out of a close examination of the particular community using it. While certain motifs can have similar interpretations in different cultures and are instantly recognizable because of the physical resemblances of the symbol to its object—for example, a wavy line symbolizing a snake, or a brilliant red suggesting blood—the true content of the symbol and its precise significance may not be obvious since they are culturally determined. Whether the snake is a symbol of evil or godhead, blood a symbol of life or death, can only be determined if one is a member of the culture or a close observer of it.

Further, it cannot be assumed that a cluster of similar motifs even if they derive from a common source will necessarily share the same meaning. As an example, a configuration composed of a triangle with an enclosed rectangle, a North American Indian motif shared by various tribes (t), takes on different meanings as the result of slight modifications to its design. Depending on the modifications, the motif can be read as a tent with poles, doorways, and pegs, or as a mythical mountain in which buffaloes are kept, or as a fort with palisades, to name a few. The different symbolic meanings attached to these variations are determined by the needs and preoccupations of each tribe. For the Pueblos the motif was a rain symbol, for the Plains Indians a mountain housing the buffalo, and for another tribe, which was probably experiencing a period of dislocation, a fort protected by palisades. The modifications to the design of a common symbol together with the different preoccupations of the tribal groups produce a whole cluster of different meanings.[24]

This methodology could have interesting applications to the elibelinde, which is widely dispersed throughout Anatolia (as well as other Asian and European weaving zones), and is found in the weavings of numerous tribal groups, in many different variations. The assumption underlying so much recent kilim scholarship is that there is a single meaning to be discovered in the many variations of this motif and that this meaning descends from Neolith-

t.

ic times. The methodology used in classifying the motifs of the Indian tribes suggests that the elibelinde more likely takes on a whole cluster of meanings depending on the point in time at which the motif was woven, which tribe produced it, the preoccupations of the tribe, and the various ways in which the motif has been modified.

Even if we are able to establish the meaning of a particular motif at one place and time we cannot generalize that it has the same meaning among other tribes or subtribes. Nor can we necessarily use this as evidence for getting back to the ancient, original meaning—if, in fact, there was one. While we usually assume the opposite, in some cases motifs were apparently created first and meanings attached to them at a later point.[25] Such a process would particularly be true for those motifs that possess symbolic potential—the cross, for instance, is an ancient motif that took on many symbolic meanings long before Christianity. Not till centuries after the birth of Christ did it begin to take on its present symbolic significance.[26] Because of its symbolic potential the elibelinde has undoubtedly evolved through many stages of meaning.

Resemblances between symbols do not necessarily establish direct influences or shared meanings or even origins from a common root. Not all motifs which look similar derive from the same source. Often resemblances are the result of coincidence because of the imperatives of the weaving technique or a shared cultural way of perceiving reality, as in the discussion of symmetries in chapter five. Certain symbols can have an extremely complicated ancestry resulting as they do from the convergence of similar forms and various meanings from a number of different origins.

Before we can accept that one symbol has derived from another, we must demonstrate that the transfer could take place, which presupposes that one version antedates the other, that communication was possible, and that the motivations and conditions existed for the transfer.[27] The resemblances of nineteenth-century Anatolian kilim motifs to Neolithic motifs, no matter how striking they may be, must be regarded only as coincidental until similar meanings and transference of meaning can be established. Obviously building interpretations solely on the shaky foundations of striking resemblances is risky with constructs as volatile as symbols. Since the meaning of the symbol is only to be found in the particular culture that is using it,

we are inevitably brought back full circle to a study of the culture of the Anatolian weaving population.

Traditional and Ritual Functions of the Kilim

How the kilims were associated with the ritual stages of tribal life, such as marriage, childbirth, and death, together with their specific functions in everyday Anatolian life offer one means by which we can establish the necessary cultural context and thus arrive at more credible interpretations of symbolic meaning.

The association of the kilim with the dowry and hence the wedding is not difficult to establish and continues in varying degrees of observance even today. The making of cloth for dowries is still commonplace in peasant and tribal societies around the world, suggesting that it was a widespread custom from ancient times.[28] Thus Anatolian weavers are part of a much larger tradition in which clothmaking is an activity associated with duty and privilege as opposed to enforced labor. Often in such societies cloths are presented by both the bride and groom's families at a wedding. In the Teke region of southwestern Anatolia a prospective bride must bring three to five kilims in her dowry, while the groom's mother must supply a kilim of her own. If the bride is unable to weave herself, she is still expected to spin the wool and to find the weaver in her own village.[29] This alternative arrangement suggests a compromise with older tradition as weaving skills become less common.

While it is clear that kilims, the requisite number depending on local custom, formed part of the dowry and were presented during the wedding festivities, there seem to be no recorded instances of how kilims might have been ritually integrated into the ceremonies or other wedding activities. However, it is known the nomads carried kilims to the yayla, their summer pasture, to make a show at weddings and other festivities.[30]

The dowry requirement implies that kilims traditionally served important functions in the tribal household, but surprisingly evidence for domestic uses of kilims is skimpy, unclear, or lacking. This is particularly so for the practices of the nomads, since their way of life began to alter long ago as they were progressively absorbed into settled life. At present there is even a debate as to whether nomads ever used kilims in their tents or reserved them only for use in the cottages that served as

Hanging kilims decorate the interior of a Bahşiş Yörük tent, near Mersin, 1939.

their winter homes.

It is now generally agreed that kilims were seldom used as tent floor coverings.[31] Instead, felt rugs served this insulating function. There is evidence, however, that the kilim served other important functions in the tent. As late as the 1930s the Bahşiş Yörük used kilims as horizontal surrounds along the inside periphery of the tent. On a practical level, one of the functions these surrounds served was to screen from view the luggage and bedding piles that lined the wall of the tent, and they probably reduced the dust, wind, and glare when the tent walls were raised. A second function was to provide added insulation during cold weather.[32] The use of kilims as insulation is corroborated by three elderly women in Kızılka near Bor, Niğde Province, who recalled that loops were sewn onto the selvedges of long kilims so that they could be hooked over the top cross-pieces of the tent wall trellises.[33] Periodically old kilims with such loops have turned up in the rug bazaars of Turkey. One of the women recalled that kilims were hung up in this way when it was very cold.[34] Undecorated weavings obviously would have been sufficient for such a practical function; however, using kilims as surrounds provided a decorated backdrop to the social, working, and sleeping activities of the tribal family. How this function may have influenced the design and character of the Bahşiş Yörük's long, horizontal kilims remains a question. Answering this question is difficult since in the last half century the Bahşiş Yörük custom of using kilims as tent surrounds has completely vanished together with almost all memories of the practice. The degree to which today's nomads have abandoned wintering in their tents may be a factor in this sudden disappearance.

However, while tent surrounds are no longer used, other traditional uses of kilims in the tents survive down to the present, even if in a debased form. Assembling the evidence from the recent past along with the remaining practices of today's nomads could take us far back in time, since the highly organized and ritualized spatial arrangements of the tents have altered little over the centuries and have in many cases been transferred to cottages by settled groups. Even though the Türkmen populations of Anatolia, Central Asia, and Azerbaijan have been separated for many centuries, they still share similar tent styles, tent organization, and tent terminology.[35] The older Anatolian practices are elucidated by comparisons with Central Asian nomadic practices, which have remained more intact and have been recorded in scholarly studies since the nineteenth century.

Because of the great variety of tent forms in Anatolia, it is not easy to generalize about its standard form and organization. Anatolia is ordinarily identified as being in the black tent zone, characterized by rectangular tents of woven goat hair. However, even the black tent takes many different forms. In addition there are trellis tents of white felt and tunnel-shaped tents of black felt. The tents usually vary in size and elaborateness depending on the wealth and prominence of their occupants. However, the similar conditions of tent living have produced certain constants. The tent door is customarily oriented to the warmth and sunlight of the south, while the major piles of baggage line the north wall, serving as a windbreak and insulator. Unlike the typical Western arrangement of living quarters in which rooms or spaces have fixed specialized functions, the tent space, except for the cooking and food processing area, is all-purpose and successively becomes the place for working, eating, sleeping, and other social activities. The taking up and putting down of rugs and kilims have been one manner in which the common space has been defined for different functions.

This use of a common space, with all the movables necessary to redefine it and to carry on the numerous domestic and animal husbandry activities, created the need for certain highly organized storage arrangements. On a daily basis bedding must be taken out and returned to the bedding pile. Clothing and artifacts are stored in woven storage bags. The paraphernalia for the spinning, weaving, knitting, cooking, and food processing activities of the women are organized on one side of the tent, while the saddles, harnesses, saddlebags, weapons, and tools of the men are stored on the men's side. The relatively small space of the tent, given the number of activities it served, needed to be highly organized and at some point in the distant past this organization evidently became fixed by tradition.

There are two typical arrangements of the tent furnishings in which kilims figure prominently. Since these practices are similar in Anatolia and Central Asia, we can only assume that they took their characteristic form many centuries ago. In both regions kilims or other weavings are used as dust covers and displayed horizontally. In one

A Sacıkara nomad woman adjusting the poles at her black goat hair tent. An auxiliary tent for storing saddles and harnesses stands nearby. Kayseri region, 1978.

arrangement the kilim is drawn over a row of brocaded storage bags, the *alaçuval*. Customarily used to store clothing, in particular items from the bride's trousseau, they are usually decoratively arranged on a ledge of rocks or a wooden trestle running along the back wall of the tent.[36] The decorative function of the arranged alaçuval (traditionally woven by the groom's mother) seems highly important. A long, narrow kilim is drawn over the top of the alaçuval and displayed horizontally, draping over but not covering the decorated faces of the alaçuval. While the kilim obviously functions to protect the household effects from the inescapable dust and grit, there may be other functions, possibly symbolic ones, having to do with the defining of social space. In the other dust cover arrangement the kilim is stretched across the stack of bedding which lines one wall of the tent. Again the kilim is seen in a horizontal position hanging down over the bedding and creates a decorative backdrop.

Decorative textiles have served in many cultures as backdrops to ceremonial occasions, in particular the visits of important persons.[37] The traditional nomadic tent has always been set up in readiness for the rites of hospitality, on the theory that guests usually arrive without warning and have been sent by Allah. The seating area, itself defined by a kilim spread on top of the felts, is customarily arranged in front of the alaçuval, which serve as convenient backrests and provide shelter from drafts. The combination of the seating kilim, the row of alaçuval, and the kilim dust cover produces

Women of the Honomli nomads seated in front of the baggage storage pile, which is covered with a kilim, Adana region, 1978.

a colorful, and perhaps meaningful, context for the social occasion. An examination of this configuration as it originated among the Türkmen of Central Asia, as will be demonstrated in the next chapter, helps to elucidate its meanings to the Türkmen and Yörük of Anatolia. One difficulty in setting up comparisons is that the dust cover kilim used by the Anatolian tribal weavers is different in character and technique from the flatweavings and pile rugs used by their Central Asian Türkmen ancestors and the other branches of Türkmen now living in Azerbaijan and other regions.

As we have seen in three instances, the long kilims used as tent surrounds, as dust covers on the alaçuval, and on the bedding pile were customarily displayed in a horizontal position and functioned as a decorated backdrop. Establishing these traditional functions enables us to determine how kilims were meant to be seen and how, therefore, we are to "read" the motifs and designs. Had these kilims been specifically designed as floor coverings there would be no fixed point of view since serving that function they would have been viewed from different angles. It has been the growing consensus among kilim researchers for some time that the long kilims were intended to be viewed horizontally, not vertically as was once thought. In contrast,

A cottage interior, Sivas Province, 1980.

prayer kilims have a definite vertical orientation as well as a top and bottom defined by the orientation of the *mihrab*. That we are still dealing with such basic matters as which way to orient a kilim in order to "read" it suggests the elementary level of our understanding.

The spatial and storage arrangements of the tent have been over the centuries transferred to the cottages of the settled populations. As is true of the tent, the cottage of the pastoralist usually functions as an all-purpose space rather than being divided into many rooms with set, specialized functions. The continuity of a way of life in which bedding is brought out and stored on a daily basis and household effects are routinely stored in woven bags explains the transference of the bedding pile and alaçuval arrangements to the cottage. Besides serving practical needs, these highly decorative arrangements undoubtedly satisfied cultural expectations that are less easy to establish.

One of the greatest contrasts between the interiors of today's cottages and tents is the degree to which the cottage walls are covered by kilims and other weavings while the role of the kilim in the tents of the nomads (now used virtually only in summer) has apparently diminished considerably. In the cottage a rough, mud-bricked, mud-floored, often windowless space is transformed through weavings into a highly decorated, insulated envelope of wool. Perhaps the degree to which the interior of the cottage is decorated with woven designs is a survival of the visual expectations created by the kilim surrounds of the winter tents. In both tent and cottage, it was during the winter season, when the tribal family was immured indoors and in need of the maximum amount of insulation, that the living environment was most dominated by the colors, motifs, and designs of kilims and other weavings. What, it remains to be discovered, did the tribal family usually see and experience as they whiled away the winter hours in this highly decorated woven environment?

In our modern society decorative motifs fill our world with such profusion that they are normally outside our attention. Are the weavings covering the walls, floors, and divans of the Anatolian cottages no different in effect than our own wallpaper, slipcovers, and drapes? Or could it be that in a world which until recently was not as visually overloaded as the West's is, the weavings functioned not as a backdrop to be taken for granted but

rather a kind of tribal screen to be studied and experienced during the long winter period? Or is it possible that only certain weavings stand out from the rest as, for example, a painting would stand out on a wall decorated with wallpaper? That is, would certain of the weavings receive the conscious attention accorded to an artefact containing a sign? Such unanswered questions illustrate how little we actually understand about the role of the kilim and other tribal weavings in daily life.

Kilims also served special functions outside of the tent and cottage. Among the Bahşiş Yörük and undoubtedly other tribal groups, kilims were used as part of the camel regalia and hence associated with migrations and journeys. A photograph taken in 1939 records the migrating Bahşiş Yörük with their camels draped with kilims, a practice which is barely a memory among today's tribal members.[38] The kilims stretched over the loaded backs of the camels kept the dust and heat out of the household effects and foodstuffs. Aside from this practical function, it seems evident that such a brilliant display also served as a kind of blazon announcing the identity and worth of the tribe. Quite possibly there is a relationship between this heraldic function and the size and boldness of the motifs so characteristic of certain Anatolian kilims (plates 39–45). Since one function of an heraldic sign is to attract attention, and to be conspicuous and clear so that it can be easily read, it is usually highly ordered and depicted in sharply contrasting colors. There is also in heraldry an extreme precision in its symbolic meaning. Further, the sign of the heraldic motif itself is set into a larger frame, the design. The function of the framing design is to enhance the power of the sign by creating the proper setting.[39] There are striking parallels between the ways heraldic and kilim motifs are rendered. These resemblances, together with the fact that we know kilims were once displayed as part of the traditional camel regalia, suggest that some kilim designs could have had heraldic origins, particularly those featuring large hexagonal medallions.

As part of a camel regalia which included elaborate bridles, harnesses, bells, and headdresses, the kilim undoubtedly contributed significantly to the colorful pageantry of highly theatrical mass movements of people and animals. Perhaps the brilliant spectacle of the ongoing migrations of the Quashqa'i, a Turkic nomadic tribal confederation in southwestern Iran, suggest what Anatolian mi-

Kilims draped over the camels of a Bahşiş Yörük family migrating to mountain pastures near Mersin, 1939.

u.

v.

w.

x.

y.

z.

grations once were. An association between the kilim and the camel is suggested by the response of an old Akkoyunlu Yörük woman who, when asked if she still wove, replied, "I used to, but we sold our camels."[40]

Outside the tribal households and caravan, the kilim has served an important ritual function as *teberrû,* votive offerings donated to the mosque.[41] The kilims, carpets, and rugs covering mosque floors all over Anatolia are irrefutable evidence of this old custom. The motives of the donors were various: To gain God's grace, to receive personal guarantees for eternal life, to honor a dead family member, or to celebrate the birth of a first-born son.[42] Inadvertently, this custom served a dual function by preserving a large collection of older kilims which otherwise would have been consumed by the rigors of daily household use. It is in this almost accidental way, not by the systematic efforts of collectors or museums, that so many old kilims have been preserved in Anatolia.

Even though we understand little about the various ways most votive functions influenced the character of kilims, there is some information that illuminates the custom of the funerary vótive offering. Now only rarely observed in a few scattered areas of Anatolia, it was the custom to weave and

reserve a special kilim for wrapping the corpse for its final journey to the mosque and burial ground. The corpse, wound in its kilim wrapping and often tied with woven tablet bands, was transported on a ladder borne by male relatives and friends (hence the Anatolian euphemism for death, "climbs the ladder").[43] Once at the mosque or graveside the kilim was removed, the body buried in its shroud, and the kilim donated to the mosque or sometimes returned to the family for future burials. Traditionally, such kilims were long, in one piece, and some are reputed to have been decorated with three blue bands. While little more seems to be known about this ritual use in Anatolia, a similar practice can still be observed in the Caucasus, where certain rugs called *sumuk* ("carpet for bones") are used to wrap the corpse. It is believed that the spirit of the dead person travels to join his ancestors only on the home carpet.[44] Possibly such a belief underlies the ritual of the funerary kilim in Anatolia.

Of all the kilims that serve ritual functions, the prayer kilim (the *seccade*) (u) and its multiple form the *saf* (v) are best understood. The sacral function of the seccade determines the size, proportions, visual lexicon, and overall design. Anatolia is unique in the importance it gives to kilims, rugs, and textiles specifically designed for prayer; most other

Men praying on tebberû *(donated kilims and cicims), Uşak Province, 1978.*

Muslim regions use kilims, rugs, and carpets which are not as specifically defined. Muslim practice only requests that *sālāt*, the ritual prayer, be performed on a clean surface. Throughout the Muslim world and even in Anatolia any covering can be used, whether it be rush matting, embroidered textiles, felt, ordinary rugs or carpets, or even pieces of cardboard. Why and how Anatolia came to create a major category of weavings specifically designed for sālāt remain unexplained. What is evident is that the size of the prayer kilim is determined by the need for a portable item readily available for the five ritual periods of prayer and also proportioned to the human body when prostrated in prayer. Although some regions, such as Erzerum, have produced outsized versions, the typical prayer kilim's scale enables the worshiper to place his knees at the base, his forehead near the top of the niche, and his two palms on either side of it. The saf, which is designed for multiple worshipers, is more likely to remain in place in a mosque or *medresseh* (religious school). Its niches are also scaled to the bodies prostrated in prayer and usually ordered in odd numbers, in rows of three, five, seven, and nine (see plates 56, 57).

Until recently, the arch-shaped prayer kilim motif, once referred to by scholars as the mihrab but increasingly as the niche, was believed to represent an architectural form, the mihrab, located in the *qibla* or the Mecca-oriented wall of the mosque. However, there is a growing sense that while there is a body of kilims, in particular those with stepped mihrabs (y, z) that take their iconography directly from the architectural mihrabs of the mosque (see plates 59, 70, 71), there is also a much older source in niche and arcaded forms that descend from the iconography of religious and cultic practices predating Islam.[45] Not all kilim prayer designs, it would appear, are necessarily from the same source. The niche, an enclosed space for housing the deity, descends from very ancient times and carries with it numerous associations, often identified with the cave of the deity and the womb of the Mother Goddess (aa). However, there is a more recent and direct influence in Muslim tradition, which itself probably inherited it from pre-Islamic times. This is the image of the niche and the lamp (bb) described in the Koran in the famous *Surah* of Light: "Allah is the light of the heavens and the earth. The symbol of His light is a niche in which is a lamp." XXXIV:35 (plate 72).

In addition to the niche form there are also versions of the motif that represent gates, arches, and arcades through which one sees flowers, plants, or the tree of life (cc–ee). Such iconography portrays a doorway or arch through which one may pass on

aa.

bb.

cc.

dd.

ee.

a spiritual journey to paradise. In Islamic art there are extensive symbolic references to *bab*, a gate or doorway, and it may be to these symbolic meanings that some prayer kilim motifs belong (plates 60, 63, 65, 66, 72, 73). Whatever its source and meaning, the central motif, whether it be niche, mihrab, or gate, establishes the orientation for prayer and serves as a frame for the prostrated body of the worshiper.

The visual character of the Anatolian prayer kilim ranges from austere, architectural constructs with little decorative imagery (plates 56–58, 61, 63) to extremely ornate designs featuring stepped mihrabs embellished with representational motifs depicting trees of life, notional ideas of flowers and vegetation, and hanging lamps. These are framed by a main field decorated with floral motifs, or water pitchers, or lamps, and enclosed by a series of guard borders lined with stylized carnations, tulips, and tendrils (plates 70–73). At the austere end of the continuum, the visual character of prayer kilims may descend from ancient indigenous origins (plate 57) or from the Selçuk Turkish period in Anatolia (plates 60, 62, 63, 65). At the decorative end of the continuum, the influence of the Ottoman court traditions, probably by way of prayer rug designs, seems to have shaped certain prayer kilim designs after the sixteenth century. It is known that there was a large commercial production of various kinds of prayer kilims in Anatolia in the seventeenth, eighteenth, and nineteenth centuries. Ottoman influences may have entered into the Anatolian tribal lexicon during this period of commercial production.

ff.

Within the larger prayer kilim lexicon there is one part of the vocabulary that seems to have a direct, conscious religious significance: the hanging lamp as a symbol of enlightenment, the water pitcher (the *iprik*) as a symbol of purification, the gate or arch as the portal to enlightenment or eternal life, and the tree of life as a symbol of life or paradise—or in its older shamanistic sense, as the axle of the universe. There is another portion of the vocabulary which is derived from the floral, vegetative images of the Ottoman court tradition: the carnation, tulip, tendril, and palmette. Both vocabularies, often seen in combination, appear alien within the context of the larger tribal lexicon. The conscious nature of the Ottoman and Islamic symbolism stands out in contrast to the vaguely conscious or unconscious symbolism of the typical

gg.

tribal lexicon. The more representational character of the prayer kilim lexicon distinguishes it from the abstract, geometric character of the typical kilim motifs. Finally, the explicitly religious nature of the imagery distinguishes it from the larger tribal lexicon. Despite the long Christian and Islamic histories of Anatolia, very little in the way of religious iconography seems to have found its way into the other kilim categories. While the religious imagery in prayer kilims is to be expected, what is surprising is that such imagery is barely found at all in the larger body of kilims, some of which served in other ritual functions such as funerary kilims which would have had religious associations.

Since designs and motifs that are indigenous and may predate Islam are often combined with elements originating in Selçuk and Ottoman times, it is difficult to establish absolute categories. However it is possible to single out those which seem to fit more comfortably into the visual lexicon and grammar we have characterized as Anatolian and those which, despite the fact that they may have been adapted to the Anatolian visual style, derive originally from sources outside it.

In addition to these traditional household, votive, and sacral functions for kilims, there is some evidence for kilims woven for public ritual functions. Among the Alevi-Bektaşı, a heterodox Islamic sect, the "red kilim" apparently served as a place for those involved in disputes to resolve their differences: "One day we will sort this out on the red kilim." Further, when the chief of the Alevi visited a tribal group, its members were expected to sit on the red kilim when presenting their accounts. Those found in debt were required to pay. Such practices suggest the red kilim became a special place of truth, judgment, and reconciliation comparable to our courtroom. The Yüncü Yörük, the majority of whom belong to heterodox sects and who weave primarily red kilims, may have traditionally used their kilims in this way; however, when asked they would not confirm it as they do not like to speak about such unorthodox customs.[46]

While it is possible to gain a general, if fragmentary, impression of the roles kilims played in the life and rituals of the Anatolian tribes, it has not been possible to reconstruct the original culture. There is little surviving evidence to suggest how the various everyday and ritual functions of the kilim shaped its visual language. How, for example, did a kilim woven to fulfill the dowry obligation differ from one woven by a married woman for household use or as a votive offering? Would the kilims displayed in the camel regalia have specific motifs associated with that function? How would kilims used as tent surrounds differ in their iconography from those used on the camel, or would the same pieces have been used for both functions?

At present, only the prayer kilim demonstrates clear connections between form and function. Similar connections need to be established for the other kilim categories. Unfortunately, it seems that prayer kilims are a late form, for the most part heavily shaped by outside influences and often commercially produced. Therefore the very category we are able to interpret best does not cast as much light on tribal practices as would be expected. While a prayer kilim has a meaning that can be interpreted, its visual language functions in a very different way from that of other kilims. Its language is more conscious in its symbolism and much of its lexicon is borrowed from the visual language of the dominant Ottoman culture.

For the bulk of kilims we are left only with a general sense of their meaning. The information provided by today's weavers and the associations with rituals and daily life that have been established suggest that the kilim both shaped and reflected the "we-feeling" of the tribe. It expressed the overpowering sentiment of belonging which bound each member of the tribe to the other.[47] But surely the kilim's roles, and hence meanings, were once much more specific. In most tribal cultures around the world, ritual textiles are filled with important iconography; the designs usually symbolize fertility, power, protection, lineage, blessings, and magical power.[48] It is reasonable to expect Anatolian ritual textiles also once did so.

Normally, organizing the extant examples of an artifact into a chronology and grouping them into separate categories lead to valuable insights into their origins, evolution, and meaning. But with kilims, working back from the present systematically does not take us very far, especially if we assume they descend from very ancient times. If we were dealing with artifacts of metal or stone, that is, things likely to be preserved over long periods of time, or if Anatolia were more like Egypt or coastal Peru where the climate and burial customs ensured the survival of representative weavings, reconstructing kilim origins would be immeasurably easier. Unfortunately, the bulk of surviving kilims date, as do most of those depicted in this book, from the nineteenth century. No one seriously doubts that the Anatolian kilim tradition is an ancient one, but it is possible to trace given kilim designs back only three or four generations. Unlike knotted pile rugs and carpets, which were collected and preserved in European collections from medieval times, kilims were never seriously collected, and therefore preserved, until the past thirty years, and they rarely survived daily use in Anatolia. The recent attention to kilim fragments that are presumed to predate the nineteenth century has pushed the record back somewhat, but even these do not take us very far back in time. As we have seen, the oral tradition of the tribal weavers does not reach back much beyond the mid-nineteenth century. Even the existence of the word "kilim" in Anatolia can only be traced back in Selçuk and Ottoman texts to the beginning of the thirteenth century. Thus far no one has been able to document when the first rudimentary Anatolian kilims appeared.

Lacking the continuous record of the artifact and facing unresolved problems in dating those that do survive, we find that rather than elucidating meaning the extant body of kilims instead cries out for interpretation. No convincing methodology for dating kilims, despite numerous claims to the contrary, has yet emerged. Unfortunately carbon-14 tests are too imprecise to use for artifacts made after A.D. 1200. The test is not only imprecise but practically worthless after A.D. 1650. It is not able to distinguish among kilims woven between the seventeenth and nineteenth centuries, the very period from which almost all kilims survive. Thus we are left with one final avenue to explore in our search for meaning: an investigation into the historical origins of the kilim.

Chapter 8

The Origins of the Kilim: A Survey of Current Thinking

The most traveled road in exploring the meaning of the motifs and designs of Anatolian kilims is undoubtedly the ongoing investigation into the kilim's origins and history. As etymology has contributed to an increased understanding of language, so a study of the origins of the kilim, it is reasoned, should lead to an expanded understanding of its visual language. The focus of this approach is on understanding how, when, and where the kilim originated, by which culture or tribe it was created, where its motifs and design came from, and how the kilim tradition and other weaving and design traditions interacted and evolved over time. For purposes of discussion most of the conflicting points of view on the subject of origins may be grouped under two general hypotheses: the Türkmen and the Goddess theories.[1]

In the Türkmen hypothesis, the Anatolian weaving tradition, including its technology, techniques, and design, is believed to be a legacy of the Türkmen tribes which started their major migrations to Anatolia from Central Asia in the eleventh century A.D. Such discussions emphasize the pan-Asian origins of the kilim, tracing its beginnings to Khurasan, historically the Central Asian homeland of the Türkmen, which lies to the east of Iran between the Amu Darya (Oxus) River and the Paropamisus, a region still occupied by the Türkmen of Iran, Afghanistan, and Turkmenistan. Some kilim motifs are traced further back to the original Far Eastern Türkmen homeland in Mongolia on the fringes of the Chinese Empire. The influences of Islam, the Türkmen having been largely converted by the ninth century, are also emphasized, as well as other religious allegiances that predated Islam, in particular, Central Asian shamanism.

The Goddess hypothesis emphasizes the indigenous origins of the Anatolian kilim, arguing that Anatolia had developed its own weaving tradition long before the Türkmen migrations. Rather than being the product of outside influences the Anatolian kilim is seen as descending in a direct line from Neolithic prototypes, presumed to have existed in the form of woven hangings displayed in cult rooms devoted to the worship of a fertility goddess. One of the attractions of this theory, and one that certainly explains its appeal, is that, if its early Neolithic origins are proved, the Anatolian kilim gains increased prestige as one of the oldest, if not the oldest, continuous design tradition in the world.

The two schools of thought are not as rigidly or neatly divided as suggested here; Türkmen proponents are willing to acknowledge indigenous Anatolian influences and Goddess proponents certain Türkmen influences. Nevertheless, underlying the present discussion on the kilim is a great divide on the subject of origins. The point in history at which these two schools diverge is A.D. 1071, when at the battle of Malazgirt in the Van region of eastern Anatolia, invading Oghuz tribesmen decisively defeated the armies of the Emperor of Byzantium. As a result of this momentous battle (occurring only five years after the Norman Conquest of England) the former Byzantine province of Anatolia was opened up to successive waves of Central Asian nomads. It is estimated that between 350,000 and 600,000 people along with seven to eight million sheep came in four large waves between 1071 and the late thirteenth century.[2] The Oghuz, the predominant tribe in the migrations, evolved in Anatolia into the tribal groups identified as Türkmen, as well as a large component of the groups known as Yörük. It is the various subtribes of the Türkmen and Yörük that have woven the bulk of the kilims we now identify as Anatolian.

At the heart of the disagreements between the two views on kilim origins are these questions: Exactly what kind of weaving technology, technique, and design tradition had Anatolia evolved by the time of the great Türkmen migrations? What kind of weaving tradition did the Türkmen carry with them when they migrated from Central Asia by way of the Caucasus into Anatolia? More specifically, was there in either or both populations a kilim tradition that could be regarded as the ancestor of what has become known as the Anatolian kilims? Finally, how did these two traditions interact in Anatolia once the various tribes began their long process of assimilation and coexistence?

The prehistorical and historical record of the indigenous weaving tradition in Anatolia is slowly beginning to emerge. Fragments of simple linen burial cloths prove that circa 6,000 B.C. weaving with flax existed in Çatal Hüyük, site of a Neolithic city in the Konya region of Anatolia. In Jarmo in northeast Iraq there is evidence of woven cloth circa 7,000 B.C., while in Nahal Hemar in the Judean desert there is proof of woven cloth circa 6,500 B.C.[3] There is no question that weaving in the Near East has a very ancient history.

Although there is no evidence for the use of wool at this early period, it is generally accepted that sheep were becoming domesticated around 7,000 B.C. and that southwestern Asia was probably their place of origin. By the fourth and third millennia B.C. there is a great deal of evidence that flocks were being managed for wool production.[4] As to loom technology, it is established that central and west Anatolia were part of the warp-weighted loom (a) tradition from at least the fourth millennium B.C.[5] The discovery at Çatal Hüyük of what may be ceramic warp weights and possibly a heading band seems to prove the existence of the warp-weighted loom in early Neolithic Anatolia.[6] Since the horizontal ground loom is composed entirely of perishable materials, its introduction into the Anatolian region is difficult to date. However, in nearby Egypt, where conditions for preservation are ideal, evidence suggests that at least by the fourth millennium B.C. a horizontal loom with shed, heddle, and beater bar was in use.[7] Establishing the period at which Anatolian weavers adopted the horizontal or two beam loom is crucial when considering the possibility of tapestry production since the maintenance of even warp tension and stability are essen-

a.

tial to this weaving technique. The instability of the warps of a warp-weighted loom makes it an unlikely vehicle for the production of tapestry weave.[8] While specific evidence for the existence of the shedding device in Anatolia at this early date has yet to emerge, it is difficult to believe that some form of it had not evolved over the eastern Mediterranean by the late Neolithic.[9] While it is possible to identify the existence of the technology necessary to produce slit-weave tapestry at these early dates, the evidence for the existence of the technique itself is much later. By the early to middle second millennium B.C. slit-weave tapestry seems to have entered Egypt from Syria, Anatolia's immediate neighbor.[10] At least one expert has associated the invention of the slit-weave technique with Anatolia.[11]

Polychromy, another prerequisite for the emergence of tapestry weave, is difficult to establish because of the carbonized state of extant textile fragments, which makes it impossible to determine whether dyes were used. However, the picture that is emerging suggests that polychromy developed gradually in the second and third millennium B.C.[12] There is evidence to suggest the stripe was in use in the fourth millennium B.C. in Susa, Mesopotamia, another region bordering on Anatolia.[13] In the third millennium B.C. there are three "hazy" indications of tapestry weave in the Near East, one of them for Anatolia;[14] however, the evidence for Anatolia is unfortunately undocumented and very controversial.[15]

The first really comprehensive view of Anatolian weaving emerges from the ruins of Gordion (Giordes), an ancient Phrygian city in west-central Anatolia remembered best as the place at which Alexander the Great cut the "Gordian knot." Preserved in several tombs and a layer of the city destroyed by fire in 690 B.C., a significant cache of textile fragments has survived, including various kinds of plain weave, felts, weft wrapping (soumak), and, significantly, scraps of slit-weave tapestry. The preserved patterns include simple stripes, quadruple lozenges, meanders, and double-barrel stripes.[16] These fragments establish that 1,800 years before the arrival of the Türkmen the weaving technology, the slit-weave technique, and simple geometric designs were already in the indigenous tradition.

Another cache of woven fabrics, dating from the late fifth and/or early fourth century B.C., also casts

Anatolia, the great land bridge between Central Asia, the Middle East, the Caucasus, and Balkan Europe.

light on Anatolian links with slit-weave tapestry. These are the Pazyryk textiles, which were preserved frozen in the ice of a chieftain's tomb in the Altai, a region in southern Siberia. Two strips of woollen cloth in slit-weave tapestry design found in this tomb are believed to have originated in Anatolia or neighboring Syria.[17] This evidence not only points to Anatolia as being in the slit-weave producing region but also suggests that at this early date Anatolia or its near neighbor was already an exporter of weavings in this technique. Therefore, fifteen hundred years before the Türkmen settled in Anatolia, examples of the technique were being exported to the East from the Anatolian region or nearby Syria.

However, it is one thing to recognize that Anatolia had a highly developed weaving tradition long before the eleventh century A.D. and that this tradition included the technology, technique, and the beginnings of a design tradition out of which a kilim tradition could have emerged. It is another to establish, as proponents of the Goddess theory have attempted to do, that Anatolia had already produced a fully developed kilim tradition in the sixth millennium B.C.

The Goddess Theory

The Goddess theory is an outgrowth of important archaeological discoveries made in the excavation of Çatal Hüyük, a site on the Çarsamba Çay River, southwest of Konya in Central Anatolia. The

excavation of what has been described as a Neolithic Pompeii was carried out in the 1960s by Dr. James Mellaart, a British archaeologist. Though never completed, it has revolutionized thinking on the nature of Neolithic civilization, which emerges as much more highly developed than previously thought. Since the abrupt termination of the excavations at Çatal Hüyük in 1965, Mellaart has gone on to put together a new theory for the origins of the Anatolian kilim—the "Goddess theory." He argues that large woven panels, some with striking resemblances to Anatolian kilims, were used as hangings in rooms dedicated to a religious cult centering on the worship of a Mother Goddess. While none of these weavings survive, nor any fragments or scraps of them, wall paintings, presumed by Mellaart to depict them, do. These murals, which have survived in various stages of preservation, are, he posits, actually copies of the weavings that were more typically used. Proof that the extant murals were copies of woven hangings is based primarily on the discovery of undecorated walls where decoration would have been expected and, in those same areas, peg holes, some with the remains of charred pegs embedded in them, suggesting the means for hanging textiles.[18] Actually of the four shrines Mellaart cites as having peg holes, in only one case was there a row of pegs feasible for hanging—and in that room there were actually traces of paint.[19] This very tenuous argument is buttressed by what Mellaart regards as very striking resemblances between the Neolithic murals and some Anatolian kilims.

The murals, Mellaart conjectures, were used in some cult rooms where woven hangings were not feasible, probably because of expense. The imagery of these murals, together with surviving plaster reliefs and terra cotta figures, has been interpreted as a codification of a number of ideas expressed in symbolic form which have been central to mankind's intellectual growth since Paleolithic times. As descendants of this tradition Anatolian kilims are by this reasoning the bearers of a repertoire of religious and symbolic motifs which date from Neolithic and even Paleolithic times.[20] The Goddess theory quickly intrigued many connoisseurs when it was introduced and captured the imaginations of many kilim gallery owners worldwide, but even its chief proponent, Mellaart, has admitted that to believe this hypothesis ". . . requires an act of faith almost as great as, and not entirely unconnected to, belief in God."[21]

A wide range of experts, including kilim and carpet scholars,[22] a professional weaver,[23] and an archaeologist-anthropologist,[24] have seriously questioned this hypothesis and shown an unwillingness to make this leap of faith. Instead they have quite reasonably asked that it be proved by the usual methodologies of science and scholarship. Their serious challenges to the validity of the Goddess hypothesis have yet to be satisfactorily answered.

To begin with, the documented evidence for the existence of the requisite wool yarns, the loom technology, the polychrome textiles, and the slit-weave tapestry technique in the early Neolithic period has yet to be produced. The historical record of the Near East established to date suggests that weavings of the sort attributed to Çatal Hüyük are not likely to have appeared before the third or fourth millennium B.C.[25]

The fragments of burial cloth found at Çatal Hüyük have been proven to be linen, not wool as Mellaart once thought.[26] Linen, because it does not take dyes readily, is not suited to polychromatic weavings, certainly not of the sophisticated type attributed to Çatal Hüyük. Further, there are additional problems with linen. While it is suitable as a tapestry warp it is not a suitable weft being deficient in those qualities that make wool so ideal for tapestry: loft, elasticity, flexibility, and compactibility.[27] Even the evidence for the use of the most basic dye, ochre, at Çatal Hüyük is very ambiguous.[28]

While the domestication of sheep was underway in the early Neolithic period, sheep at this date were still in their primitive, kempy form rather than the white woolly domesticated animals we know. The kempy coats of primitive sheep were coarse, hairy, and hence unsuitable for spinning or weaving. At the most there may have been a short, skimpy, woolly undercoating that would evolve over the millennia through selective breeding into full woolly coats. Further, these primitive coats ranged in color from black and dark brown through reddish and buff or gray colors, with very little white, colors typical of wild goats. These naturally pigmented fibers would have been unsuitable for dyeing and thus for polychromatic weavings—other than for weavings using animal fibers in their natural colors.[29] Not until the fourth or third millennium B.C. does evidence begin to appear for managed flocks of sheep suitable for wool production.[30]

While there is evidence suggesting the existence of the warp-weighted loom at Çatal Hüyük,[31] the loom at this early period would have been at a very primitive level of technology lacking the necessary warp tension and stability and hence not equipped to weave fabrics consisting of discontinuous wefts or eccentric wefting. While fragments of burial cloth survive from Çatal Hüyük, these seem to be the product of extemely elementary constructions. The cloths are either the result of weft-twining or transverse wrapping, simple techniques more related to basketry, or in the case of tabby cloths, to darning, a laborious method of weaving in which alternative warps were picked by hand. In all cases the cloths are the product of slow, tedious work. From a technical point of view it is an enormous leap from these simple burial fabrics to the sophisticated, large scale tapestries claimed by Mellaart.[32] Further, it seems very unlikely that a slit-weave kilim tradition would have first developed on a primitive warp-weighted loom and then been transferred to the ground loom tradition that has come down to us.

Not only is 6,000 B.C. impossibly early for the existence of the kind of weavings Mellaart attributed to Çatal Hüyük, but what strains credulity even further is the impossibility of the existence of the much earlier weaving tradition out of which such sophisticated weavings would have evolved. Furthermore, if a full-blown kilim tradition existed in the early Neolithic period, it is impossible to explain how a kilim tradition which still showed considerable vitality as late as the nineteenth century had remained virtually static, seemingly frozen in time for approximately eight thousand years.[33]

In addition to these serious questions about whether Çatal Hüyük had the necessary level of weaving technology to produce kilims, there are questions regarding the primary evidence that Mellaart presents to support his theory. The wall paintings as recorded in photographs, scale drawings, and what are described as "sketched reconstructions" have come under serious scrutiny. The bulk of the evidence chosen to demonstrate striking resemblances between the Neolithic murals and Anatolian kilims is drawn not from the photographed paintings and scale drawings included in the official archaeological reports published in the 1960s, but from the forty-four examples of sketched reconstructions which did not appear in print until twenty-five years later. These are not, as would be expected, supported by photographs taken at the site or by scale copy drawings executed by trained artists, nor has their authority been corroborated by anyone associated with the original excavations. But what is most damning and calls the credibility of the sketched reconstructions (and hence Mellaart's entire argument) into question is that in many cases the information in the official archaeological record contradicts the very existence of some of the murals depicted in the sketched reconstructions, their locations, and their content.[34] The suspicion aroused regarding Mellaart's methods and motives is understandable given the lack of any documentary evidence for materials which have since been destroyed or covered up. Leaving aside the sketched reconstructions, Mellaart's only credible evidence is reduced to a few photographs of wall paintings that have simple designs of triangles and rhombs that are not especially striking in their resemblances to Anatolian kilims.

Not only is the authenticity of these undocumented sketches very doubtful, but their plausibility as painted copies of weavings has been carefully examined and found wanting. From a weaver's point of view the sketched reconstructions of the painted murals are not convincing depictions of weavings. Given the technical restraints of the slit-weave technique, most of the designs could not have been produced using this method. Some of the designs (those shown in the photographs) are more akin to those of basketry or feltmaking. In slit-weave tapestry some designs would be impossibly weak in structure. Nor is the way that some designs

are organized convincing, consisting as they do of non-objective geometric forms scattered randomly rather than arranged in the aligned, regular fashion of woven patterns. Some designs could not have been executed in weavings, depicted as they are with the designs turned the wrong way in relation to the warps.[35]

There are even more problems with the sketches. The ideational content of the authenticated and the reconstructed evidence is markedly different. Mainly these differences have to do with the presence of the Mother Goddess. There are figures in the authenticated plaster wall reliefs and small terra-cotta figurines from the excavation that could be interpreted as Mother Goddesses, but such images appear only twice in the photographed murals. In marked contrast, "Goddess figures" appear in no less than twenty-five of Mellaart's forty-four sketched reconstructions.[36] In light of the very serious and legitimate objections to this undocumented evidence, it seems very lame indeed to argue that sketches had to be used since photography proved impossible because of the poor condition of the murals.[37]

It is also doubtful whether there actually was a Goddess cult at Çatal Hüyük. Since the civilization in question had not produced a written language, the evidence for its religious practices rests entirely on archaeological artifacts. Anyone, therefore, who attempts a reconstruction of the religious practices of this unknown people who inhabited a still-unnamed city is working in the realm of the speculative, since the archaeological evidence is open to a number of interpretations. An archaeologist-anthropologist, who left aside the suspect sketched reconstructions and focussed on the documented evidence, has concluded that Çatal Hüyük most likely had a religious pantheon of deities and spirits, not a fertility cult built around a Mother Goddess. There is, according to this scholar, no evidence for a Goddess who served as a preeminent figure, to say nothing of one who was dominant. While it is true that a Mother Goddess figure has been present throughout much of Anatolian history, the first convincing evidence for such a cult is no earlier than the fourth millennium B.C.[38]

In light of this evidence, belief in the Goddess theory requires, as Mellaart concedes, a considerable leap of faith. Certainly it is the romantic nature of the hypothesis rather than the convincing nature of the case made for it that explains why many in the kilim world have embraced it so readily. These converts argue that the resemblances between the extant Anatolian kilims and the Çatal Hüyük murals, as recorded in the sketched reconstructions, are too great to be merely coincidental. But what if the influences have actually flowed in the opposite direction, as sketched reconstructions of murals so badly damaged they could not be photographed were carried out years later by someone familiar with Anatolian kilims? Or, as has slyly been suggested, by someone working with an Anatolian kilim book at his elbow?[39]

For those who have nevertheless made the leap and believe in the Goddess theory there is yet another major difficulty. There is virtually no evidence of the kilim tradition between its supposed Neolithic origins and the kilims surviving from the last few centuries. Proponents of the Goddess theory, when faced with this hiatus of almost eight thousand years, argue that possessing the head—that is, the supposed Neolithic weavings as recorded in the sketched reconstructions of the Çatal Hüyük murals—and the tail—the surviving body of Anatolian kilims—we should be able to infer the existence and character of the missing body. Or using an analogy drawn from paleontology, if one discovers an ancient fossil prototype of a still-living fish, then the stages in between are not important; they must have existed even if they have not been found and thus are bound to turn up sooner or later.[40] However, if the head is proved to be false or the wrong one, then we are left with only the tail. We thus seem to find ourselves right back where we started, with the very end of a tradition and little sense of its origins or evolution. But not quite.

Even those who question the validity of the Goddess theory do not find it unreasonable to expect some elements of Neolithic imagery to survive in Anatolian kilims. However, to accept the possibility of some Neolithic survivals in the Anatolian kilim tradition is quite different from arguing that the Anatolian kilim is an artifact that originated in the early Neolithic and maintained its essential character over eight thousand years. While the original hypothesis of the Goddess theory may not hold up under scrutiny, the research it engendered has stimulated interest in the indigenous origins of the kilim. This new emphasis strikes a responsive chord in kilim studies since it accords with the growing perception that the kilim may have origins different from those of other flatweaves and the

knotted carpet. The old assumption that the kilim was brought to Anatolia wholesale by Türkmen nomads is no longer entirely convincing.

The Indigenous School

A more modest version of the Goddess theory, probably best called the "indigenous school," argues that most Anatolian kilim designs have developed from the earliest and longest-lived repertoires of Near Eastern symbols.[41] Belkis Balpınar and Udo Hirsch, the chief proponents of this more cautious theory, are heavily influenced by Mellaart's hypothesis, though curiously noncommittal about his argument for the existence of early Neolithic kilims. While they subscribe to his theory of the Mother Goddess cult and cite his sketched reconstructions of the Çatal Hüyük murals in their discussions, the main thrust of their arguments is to establish that most motifs found in Anatolian kilims descend from Neolithic and possibly even Paleolithic times.

Since no kilims, kilim fragments, or even evidence of kilims survive from the early Neolithic period down to long after the arrival of the Türkmen, the case for the continuity of ancient motifs and designs has necessarily been made using artifacts culled from ancient pottery, sculpture, and jewelry. An impressive array of evidence has been assembled, including "goddess" figurines, plaster reliefs, and clay seals from Çatal Hüyük; "goddess" shaped pots and painted bowls from Hacılar, another Anatolian Neolithic site; Phrygian rock tomb facades; Aegean island painted pottery; early Bronze Age figurines; and Roman and Byzantine sarcophagi and tombstones. Photographs and sketches of these items, together with Mellaart's sketched reconstructions, have been juxtaposed with kilims bearing similar looking motifs and designs.[42]

The cumulative effect of this rather simple methodology does tend to beguile the reader and seems to transform what is actually a rough, working hypothesis into established canon. However, now that the initial enthusiasm for the Goddess theory has begun to subside, it remains to be proved through careful scholarship that these perceived resemblances between kilim motifs and those of ancient art forms are the result of direct influence.

It is yet to be established how these ancient motifs, presumably produced mainly by urban high cultures, found their way into the Anatolian rural weaving traditions. No convincing evidence has been adduced that kilims were produced contemporaneously with these art traditions of ancient civilizations. In fact, the general picture that emerges at present suggests a great hiatus between the time that these ancient traditions faded away and the emergence of the Anatolian kilim. Further, while some broad similarities in form have been observed, the differences seem as prominent as the similarities in many cases, and in some instances the similarities seem at best fortuitous. A careful case by case analysis needs to be undertaken, followed by a great winnowing. Hopefully, what would remain is a small body of kilim motifs of authenticated ancient origins.

As this process is carried out, it should be recalled that there are ways of explaining resemblances other than direct influence. For one, the imperatives of a culture's characteristic symmetries, as we saw in chapter five, can powerfully shape the manner in which motifs and designs are rendered. In depicting the human form, for instance, a propensity for bilateral symmetries results in anthropomorphic forms shown in rigid frontal positions posing in a number of conventionalized symmetrical positions: arms at rest, hands on hips, arms extended out from the shoulders, or forward, or over the head. The elibelinde is one such figure presented frontally and symmetrically with hands on hips. While little attention has been paid to them, there are other related, seemingly anthropomorphic kilim motifs with symmetrical arm positions: hands on the breast (elibogründe), arms extended out from the shoulders, and arms raised above the head, and arms extended forward in supplication. The imperatives for symmetry that produced these poses, together with other conventionalized modes of schematizing the human form as base, trunk, and head (f), of exaggerating the indentation of the waist and rounding the female form, and of delineating in a linear style the male form, are bound to produce numerous coincidental resemblances over the millennia. The strikingly similar way in which Western children first draw their parents is a product of the common way they perceive, understand, and depict their world, not the result of copying drawings made by children in the past.

Another example that illustrates how certain imperatives shape design and create resemblances is the so-called pottery version of the Mother Goddess. Neolithic pots found in another Anatolian site, Hacılar are characteristically shaped in the conven-

tional base, trunk, head configurations and have hooked handles suggesting arms (h). These pottery goddesses, it is believed, were filled with grain to encourage germination. A prayer kilim motif composed of three stacked hexagons and a pair of hooks set within the frame of a tapering niche (i), it is argued, descends from these ancient pottery goddesses. Designs formed of stacked or conjoined hexagons are typical of Anatolian kilims, particularly those woven by the Türkmen tribes in the Konya region (plates 27, 29). Since the hexagons in these designs are usually equal in size, these configurations do not take on an anthropomorphic character. It is only when the hexagons are stacked inside a tapering niche in a combination of three that they do so. These stacked hexagons do vaguely resemble the goddess pots of Hacılar since the tapering niche necessitates that the stacked hexagons be arranged with the largest at the bottom and the smallest at the top, and this configuration is embellished with a pair of downward turning hooks.[43] However, there are also prayer kilims with niches containing hexagons in stacks of two or five (j). Even though the hexagons in these arrangements also taper they do not create a convincing resemblance to a pottery goddess, largely because they lack the conventional base-trunk-head configuration of simple anthropomorphic forms.

Even the basic assumptions that underlie the way we perceive elibelinde motifs need to be scrutinized. As an example, let us examine what appears to be the most obviously anthropomorphic of the elibelinde motifs, the so-called "deity motif with a long-skirted shape" (k). First it should be noted that there is no authenticated motif in the Çatal Hüyük pictorial evidence that resembles this long-skirted version. As characteristically handled in the kilim, the motif is formed of what is either half of an irregular hexagon or a triangle lacking its apex (the body), a small hexagon or diamond (the head), and a pair of downward turning hooks (the arms). With this version of the elibelinde are we looking at what was once a representational human form which has because of certain cultural and weaving imperatives become a geometrical motif? Or was it originally a geometrical form which over time, and particularly because of the downward turning hooks, became vaguely identified in the weavers' minds as anthropomorphic?

It should be recalled that Anatolian weavers only refer to the motif as elibelinde, "hands on hips," and

b.

c.

d.

e.

f.

g.

h.

i.

j.

k.

that no weaver has ever been reported to identify it as a goddess. Is it, therefore, possible that the weaving term "hands on hips" is no more related to meaning than the rest of the language of convenience weavers use? Is it possible that as weavers gradually lost touch with the original significance of their motifs, they subtly began to move them in an anthropomorphic direction? The history of weaving is, after all, filled with such metamorphoses as over time motifs that were originally birds have become airplanes, hanging lamps have been transformed into evergreens, and *botehs* (paisley shapes) have become roses.

Underlying the particular questions about the elibelinde motif is the larger question: Is the kilim lexicon composed of geometric motifs which were originally representational, or was the language originally geometric and abstract but evolving in the direction of the anthropomorphic, or absorbing anthropomorphic elements over time? At one time it was generally agreed among theoreticians that in the evolution of design the recognizable image must have been the original creation and that geometric forms were the end result of an evolution in which a naturalistic image was simplified and abstracted beyond recognition. But it is now accepted that the opposite can also occur. One such convincing example of the transformation of a geometric into a naturalistic image (l) is the acanthus motif.[44]

l.

The assumption underlying the argument of the indigenous theory is that the visual language of the kilim derives from a representational tradition and that this character originated and took form in the early Neolithic period in such cities as Hacılar and Çatal Hüyük. But, as we have seen, many of the basic tenets of this hypothesis have been called into question. The sketched reconstructions of the Neolithic murals are suspect, the existence of the Mother Goddess cult in the early Neolithic is doubtful, and the figurines, plaster reliefs, and goddess pots are archaeological artifacts open to various interpretations. When all is said and done, the original source of the kilim design tradition is still very much an open question.

For purposes of discussion we have focused on only a few examples of the elibelinde. This central icon of the goddess school is actually identified in many different forms, including the double-headed goddess, the goddess with leopards, the goddess with vultures (n), the goddess giving birth (o), the goddess of the mountain, the goddess in the cave,

m.

n.

o.

p.

q.

r.

and so forth. These versions range from seemingly anthropomorphic styles to extremely abstract, minimal hooked forms (r). Indeed, one of the great difficulties with the classifications is that there seem to be few guidelines that help to delineate what is and what is not a goddess image. In particular, in the more abstract versions there is no clear division between hooked forms identified as goddesses and those identified as rams' horns. Any downward turning hooked form or any geometric form with these embellishments is indiscriminately catalogued as "The Mother Goddess, mistress of leopards . . . with her hands cupping her breasts as an offering of fertility."[45]

At its best the study devoted to the elibelinde has increased our awareness of the distribution of these motifs throughout Anatolia, the Middle East, the Balkans, the Caucasus, Central Asia, and the Far East. At its worst it threatens to become a dead end since attaching downward turning hooks to almost any motif is a standard feature of Anatolian design and all such configurations seem destined to be catalogued as variations of the Goddess.

The indigenous school has built its case for design continuity in Anatolia not just on the continuity of motifs and designs in other art media but also on two related arguments. One is a historical study that argues for the survival of indigenous populations who preserved the old beliefs and ways, including a weaving tradition, despite all of the cultural transformations Anatolia passed through over the millennia. The other is the study of an existing population which describes itself as *yerli*, the native or settled population. The theory is that ancient Anatolian populations periodically were driven into remote mountainous areas, leaving the rich lowland areas to the new occupiers, whoever they were at a given period. These enclaves of indigenous people, it is argued, resisted all attempts at religious and cultural assimilation as Anatolia passed through its Hittite, Phrygian, Hellenistic, Byzantine, and Islamic stages.

It is plausible, given the long history of Anatolia, its rugged terrain, and its cultural, linguistic, and religious complexity, that numerous ancient cultural survivals have always coexisted with the dominant culture. For example, it is an open question how thoroughly the different ruling groups of a given period managed to acculturate the populations in the remote regions. Until recent times the nomadic and peasant populations of the interior and eastern regions have largely maintained a cultural identity quite apart from that of the urbanized and coastal regions. However, accepting the probability of such limited cultural survivals is not the same as arguing for the continuity of an eight thousand-year-old culture preserved by an isolated, almost underground, Anatolian population. The story-book-like arguments put forth to support this theory suggest more the assembling of evidence to prove a preconceived theory than dispassionate scholarship in search of historical truth.

The search for ancient cultural survivals has, however, had the positive effect of initiating a serious examination into the ethnic makeup of the Anatolian population, in particular of the yerli, who perceive themselves and are perceived in turn as different from their Türkmen and Yörük neighbors. They have maintained a strict separation from the tribal groups around them and do not mingle or intermarry. They adhere to what they perceive as the old ways and their architecture, customs, and weaving traditions are different from those of their neighbors. For these reasons, it might be argued they could be an indigenous population.[46] But they are also, it should be emphasized, Turkish speaking and Muslim, and have been so for a long time.

One group of yerli, living in a remote mountainous region of western Anatolia bounded by the towns of Eskişehir, Kütahya, Afyon, and Bursa historically part of ancient Phrygia, has been studied primarily because of its distinctive kilim, the *parmaklı*, which means "with fingers" (Plates 32–33). The unusual nature of its "fingered" designs and its uncharacteristic weaving technique, which de-emphasizes the slit-weave technique and employs considerable eccentric wefting, set these kilims apart from other Anatolian kilims. The fieldwork carried out in these remote villages has contributed to an expanded knowledge of kilim design and toward building a strong case for an indigenous tradition with historical continuity, possibly as far back as a thousand years before Christ in Phrygian times.

However, accepting at face value the villagers' descriptions of themselves as yerli without the support of thorough anthropological and historical investigations seems risky. Such claims may be ideological rather than historical. Also the testimonies of the yerli can be somewhat contradictory. For example, one elderly villager from Ayazın proudly identified himself as a yerli, boasted that his people were the oldest inhabitants of the region, and insist-

ed that they had always lived there. When pressed on the origins of his people he saw no contradiction in claiming both that they inhabited the region prior to the Türkmen and that his people originally came from Khurasan, the homeland of the Türkmen![47] It is possible the yerli of the "Phrygian highlands" predate the Türkmen tribes settled around them and that their lineage stretches back to Phrygian times. However, it could also be they only predate the arrival of the Türkmen into their own immediate region. The hypothesis that they are an ancient population deserves further study, but the point of view should be broadened to include other major "yerli" populations, among them, the Armenians, the Kurds, and the Assyrians. To exclude from a study of indigenous origins these ancient populations, which have maintained their cultural identities, their religions and languages into this century, seems very myopic indeed.

The identification of a yerli population with its own distinctive parmaklı weaving tradition has raised more problems regarding the indigenous theory than it answers. The dilemma of the indigenous school is that the vast majority of typical Anatolian kilim motifs and designs (including even the eli-belinde) are most typically found not in the weavings of the yerli but in the repertoires of the Türkmen and the Yörük. A new hypothesis is required to explain why so much of what is identified as the indigenous repertoire is more likely to be found in weavings of descendants of the tribal populations that only began to arrive in the eleventh century.

The very reasons put forward to explain the survival of the yerli—their conservatism, their hermetic, inward-looking tradition, their refusal to intermingle and intermarry with other groups—make it unlikely they would have drawn the new populations into their culture. In contrast the newly arrived Türkmen are characterized (obviously for purposes of explaining transference) as being open to new ïdeas and having a propensity to intermarry.[48] However, arguments of this sort lead to apparent contradictions in the ways tribal cultures are characterized. When the need is to prove cultural survival, the emphasis in the indigenous school's argument is placed on the hermetic, closed, insular nature of the tribe, but when the need is to prove transference the tribal inclinations for interaction and intermarriage are underlined.

Historically, transferences have been known to take place in Anatolia when a weaker tribe has been subjugated by a larger one. There are documented instances in which forced conversions and assimilations were carried out by Türkmen tribes. The forced conversion of the Şabanlı, thereafter known as *kiliç* Türkmen, that is, converted by the sword, is one such example.[49] However, given that the Türkmen were the invaders and the indigenous population the subjugated, any transferences were as likely to have been in the opposite direction—from the Türkmen to the indigenous population.

Another hypothesis on transference posits that kilims served heraldic functions associated with fixed territories and that as Türkmen tribes displaced the indigenous populations they adopted their kilim designs as a means of legitimizing their territorial claims. Historically, the newly established Selçuk principality in Konya did appropriate the Byzantine emblem of the double eagle as its own; therefore, it is argued, the various Türkmen tribes could have done likewise in the regions they usurped.[50] While there is some plausibility to the argument especially given certain resemblances between heraldic and kilim motifs, at present too little is known about the interactions between the indigenous and new populations during a turbulent period to reach a definitive conclusion.

The case for the indigenous origins of the kilim has neither been proved nor disproved, but the debate has clarified a number of issues. There is no doubt that, starting in Neolithic times, Anatolia evolved its own distinctive weaving tradition. It is incontestable that long before the arrival of the Türkmen, Anatolian weavers had invented the weaving technology and technique necessary for the creation of the slit-weave kilim. What fails to stand up is the hypothesis that the kilim already existed in early Neolithic times at Çatal Hüyük, where it served as cult textiles in rooms devoted to the worship of a Mother Goddess. Nor is it convincing that when the Türkmen reached Anatolia they encountered a fully developed indigenous kilim tradition which they adopted wholesale.

The Türkmen Theory

Those who subscribe to the Türkmen theory argue that Anatolian kilims are not primarily indigenous in character but are an outgrowth of a cultural continuum which, while it may also include other influences, has as its center the culture of Turkic people.[51] The indigenous school counters by arguing that the notion that kilims were brought to the

West by Turks is no more supportable than the once widely held contention that Turks brought the carpet to the West.[52] As polarized as these positions seem, there is some common ground. Both sides agree that the Anatolian kilim occupies a special niche in the larger weaving tradition. Even those who most vehemently insist on the Turkic origins of Anatolian weaving acknowledge that Central Asian design in its purest form is not found in the kilim but rather in the other flatweavings, felts, and the pile carpet.[53] No one seriously argues that the Anatolian kilim as we know it arrived full blown with the Türkmen, nor are Central Asian kilims offered as convincing prototypes.

The contrast between the unusually predominant role the kilim plays in Anatolian weaving traditions and the relatively minor role it plays in those of Central Asia argues forcefully against direct Türkmen influence. It is logical to expect that if the kilim was originally a Türkmen artifact brought from Khurasan, something similar to it would still be found in use among the present Türkmen population in Central Asia, or there would be evidence for its having played such a role in the past. This is not the case. Instead, it is feltmaking, the knotted pile rug, and forms of flatweaving other than the kilim that are primary among the tribal peoples of Central Asia. This weaving region has produced relatively few varieties of kilims, and the design and technique of these kilims differ markedly from those of Anatolia. If the Türkmen did arrive with a slit-weave kilim that resembled the Anatolian kilim, it was probably adopted as they moved through the Caucasian regions on their migrations. However, little is known about this period of their history and therefore such an adoption of the Caucasian kilim remains speculative.[54]

This is not to say that certain Turkic influences could not have played a large, even predominant, role in reshaping the character of whatever Anatolian or possibly Caucasian kilim traditions they encountered. Proponents of the Türkmen hypothesis argue that these influences flow from other Central Asian weaving forms, as well as the felt and reed screen traditions.

Discovering the nature of these Central Asian Türkmen influences in Anatolian weaving is complicated by the long period between the thirteenth and the present century when there was little direct interaction, and the two weaving traditions developed independently. The Türkmen design tradition that originally entered Anatolia undoubtedly was not only influenced and modified by whatever traditions it encountered en route to Anatolia but by whatever indigenous design tradition, the nature of which is still to be established, it encountered in Anatolia. Subsequent to their settlement in Anatolia, other layers of influence, chiefly Selçuk and Ottoman, also overlaid the original character of the Türkmen tribal designs. However, since new influences in a traditional activity like weaving rarely displace the old, the new influences instead combining with and overlaying the old, a residue of basic motifs and designs (the old core design vocabulary) still survive and can possibly be rediscovered. This ancient core of design, once identified, not only establishes links to the original source but also additional links with the weavings of other peoples who share with the original source a common ancestry or ancient contacts.[55]

Current thinking in the Türkmen school is that core motifs found in the weavings of Western and Central Asia derive from a pre-Islamic iconography of great antiquity, perhaps of shamanic origin (s). In the Central Asian shamanic worldview the universe is divided horizontally into three levels: the upper, the middle, and the lower. The upper world, signified by the sun, the circle of light, is the source of all outer and inner illumination. Contact with the world takes place along a vertical axis usually represented as a tree, a pillar, or a post (the axle of the universe), hence the sacred tree or tree of life.[56]

The tree-like motifs of the Yüncü kilims (plates 2–7) as well as the trees of life typically depicted in prayer kilims (plates 67, 70, 71, 73) may descend from such influences. Similarly the tripartite designs (plates 26, 36) could reflect the Shamanic view of the cosmos. It is, however, too soon to be certain in such matters since the study of the core motifs and their meanings is still in its infancy.

The search for Türkmen influences leads not only to Central Asia but beyond to their homeland in Mongolia on the borders of the Chinese Empire. The first record of the Turkic peoples is in the Chinese Annals of A.D. 545, which refers to them as the *Tiou Kioue.* At this period they were a nomadic people indistinguishable from the Mongols. Their shared heritage is captured in the legend that the two peoples descended from Tatar and Mongol, twin sons of the Oghuz king, Alindje Khan.

The Turkic and Mongolian tribes adopted certain motifs from the dominant Chinese culture,

made them their own, and brought them westward, dispersing these influences as they migrated to Khurasan and on to the Caucasus and Anatolia. The imperial insignia of the Han Dynasty (206 B.C. to A.D. 220), the *Yün-chien,* which has become known as the cloud collar, is one such motif. A case has recently been made that it (not an indigenous Anatolian fertility goddess) is the actual source for what Anatolians call the elibelinde.[57] The cloud collar, believed to have cosmogonic significance and displayed on the collars of princely garments, is a circular form punctuated with images that are similar to the elibelinde. It is still to be found on contemporary Mongolian and other steppe nomad tent decorations. In fact, elibelinde-like images are found in almost all categories of carpets made by Turkic peoples and are not, as some discussions of the Goddess school would lead one to believe, unique to Anatolian kilims.

Ironically, the search for origins has brought the two schools of thought into direct confrontation over one of the central kilim motifs. Is the elibelinde an ancient Anatolian fertility motif that spread into neighboring regions along with religious practices, agricultural innovations, and weaving technologies? Or is it an ancient Chinese imperial motif, the yün-chien, descending from the Han Dynasty and brought to the Near East and Central Asia by the Türkmen?

In both cases, the arguments assume an incredible period of survival. To have reached the present, the yün-chien would have had to survive through 80 to 100 generations and movements across vast regions from Mongolia to Khurasan and then on to the Caucasus and Anatolia. If the elibelinde originated in the Mother Goddess cult, the motif would have had to survive through 350 to 400 generations and dispersion from Anatolia throughout the Near and Middle East as well as the Caucasus, Central Asia, and Balkan Europe.[58] It is too soon to make a definitive case for either hypothesis. And there is, as we have seen, always the alternative that similar motifs originated in a number of regions and merged into a single entity, a not uncommon occurrence in the history of ancient symbols. While it is conceivable that the motifs might have survived over such huge spans of time and space, the likelihood of there being continuity in meaning, given what we know about the volatility of symbols, is virtually nil.

The present impasse in thinking on the eli-

s. *The Shamanic Cosmos*

t.

u.

v.

w.

x.

y.

belinde/cloud collar motif demonstrates the difficulties in establishing influences and origins by relying primarily on an examination of individual motifs. Such a methodology might bring clearer results if mutually exclusive cultural zones were involved, as with Europe and the New World at the time of Columbus. However, Anatolia and Khurasan were emphatically not mutually exclusive cultures at the time of the Türkmen migrations.

From ancient times the Near East was the center of an advanced culture which dispersed its agriculture, religion, and art to the regions around it. Anatolia was the great land bridge for the mass movements of peoples and cultures to the East and West. From early Neolithic times Anatolia was a crucial transitional zone between the weaving regions of Europe and the Middle East and Egypt. Its history is one of ancient, continuous interactions between the Near and Middle East and Central Asia as well as the Caucasus and Balkan (European) regions. Influences and populations from Central Asia had entered Anatolia long before the Oghuz tribes migrated in the eleventh century, so when the Türkmen arrived Anatolia and Khurasan already shared certain religious and cultural traditions.

Another significant design link has been posited between the octagonal motifs characteristic of Central Asian Türkmen weavings and the hexagonal motifs prominent in Anatolian kilims. The octagon appears in many variations, in particular in the numerous Türkmen tribal *göls*, emblematic motifs which express the identities of the various tribes. It is generally accepted that the octagon represents the circle, an ancient Türkmen motif referring to the sun and of great symbolic significance. The translation of this ancient motif into octagonal motifs, it has been argued, resulted from the technical constraints of the Türkmen knotted pile weave, which could not produce curvilinear forms because of the size of its knots. (However, this explanation is not entirely convincing since a reasonable circle can be executed in the tiny knots typical of the older Türkmen pieces.) The more orthogonal technique of the kilim, together with the imperatives of the slitweave technique, it is conjectured, caused the Central Asian octagon to metamorphose into the Anatolian kilim hexagon. Thus, the Anatolian hexagon refers to the Türkmen octagon, which ultimately refers to the circle.

While it is difficult to believe that the indigenous Anatolian weaving tradition would have been dependent on the Türkmen for the introduction of forms as basic as the octagon or hexagon, it is conceivable that the prominence of the hexagon in Anatolian design was a result of the octagon's role in the pile weavings of Khurasan. Since it was the descendants of the Central Asian Oghuz, the various Türkmen and Yörük tribal groups of Anatolia, who created the bulk of Anatolian kilims, such an influence is very likely.

There is no evidence, however, that the symbolic content of the Türkmen octagon passed into the hexagonal adaptations of the Anatolian weavers. Further, the supposed common motif (the hexagon/octagon) is handled quite differently in the designs of Anatolia and Central Asia. The Central Asian Türkmen weaver characteristically arranges relatively small octagonal göls in ordered rows on a plain field (v), creating a repeat pattern in a restrained palette of red and blue with a minor use of yellow or white. In contrast, the Anatolian weaver typically creates very large, central hexagonal motifs which are usually regular in form (w). The Anatolian motif functions as dominant medallions in a design featuring numerous other minor motifs. These oversized hexagonal medallions are typically ordered or conjoined in a single or double row down the center of the main field. The palette of Anatolian kilim weavers is more brilliant, employing a much wider range of colors in combinations with very high contrasts. Indeed, despite a shared preference for red, the flamboyant Anatolian kilim palette is one of the features that most differentiates Anatolian weavings from those of Central Asia.

Another obstacle to postulating a transference between the two traditions is that the Central Asian Türkmen characteristically used the octagonal motifs in knotted pile and brocaded weavings, not in kilims. Türkmen kilims of Central Asia usually consist of narrow banded designs with small motifs.

The difficulties involved in establishing influences between traditions by identifying shared motifs are illustrated by a recent study of the relationship between the Türkmen *ak kaz* (white goose) motif and the Anatolian *çomçalı* (ladle) motif.[59] The Central Asian ak kaz is composed of a pair of bird-like forms (x), often sharing the same body, their wings and necks outstretched, flying in opposite directions. The Anatolian *çomçalı* (y) similarly consists of two bird-like forms flying in opposite directions (plate 11). Slightly different versions are to be found in the flatweavings of Central Asia and Anatolia. Further they are found on artifacts in both traditions, chiefly dust covers and storage bags, that serve similar functions in the tents and cottages of the two regions.

The populations of both regions, despite their conversion to Islam, have retained vestiges of shamanism down to the present. Anatolia and Central Asia share a common shamanic symbol in the white goose. Like the swan, it is regarded as an auspicious bird and as the shaman's familiar. The white goose is a symbol for the reconciliation of opposites (fire and water) and an archetype of bisexuality. Its whiteness stands for purity, strength, and grace, and represents an incarnation of light, which is seen in two forms: one diurnal, solar, and male; the other nocturnal, lunar, and female. While the wild goose visits the earth, it also belongs to the heavens, and like the migrations of the nomads its movements are seasonal and two-directional.[60]

However, the Sarıtekeliler weavers of Anatolia identify this motif as the çomçalı (ladle) and not ak kaz (white goose), which suggests that if the motif was ever identified as a bird-form in Anatolia the memory of its significance vanished some time ago. While the motifs resemble each other, they are handled in the two design traditions in markedly different ways. Characteristically, the ak kaz appears as a small motif in narrow banded designs, while the çomçalı appears in enlarged medallions as a central motif. Further, the ak kaz is worked out in muted colors as part of a repeat design, while the çomçalı is very colorful and dramatic in its effect.

Attempting to identify relationships between design traditions by singling out shared motifs differs little from arguing that languages belong to the same family because they share a small body of vocabulary. A common grammar is obviously more convincing. Likewise in a visual language shared designs and structural principles are the more convincing indicators of direct influences or common origins, since it is always possible for individual motifs to be absorbed into preexisting languages. As a general rule, designs are older than some of the individual motifs they contain. For these reasons, focussing on motifs in isolation from the larger design is not usually the most effective methodology.

Rather than being isolated, a motif should be viewed as a component of a design and discussed in that context. Design is created through the relationship established between a major motif and a group of either similar or dissimilar motifs. An oc-

tagonal medallion centered in a rectangular field and embellished with pairs of ram's horns and surrounded by rows of triangles and small hexagons becomes the major image of a larger design.

The design itself is organized on the surface of the kilim according to certain structural principles.[61] As we saw in chapter five, the oldest structural principle operating in the Anatolian kilim is the horizontal banded arrangement, which had its origins in the simple stripe designs (plates 13–25). A variant is the vertical banded design. Other major structural principles shaping Anatolian kilim design include the rectangular grid (plates 20, 29, 30), the repetition of hexagons (plate 47), the diamond grid, concentric diamonds (plates 31–38), and diagonal bands. One additional important structural principle is the undivided central field dominated by large, central hexagonal medallions and framed by a border (plates 39–50).[62] As we suggested in chapter five, this is a structural principle that does not seem to have its origins in the indigenous tradition. Discovering where this category of kilim originated depends upon locating other design traditions that share this design and structural principle.

A convincing case has been made that certain categories of kilims share their structural principles with types of medieval Turkish carpets, which were the outgrowth of Central Asian Türkmen influences. However, these correspondences do not extend to the individual motifs themselves. One medieval Turkish carpet type consists of a single unbroken field dominated by a row of large octagonal medallions. A variety of Anatolian kilims has the same structural principle (see plates 39–49) and a similar design, but the medallion is hexagonal rather than octagonal. While a number of other striking parallels have been established between various carpet and kilim categories, such comparisons do not purport to establish the carpet as the source for kilim designs. Instead the correspondences between the carpet and kilim traditions are more likely the result of a common source, such as earlier Turkic textile or felt-making traditions.[63]

These ancient precursors are presently the subject of much speculation. One of the most convincing candidates as a source for certain kilim designs is the reed screen tradition of Central Asia.[64] An important feature of the round felt tent, the reed screen is composed of steppe grass, *Lasiagrostis splendens (graminea)*, the canes of which are cut to size, twined together into a screen, and run around

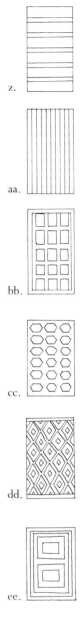

z.

aa.

bb.

cc.

dd.

ee.

ff.

gg.

hh.

ii.

jj.

kk.

ll.

the perimeter of the tent interior. This screen, with the reeds in a vertical position, acts as a lightweight floor to ceiling wall which keeps out the glare and dust as well as small animals and chickens when the tent sides are raised, and also probably (although this is a matter of some debate) provides added insulation when the tent sides are down. Some tribes cover their screens with designs, transforming them into the primary decoration of the social space, while others leave them plain except for the zigzag lines created by the binding yarns.

The Qirgiz and Qazak are nomadic tribes in the steppes north of Turkmenistan who still live in round felt tents fitted out with decorated reed screens. Numerous examples of their screens have been preserved in museum collections.[65] To achieve their elaborate designs, the reed screen makers place the cut reeds in order and mark them in such a way that when the reeds are wrapped in different configurations of dyed wools and then twined together, an elaborate overall design is created. The technique is not unlike that of ikat weaving, in which predyed threads in preplanned patterns are woven together to create a designed fabric. However, since no loom in the usual sense is used in the process, reed screen making is closer to basketry than to weaving.

The Qazak and Qirgiz reed screens (hh–ll) bear an uncanny resemblance to Anatolian kilims in their motifs and designs and particularly their structural principles. The spaciousness of the reed screen designs—their large, bold, geometric motifs embellished with hooks and horns—and the hard-edged clarity of the designs make these screens infinitely more convincing as precursors of Anatolian kilim designs than the suspect sketched reconstructions of Çatal Hüyük murals. Even the technical constraints of reed screen making and kilim weaving are similar. Motifs in both techniques are worked out by subtly stepping the designs up and down a rigid foundation, canes in the case of the reed screen and warps in the case of the kilim. In both, the numerous hooked and horned embellishments, which obviously descend from a curvilinear design tradition, become angular, almost linear, in character. Diagonal lines are preferred over vertical and are actually serrated rather than straight. Motifs are predominantly linear, geometric, and nonrepresentational in character. Both the motifs and designs favor configurations that are bilaterally and horizontally symmetrical. The structural principles on

which so many reed screen designs are arranged accord with many of the typical Anatolian design structures.

Besides these design similarities, there are significant correspondences in terms of function and characteristic sizes. As we have seen in the previous chapter, kilims were once used by some Anatolian nomads as tent surrounds serving practical and decorative functions comparable to those of reed screens. The reed screen used around the inner periphery of the outer walls of the tent is similar in size to the typical Anatolian main or long kilim (plates 39–49). The medium-sized reed screen, used to separate the living area from the milk-processing area, approximates the medium sized kilim (plates 2–8). The small reed screen, used as tent door panels, is comparable in size to the standard prayer size kilim (plates 58–73).[66] Given the striking resemblances in design together with these correspondences in function and size, the case for the decorated reed screen as precursor to the Anatolian kilim has great plausibility; however, there remains the tricky problem of transference.

How it needs to be established did the Central Asian decorated reed screen designs find their way into the Anatolian kilim? The hypothesis is that during the great migrations between the eleventh and thirteenth centuries components of the tribal confederations arrived bringing the decorated reed screen tradition with them. In their new environment they were unable to maintain the tradition in its original form since Anatolia lacked the steppe grass they were accustomed to using. Further, they found themselves in a region in which they could make limited migrations, up to the mountains for the summer and down to the lowlands in the winter, and thereby live year round in a relatively mild climate. Reed screen making, therefore, fell into disuse. However, the visual decoration and, perhaps, its symbolic content were missed and, therefore, transferred to kilims, which replaced the reed screens as tent surrounds, partitions, and doors.[67]

The difficulty with the argument is that the decorated reed screen does not seem to have been a Türkmen tradition and there is as yet no evidence that appreciable numbers of the Qazak and Qirgiz were ever part of the great migrations into Anatolia. The only evidence for their presence in Anatolia is very recent, when they arrived in 1953 and 1982 as refugees. The present day Türkmen of Central Asia and Azerbaijan make reed screens but do not decorate them. Nor is there any evidence that Türkmen decorated reed screens in the past.[68] It has been argued, however, that the Qazak and Qirgiz could have participated in the migrations since the great tribal confederations were constantly in flux and were more temporary political groupings than ethnically homogeneous entities. The Qazak and Qirgiz, with their strong cultural affinities to the Türkmen, could, therefore, have been included.[69] Only a more complete historical record and a thorough study of the ethnic makeup of Anatolia's complex tribal populations can resolve this dispute.

There is, however, another way of explaining why the designs of the reed screens and certain Anatolian kilims resemble each other. Both may derive their designs from a common source in an older design tradition. Discussions of the origins of carpet design, kilim design, and reed screen design invariably lead to speculation about an older common source, the most likely candidate being feltmaking.

Felt was the predominant covering fabric among the Central Asian nomads. It is generally accepted that felt is the invention of the nomads of the steppes and that it was dispersed from these regions.[70] It was used for every conceivable purpose, not just for rugs, clothing, foot coverings, horse trappings, and baggage, but even dishes and idols, and, of course, for the tent. As an indication of the importance of its role, while feltmaking could be removed from most cultures with no serious disruption to their way of life, it is no exaggeration to say that its removal from traditional Central Asian nomadic culture would have threatened life itself. While Anatolia by the time of the arrival of the Türkmen in the eleventh century A.D. was already engaged in feltmaking, unquestionably the role it played there and the influence of the associated design traditions increased markedly with the arrival of new populations from Khurasan.

How the transference from the feltmaking tradition to the Anatolian kilim took place remains to be established. The transference from feltmaking to the reed screen seems clearer. There is what seems to be an intermediate, decorated reed screen tradition in which felt-type designs are painted onto the screens. Conceivably the next step was improving on the designs and the insulating qualities of the screens by wrapping them with dyed wools. Unfortunately, there are no similar clues for the transference to kilims. It has, however, been conjectured for some time that Yüncü kilim designs were di-

rectly transferred from earlier felt designs. There are still felt rugs in use in Central Asia that strikingly resemble the classic Yüncü kilims. However, the investigation into the relationship between the felt and kilim traditions has barely begun.

Obviously at present the investigation into origins is a field very much in flux. Although a clearer picture is slowly emerging, it remains to be seen whether elucidating the history and origins of the kilim will establish what the meaning of the kilims were to the Anatolian tribal cultures that wove and used them. It would be one thing to establish the historical meaning of a motif or design in its host culture, whether it be Khurasan or ancient Çatal Hüyük, but quite another to discover what it meant and how those meanings evolved among the weavers of Anatolian kilims. It may be as in linguistics where the quest for the "spirit" of a language has been largely abandoned, that the quest for the origins of kilim images and meanings may finally prove to be similarly inconclusive. As contemporary studies of language have shifted their focus from the search for ancient origins to an analysis of how language actually functions in any one community, so we might follow suit and concentrate on the known functions of kilim designs in the past and present. Unfortunately, such a focus might not take us very far back in time since so few kilim artifacts have survived from before the nineteenth century.

Whether or not kilim meanings and origins are ever elucidated, research on the kilim nevertheless continues to increase our understanding of it as a major artifact of tribal culture. And with increased understanding comes greater appreciation. It is, however, still too early to arrive at hard and fast theories. We are presently at a stage of inquiry where it is better to consider carefully all of the possibilities. The kilim is after all probably thousands of years old and our attempt to understand it spans not much more than thirty, and only in the last decade of these thirty years has intensive investigation been carried on. It remains to be seen how the Anatolian kilim will be perceived in the twenty-first century.

Chapter 9

The Horn and the Hexagon

The study of design origins and evolution is, as we have seen, difficult for an artefact like the Anatolian kilim. The climate of Anatolia is not ideal for the preservation of textiles, and until recently no effort has been made to preserve kilims as historical artefacts. Also, huge gaps in the historical record of Anatolia complicate this problem. The relatively few surviving kilims that predate the eighteenth century are very fragmental because older kilims deteriorated gradually from being buried beneath the layers of votive rugs and kilims that have typically carpeted the older mosques in Anatolia.

While the West has collected and preserved examples of Oriental rugs and carpets since the fourteenth century, a serious interest in the kilim has only developed over the last few decades. Rugs and carpets that were originally exported to Europe during the Renaissance were luxury items only within the means of royals, aristocrats, the high bourgeoisie, and church dignitaries. Because these rugs and carpets were regarded as prestigious items from what was then the superior culture of the Mediterranean world, they were kept in protected environments, recorded in inventories, and carefully preserved. While relatively few survived, we have pictorial evidence of them in royal and aristocratic portraits as well as in paintings with religious themes, particularly those treating episodes from the life of the Virgin Mary.

From the early Renaissance, Oriental rugs and carpets were stock props in the mise-en-scène of painters and also appeared in nineteenth-century paintings as Romantic accoutrements of Orientalism. No comparable pictorial record exists for the Anatolian kilim.

The problems posed by the lack of a continuous historical record of kilims have been further compounded by political factors as researchers, collectors, and curators of Turkish backgrounds or sympathies on one side and Armenian and other minority Anatolian populations on another side establish their cases. As expected, Turks and Turcophiles prefer to see the kilim as a Türkmen artefact while Armenians favor theories that stress the indigenous contributions of their own ethnic group.

As seen in the last chapter, Turks and Turcophiles, together with some Western dealers, have favored a new indigenous theory—the now discredited Goddess theory. This theory seemed to have the advantage of leapfrogging over the counterclaims of the Turk's ancient adversaries by focusing on origins in Neolithic times. This focus, interestingly, parallels the way the politically motivated Ankara government in its state museums and touristic literature prefers to focus on Anatolia's Hittite past (there are no contemporary Hittites with territorial claims) rather than its Greco-Roman past. The Goddess theory serves similar ends by crediting the Anatolian kilim design to an ancient Anatolian culture that predates the emergence of the Armenians, Greeks, and Kurds.

Not only nationalistic concerns but also the interests of the marketplace have come into play to skew the arguments favoring such theories as the Goddess theory. The effect of this theory, and possibly the conscious aim of some of its promoters, was to remove the kilim not only from the realm of nationalistic territorial claims and rivalries but also to remove it from the category of the Oriental rug, thereby elevating it to a higher status as an ethnographic textile of great antiquity. This elevation not only would have given the kilim greater cachet but also terminated its status as a poor cousin of the knotted rug and carpet, allowing for significant mark-up potential. After all, if it were possible to prove that the Anatolian kilim descended from an eight-thousand-year-old tradition, it would be seen as a part of the most ancient, continuous design tradition in the world—and priced accordingly.

Thus ancient enmities, territorial disputes, national pride, and mercenary considerations all serve to obfuscate and confuse what is already a difficult area of study. Rather than attempt to discuss how the entire Anatolian kilim design tradition came to be, it might be more productive, given how limited our knowledge is at this point, to narrow our focus to an examination of how several motifs and their combinations may have evolved and, from that endeavor, to gain more general insights into the evolution of kilim design.

The Strange Horn / Hexagon Combination

Two of the most ubiquitous motifs in the Anatolian kilim repertoire are the hexagon (a) and the ram's horn, in Turkish the *koç boyunuzu* (b). As often as not these two motifs are seen in combination in the form of hexagons bracketed or decorated with ram's horns (c). Indeed, so common is their combination that we might regard the pairing as a single motif—the horn/hexagon combination. In fact, if one were asked to choose the motif that is most typical of Anatolian kilim design the horn/hexagon combination would probably be it. For instance, if we examine the plates in this book the motif in one form or other is present in fifteen out of the thirty-five nonprayer kilim examples.[1]

Because the horn/hexagon combination is so prominent in the Anatolian kilims that survive, it is regarded as a natural part of the design repertoire. However, closer examination reveals that the two motifs appear to come from very different worlds. It becomes clearer on reflection that the pair are not really as natural a combination as they first appear. In fact, in many important respects this seemingly natural combination represents the fusion of opposites. I would argue that the ram's horn motif is a borrowed motif from another textile tradition, while the hexagon is a motif that naturally emerged from the slit-weave tapestry technique.

Why the hexagon is such a natural kilim motif was demonstrated in chapter 5, where I made the argument that the structural limitations of the tapestry weave typical of the kilim, together with the propensity of Anatolian weavers to favor an orthogonal technique, produced motifs that are rectilinear rather than curvilinear. These constraints shaped a repertoire of kilim motifs largely consisting of geometric forms: triangles, diamonds, and hexagons, rather than one of representational forms.

The ram's horn, on the other hand, is a quintessentially curvilinear motif (d) and, therefore, would not have naturally emerged from the Anatolian tapestry weaving tradition. As established earlier, any curvilinear motif found in Anatolian kilims would have originated in other design traditions. The alien nature of the *koç boyunuzu* is shown in the typically awkward, angular rendering this motif receives in kilims. These renderings result from a process of translation in which the curved lines of the original motif are necessarily approximated in the orthogonal kilim weave by fracturing the curve into short broken straight lines (e).

The result is a rough translation of what was a curvilinear motif into a medium not suited to it. The accidental result is that the awkward renderings give Yüncü kilims an archaic look, a factor that may explain part of their appeal to Western collectors (see plate 2). While the remedial technique of eccentric wefting would have accommodated the motif better, the propensity of the Anatolian weaver, as we have seen, has always been to remain with the orthogonal character of weaving.

a.

b.

c.

d.

e.

Hexagon and Horn Compared: Function

The hexagon is an abstract geometric form while the koç boyunuzu is believed to be a stylized representation of a natural form—the ram's horn. While the hexagon may function in a heraldic way, it does not seem to have an identifiable symbolic meaning, and the ram's horn has traditionally been regarded as an ancient fertility symbol amongst Turkic pastoral peoples.

In terms of cultural preferences for symmetries, the ram's horn in its original form is basically a bilateral symmetrical motif, while the hexagon fulfills what seems to be the Anatolian world's clear preference for double symmetries. Significantly, it appears that in the Yüncü kilims, and in combination with hexagons in other Anatolian kilim designs, this bilateral motif is always doubled by either placing them so that they flank the tree trunk as in the classic Yüncü kilim (plates 2 and 3) or by having them flank or embellish hexagons in the kilims of the Konya region and by the Aydınlı (as in plates 39–46 and 48–50).

The Origin of the Combination

As different as these motifs are in their genesis, structural requirements, character, and function, they constitute one of the most characteristic of Anatolian kilim motifs: the horn/hexagon combination. How this combination evolved is an intriguing question; its answer may cast a great deal of light on the origin of certain major Anatolian kilim designs as well as giving insights into their visual language.

While we cannot turn to extant examples of kilims from the far distant past, we can examine kilims of the past few centuries that contain ancient designs that have been perpetuated to the present. The classic Yüncü (g) is, I believe, one such kilim design tradition (it may extend back almost a thousand years) that seems to lead back ultimately to even older textile design traditions in a region thousands of miles from Anatolia—Central Asia.

The Classic Yüncü Kilim

The classic Yüncü kilim (plates 2 and 3) is one of the best-known Anatolian kilim designs and one of the most-sought-after by collectors, but it is actually the least characteristic of the repertoire.[2]

When the classic Yüncü is carefully examined in the context of the larger Anatolian repertoire, it appears very different. The design structure of the classic Yüncü kilim is an undivided central field dominated by an overall design of large motifs (the trunk and ram's horns) framed by a border. As seen in chapter 5, the vast majority of the structural designs of Anatolian kilims derive from the horizontally banded format, as well as the vertically banded format, the rectangular grid, the repetition of hexagons, the diamond grid, concentric rectangles, and concentric diamonds (f). The classical Yüncü, by contrast, is an undivided overall design consisting of three trunklike forms bracketed by ram's horns and framed by a serrated plain border (g). The structural designs that most resemble this in the Anatolian repertoire are in the kilims of the Karakeçeli, the Hotamış Türkmen of the Konya region, and the Aydınlı. These designs also have an undivided, overall design but the large motif consists of a column or columns of stacked hexagons bracketed with ram's horns framed by either a serrated border or one of geometrical motifs (h) (plates 39–46 and 48–50).

This undivided, overall design structure, as pointed out in chapter 8, does not seem to have the same origins as the others. The structural principle of the Yüncü and Konya and Aydınlı kilims, though incorporating different major motifs, are basically similar in format.

f.

g.

h.

The classic Yüncü kilim is, in the context of Anatolian kilim design, uncharacteristically minimalist in every way, consisting of only the three trunklike forms bracketed with koç boyunuzu, with none of the elaborate geometric forms that are more typical. Significantly, the trunklike motif is like the koç boyunuzu—a motif unsuited to the structural limitations of kilim weave. Hence, it also seems to have originated in another design tradition. Vertically oriented motifs require long, straight lines and, like curvilinear forms, undoubtedly originated outside the Anatolian tapestry tradition. Vertical motifs are decidedly an uncomfortable fit: the trunk motif can only be approximated by fragmenting what would be a pair of straight parallel lines into a series of short, straight lines that zigzag (i). As mentioned in chapter 4, motifs created by long, straight vertical lines are technically impossible in tapestry weave without compromising the structural integrity of the weaving. Remedial techniques, such as fragmenting or crenellating the long verticals, are necessarily brought into play. Curvilinear and vertically oriented motifs, however, pose no structural problems in felting, as we have seen, since the motifs are not woven on a framework of warps but cut

out and quilted together or arranged into a design and pressed into a base fabric.

Another Yüncü design variant, obviously a later solution, is the crenellated Yüncü design (j). The trunk verticals in this version are executed in the typical crenellated manner that verticals are handled in Anatolian kilims. In this treatment the ram's horns move even further into abstraction as they are handled in a completely rectilinear manner.

But to return to the classic Yüncü design, the ram's horn and trunk are not only alien kilim motifs in terms of the technical limitations of orthogonal tapestry weave; both are also atypical in that they are not geometric forms. As demonstrated in chapter 5, geometry is the very heart and soul of Anatolian kilim design. Indeed, it is one of the chief elements that defines the Anatolian tribal eye. The absence of geometry in Yüncü design is certainly one of the major factors that gives it a decidedly foreign look.

The typical palette of the classic Yüncü is also unlike most Anatolian kilims. In comparison with the rather flamboyant palette typical of Anatolian kilims the Yüncü's is very limited and quite somber. The typical classic Yüncü kilim consists of a red field framed by a blue or brown serrated

A crenellated version of the classic Yüncü kilim design (19th-century fragment).

edging; it is decorated with trunk and ram's horn motifs in dark blue outlined in white (plates 2 and 3). Significantly, the palette of red and blue with a minimal use of white is also typically Central Asian.[3]

The character of the Yüncü motifs also differs from those found in most Anatolian kilims. The Yüncü motifs of the classic design have a cut-out quality—like silhouettes—because they lack the kind of elaboration and color changes typical of the motifs of most Anatolian kilim motifs—for instance, the typical Aydınlı, or Konya, kilims (plates 39–46 and 48–50). Silhouette-like motifs are typical of felt pieces, in particular those created by quilting together a design from cut-out felt pieces (k).

By contrast, the hexagons of the Hotamış Türkmen and Aydınlı are not simple silhouettes, but elaborate motifs in which hexagons appear within hexagons in diminishing sizes and in different colors; some are outlined in barred designs, others are elaborated with hooklike forms (l). The elaboration of these motifs often requires a palette of eight or more colors. The ram's horns bracketing the hexagons are similarly elaborated with outlines in barred designs or different colored edgings and are decorated with minor motifs (m) (plates 39 and 40).

In addition to the major geometric designs, the main field is decorated with a variety of motifs of different sizes, while the borders and skirt bands contain their own repertoires of motifs. In contrast to the Aydınlı and Konya kilims, which are filled with dozens of motifs, the classic Yüncü is built around just two major motifs and virtually no minor ones other than the tiny floating weft motifs that seem extraneous to the main design and largely due to the improvisation of the weavers. The absence of infill creates what seems, for an Anatolian kilim, to be an uncharacteristically generous use of negative space. However, more prolonged examination reveals that in many cases what appears to be negative space actually functions to create reciprocal designs.

Reciprocal design is one of the chief visual effects of felt pieces, particularly those of the quilted variety. The degree to which the classic Yüncü kilim emphasizes reciprocal design and deemphasizes a proliferation of smaller motifs is another clue to the origins of this design.

The differences in design between the classic Yüncü and the Aydınlı and Konya kilims are also reflected in the weaving technique. While the Aydınlı and Konya kilims, like the majority of Anatolian kilims, are in the slit-weave technique, the weavers of the classic Yüncü kilim have conspicuously avoided the technique. Both the ram's horn and trunk motifs of the Yüncü are effected by breaking curves and vertical lines into short, broken diagonals that step their way up and down the warps and horizontal lines (n). Since there are no verticals, the need is obviated for the slitting that ordinarily separates color fields meeting on the vertical.

Genesis in the Feltmaking Tradition

The characteristics that differentiate the Yüncü from most Anatolian kilims—a limited palette; a few, large silhouette-like motifs; a predominance of curvilinear and vertical motifs; large areas of negative space functioning as reciprocal design; a palette of red and blue; and the outlining of motifs in white—give the Yüncü classical kilims a striking resemblance to certain felt pieces of Central Asia (see p. 84).

How has this amazing resemblance come to be? It is known that the Yüncü Yörük tribes, now located in the Balıkesir region of northwest Anatolia, trace their origins by oral tradition to Central Asia. It is also established that feltmaking was a major textile tradition in Central Asia and an artefact central to nomadic life there. Indeed, when Turkic tribes came into what we now call western Turkestan in the fifth and sixth centuries, they remained (as documented in accounts made by Chinese Buddhists traveling the Silk Route on pilgrimage to India) true to the felt carpets brought with them from the East. One very detailed report from 630 A.D. recounts that the Great Khan's yurt was only furnished with felt carpets. Significantly, while evidence of felt carpets is plentiful for this period, there is no evidence for kilims or knotted carpets.[4]

Thus, for cultural reasons as well as the need for an insulating fabric in a region with extremely cold winters, felt was the primary textile produced by Türkmen in Central Asia. Feltmaking undoubtedly appeared long before woven rugs and kilims because it did not require the invention of spinning. Therefore, much of its design tradition would have predated the knotted and tapestry weaving tradition, which the Türkmen apparently adopted during their stay in Central Asia. The flow

l.

m.

felt motif

n.   kilim motif

of influence in textile design is more likely to migrate from felting to woven rugs and kilims rather than vice versa.

While felting was important to the life of Central Asian nomads, there is no evidence that kilim weaving ever played a prominent role amongst its weavers as it has in Anatolia. There is no evidence that the Central Asian kilim weaving tradition produced more than the limited range of designs that have survived to the present. Central Asian kilims usually have motifs, designs, and palettes that bear little resemblance to those of Anatolian kilims. It is flatweavings of the brocaded variety that were more characteristic of the Türkmen repertoire in Central Asia. The brocaded flatweavings of Anatolian Turkic groups resemble those of Central Asian weaving groups in design and palette.[5]

It is very probable that when the Yüncü Yörük migrated into Anatolia and finally settled in the Balıkesir region their textile tradition was heavily focused on felting; they may have brought the koç boyunuzu–oriented design tradition in their felt pieces and memories. If their oral history is accurate, the ancestors of the Yüncü Yörük, as part of the larger Türkmen migration, arrived in Anatolia sometime around the twelfth century. As established in the preceding chapter, they would have entered a region with a slit-weave tapestry tradition dating to at least 1,800 years before their arrival. Certainly the Türkmen invaders settled amongst a much larger indigenous population with a highly developed weaving tradition in which slit-weave tapestry was a major part of the repertoire.

The Yüncü Yörük also ultimately settled into a region—the Balıkesir region of northwest Anatolia—that had much more temperate winters by Central Asian standards. The region's topography allowed for short migrations from lowlands to highland and enabled this nomadic, pastoral people to avoid the extremes of climate. Further, the Türkmen found themselves a tiny minority amongst an ancient indigenous population. It has been established that the proportion of Muslims to non-Muslims in Anatolia was about 1 in 10 during the time of the Selçuk state; before that time the proportion was even smaller. With the conquest of the western Byzantine part of Anatolia in the fourteenth and fifteenth centuries, the Muslim proportion barely increased despite frequent Türkmen migrations.[6] Thus, a small conquering group found itself surrounded by a much larger indigenous population of Byzantine culture. Not only was this group small but, in many cases, the armies of this invading group came without families, which required considerable intermarriage with the indigenous population.[7]

The taking of wives from the local population would be an important factor in the assertion of Anatolian culture, particularly when it comes to textile production, since weaving was the province of women. It seems obvious that the women would have continued to cultivate Anatolian traditions and pass them on to their daughters. A similar major transition is documented whereby the Türkmen abandoned their Central Asian felt tents at this period for the Near Eastern black goat hair tent.[8] It seems to be the consensus of ethnological anthropologists that the Turkic tribes from the steppes brought organization, patriarchy, and language to Anatolia but not culture.[9] Studies of Anatolian population figures suggest that what we categorize as Anatolian Turks are for the most part Anatolians who became "Turkified."[10]

Thus, the Türkmen entered a region with a highly developed slit-weave tradition and were influenced by this more advanced culture. No longer requiring the insulating qualities of felt to the same degree and becoming acculturated to this ancient Anatolian indigenous tradition, the Yüncü Yörük conceivably began to shift the emphasis of their textile production from felting to kilim weaving.

However, they probably would not have discarded their traditional designs, an important element of tribal identity, which, since they were only recent Muslim converts, probably still had shamanist significance to them. As explained in chapter 8, the tripartite trunks of the Yüncü design may represent the shamanist axle of the universe that passes through the three worlds (o) while the koç boyunuzu symbolizes fertility and prosperity. The ritual significance of certain textiles undeniably acts as a powerfully conservative force.

The classic Yüncü kilim may be a transitional design descending from the first phase of the Yüncü Yörük's transition from felting to kilim weaving. In other words, it seems to be a direct translation into tapestry weave of a traditional Central Asian felt design.[11]

The classic Yüncü was only the first stage of an ongoing process out of which later versions of the

o.

koç boyunuzu design emerged, versions that became increasingly Anatolian in character. These would include the polychrome Yüncüs and polychrome Yüncüs with a highly centralized design. Even though these later more Anatolian-influenced designs emerged, the original transitional design, the classic Yüncü, continued to be perpetuated by Yüncü women to the present. Conceivably, this cultural conservatism derives from the Yüncü Yörük's uneasy position as a member of a small heterodox Islamic sect (the Alevi-Bektaşi) amongst a largely Sunni population.[12]

As established in chapter 7, the Yüncü Yörük, even today, characteristically maintain secrecy about their kilim designs and customs. Possibly the ritual associations of the kilim, which was a textile associated with truth, judgment, reconciliation, and binding agreements, ensured the design's continuity. Further, the Yüncü Yörük, probably because they were a heterodox sect, have survived as an endogamous society. Thus, the evolution of weaving design commonly produced by intermarriage with other tribes has not occurred.

The Polychrome Version

The polychrome Yüncü (plates 4–8) is undoubtedly a later transitional design representing the beginning of the Anatolianization of what was originally a Central Asian felt design.[13] Over time, the classic Yüncü kilim apparently absorbed more characteristics of the indigenous Anatolian weaving repertoire. In this version, the basics of the design, motifs, and overall layout are still preserved—it has the three tree trunks bracketed with koç boyunuzu, the red field, the blue trunk and horn motifs, and the outlining in white. While remaining faithful to the basic elements, the polychrome version has nevertheless undergone a considerable transformation. The most obvious change is the infilling of geometric motifs into the trunk forms and borders, which establishes a real kinship with typical Anatolian kilim design. The geometric motifs that fill the trunks at this stage are miniaturized to fit into the narrow silhouettes of the trunks and borders.

Accompanying these introduced geometric forms is a change that also alters the character of the design. The palette is considerably expanded, to include the additional colors needed to depict these more elaborated motifs, beyond the typical red, blue, and white to pale terra cotta, abrashed dark blue, mid-blue, blue-green, ivory, and brown. The major effect of this introduction of motifs and colors is to diminish the silhouette-like character of the trunks. Thus the polychrome design emerges as a transitional design in which the original felt design in flatweave translation (the classic Yüncü kilim) is hybridized with the geometric visual vocabulary typical of the indigenous Anatolian weaving tradition.

In both stage one, the classic Yüncü (plates 2 and 3), and stage two, the polychrome Yüncü (plates 4 and 8), there is an equal, overall focus to the design in the sense that the three trunklike forms are nearly identical and of equal value. The identical nature of the trunk forms may very well be a vestige of the shamanic symbolism—that is, of a single trunk running through the three worlds (the trunk being, perhaps, segmented into tripartite form to fit into the format of a textile design).

In contrast, in the centrally focused polychrome Yüncü—the third stage—the small geometric forms of the central trunk become significantly enlarged and more hexagon-like. These changes are prefigured in the polychrome Yüncü version and gradually appear as certain differentiations between the central trunk and the pair that flank it. These differentiations take a number of forms: coloring the central trunk green rather than blue, introducing brocaded or geometric motifs into the central trunk but not the ones flanking it, or introducing different kinds of geometric motifs from those in the flanking trunks into the central trunk.

This transitional design also has survived in extant kilims (plates 5, 6, 7, and 8).[14] In this third stage two things have happened: the central trunk has become predominant as a result of the considerable enlargement of the hexagonal motifs, and the geometric forms incorporated into the central trunk differ from those of the two flanking trunks. The changes in the character of the central trunk transform it into a motif that resembles a column of stacked hexagons. The relatively equal focus of the classical and polychrome designs on the three trunklike forms as a unit has vanished. Indeed, how this metamorphosis transpired is suggested by comparing the imprecise rendering in plate 8 and the much more precise geometric rendering in plate 7. The fit of the hexagonal motifs into the trunk form was facilitated (and possibly even suggested) by the zigzag rendering of the trunk. The p.

q.

r.

zigzag of the verticals, when enlarged, creates a perfect fit for the outline of the hexagon (p).

The new predominance of the central trunk (or stacked hexagons) in this transitional design is heightened by the more important role the horizontal bars of geometric motifs that connect the tops and bottoms of the flanking trunk forms gradually take on. This appears to begin an evolution in which the left and right trunks increasingly function less as equal trunks and more as a frame to the primary central trunk (q). We see this process at work in the polychrome versions of plates 4 and 5. Another element that moves the Yüncü in the direction of more typical Anatolian designs is the introduction of the banded designs in the emerging skirt border (see plate 4). While the classic Yüncü kilim was framed with a simple serrated edging, the centrally focused polychrome version not only has side borders decorated with geometric motifs but also skirt borders at each end decorated with bands of geometric motifs, a treatment typical of Konya main kilims (plates 42 and 45).

The introduction of certain geometric motifs (r) necessitates a technical transformation as the weavers shift to slit-weave tapestry technique. Instead of a design exclusively executed by diagonal and horizontal lines, as in the classical and polychrome versions, short verticals appear in minor motifs that require the slit-weave technique. However, the design is still executed almost entirely in diagonals and horizontals since most of the geometric motifs introduced do not require verticals. The glacial pace at which slit-weaving seems to have entered into the weaving of the Yüncü design also serves to emphasize its foreignness.

The centrally focused polychrome version provides evidence that helps to answer two questions posed at the beginning of this chapter: How did the horn/hexagon combination motif come to be? And where did the overall design of a column of stacked hexagons bracketed by ram's horns originate? It would seem that the insertion of the hexagonal motifs into the trunk forms (which were already bracketed with horns) gave birth to the horn/hexagon combination, a motif that would become a major element in the design vocabulary of the Anatolian kilim. Thus, this very unlikely combination has a perfectly logical explanation. Further, the filling of the Yüncü central trunk with

hexagons (in a design that already was an overall design) created the central column of stacked hexagons bracketed with ram's horns that becomes the central feature of kilims such as those of the Karakeçeli, Aydınlı, and the Hotamış Türkmen of Konya, to name a few, giving birth to a kilim design that we now recognize as distinctively Anatolian.

If the centrally focused Yüncü polychrome is modified by editing out the trunks left and right (or they are absorbed further into framing devices or borders), if the red background is changed to white, and if more infill in the way of small geometric motifs are added, what emerges is a distinctive Anatolian kilim design (plates 39–46 and 48–50). The transitional stage is apparent in plates 39 and 44.[15] In these pieces there is typically an overall design created by a column of stacked hexagons bracketed with koç boyunuzu running vertically in the center of the kilim.

There has been much speculation in kilim research as to where this unique Anatolian structural design came from. As discussed in chapter 5, the vast majority of Anatolian kilim designs appear to have distinctively different structural principles ordered on the banded forms that derive from primitive striped designs. It would seem that the marriage of the Central Asian felt design to the indigenous Anatolian geometrical design is the genesis of this Anatolian structural design.

The process of hybridization, as Central Asian and indigenous Anatolian influences coalesced, was not unique to the Yüncü Yörük. Indeed, there are numerous kilims surviving from other weaving groups in the neighboring region—in particular, the kilims of the nearby Karakeçeli tribe (see plate 50)—that suggest a similar process at work.[16]

The direct influence of the Yüncü weavers could explain some of the spreading of this design tradition, particularly in the Balıkesir/Eskişehir/Kuhtayha region. Some of the broadcasting could have been the result of the fragmentation and movement of tribal groups (as with the Aydınlı who are found in a swath of territory extending across Anatolia from Aydın to Adana). It also is evident that a design evolution similar to the one that seems to have taken place in the Balıkesir region with the Yüncü could have happened spontaneously in other parts of Anatolia through similar interactions between arriving Türkmen groups and the indigenous Anatolian population. It seems unlikely that this design influence would have spread solely from the Yüncü of the Balıkesir region.

A similar process is evidenced in one variety of kilims woven by the Azeri Turks in the Caucasus. Forming the overall design of this Azeri kilim is a trunklike form composed of hexagonal forms bracketed with large ram's horns. While the central motif has been fragmented and obscured by an additional banded format, the ghost of the original trunklike motif bracketed with ram's horns still functions as the superstructure of the design.[17]

What would differentiate the Yüncü Yörük from other Turkic groups is that the Yüncü Yörük seem to have conservatively preserved the transitional stages of the design evolution, perpetuating them to recent times. Among other Anatolian weaving populations, and apparently the Azeri Turks as well, only the intermediate and final versions have survived, while the earlier stages of the design evolution have not.

The process described above suggests that the tribal eye of Anatolia—the distinctive visual expression of its nomadic and peasant weaving cultures—is in good part the product of the fusion of the slit-weave tapestry design traditions of the indigenous weaving populations of Anatolia and the felt design traditions carried from Central Asia by Türkmen nomads. This fusion has not only created a major kilim motif and a distinctive kilim design but also an important part of the vocabulary of the underlying common visual language. This fusion has been so successful and effected so completely during the almost one thousand years of its evolution that we now perceive this hybridization to be one of the most characteristic of Anatolian kilim designs.

A Caucasian Azeri kilim with a koç boyunuzu–type design (19th century).

Chapter 10

Towards an "Ethno-aesthetics" for the Anatolian Kilim

natolian tribal weavers, as seen in chapters 6 and 7, are not usually able to respond to questions posed from the point of view of Western aesthetics. Nor are these rural women able to deal with the esoteric preoccupations of rug scholars, connoisseurs, and ethnographers. There is not much evidence that the kind of pop-Jungian symbolism, so beloved of rug enthusiasts, has much to contribute to an understanding of Anatolian kilims.[1] Rug and kilim scholars, in emulation of musicologists (who have formulated an ethno-musicology), need to construct an "ethno-aesthetics" of Anatolian weavings.

As a start, I propose to examine three aspects of such an ethno-aesthetics: (1) the kilim as a potent expression of the nomadic and peasant cultures of Anatolia, (2) the kilim as a highly personal expression of the rural women of Anatolia, and (3) the kilim as an expression of a Turkic aesthetics which rural Anatolian culture shares with the dominant, high Ottoman culture. I would argue that the unique tribal eye that has given expression to the Anatolian kilim during its long evolution is a composite of these powerful cultural and personal facets.

Anatolian Nomadic and Peasant Culture

Unfortunately, the anthropological fieldwork in Anatolia that would enable us to fully understand its ancient tribal and village cultures has not been done. Recent fieldwork carried out by anthropologist Patricia Daugherty[2] suggests that it might not be too late. Using the indirect method in studying an Anatolian yörük population, she observed and analyzed the "aesthetic discourse" of the weavers as they wove at the loom and as they evaluated photographs of flatweavings. From listening to their undirected conversations, she determined that the way in which these yörük women saw their world emerged from what is called "embodied experience"—that is, a projection of their awareness of the body as a container with a mouth as entry—into the activities and structures of their daily life. This sense of embodied experience, Daugherty discovered, not only shaped their household arrangements, social organization, rituals, and customs, but also their experience of the weaving process and their shaping of design itself.[3]

As they weave, the yörük women use the term "mouth of the loom" (ağzi). When nothing is being woven the weavers say, "the mouth of the loom is empty." When the loom is being warped they say, "they are making the mouth of the loom now." When a kilim is being woven they say, "there is a kilim in the mouth of the loom now." The mouth of the loom, the ağzi, is, for them, the place where the shed is opened to receive the weft. As they insert the wefts through the warps they "fill the mouth." Figuratively speaking, the ağzi moves as the weaving progresses.[4] The weavers perceive the loom as a three-dimensional container that can be filled through a mouth-like opening. As they would nourish their men, children, and baby lambs they also nourish the loom. They are doing the "women's work" of their culture.[5]

Not only do these women perceive the weaving process in terms of the human body but the way in which they perceive, create, and execute weaving design is similar. One of the most pervasive, underlying ways of organizing design in this weaving culture is center-periphery structure. That is, they extend the idea of the body as a separate, enclosed container—something separated into inside/outside areas—into the way they perceive,

a.   top

eye

stone

b.   flower

c.   sürme

d.   line separating
       and coming together

organize, and shape motifs. The terms they use—*top*, *sürme*, and *göbek*—derive from the way they perceive center-periphery structure.[6]

Top literally means "ball" in Turkish but it also can mean something roundish or a constellation of grouped things. In weaving it does not refer to a specific design but to the design element that includes the outline and all the motifs and design elements inside the enclosed area (a). The top can be a major or minor motif such as a *göz* (eye), *kabataş* (large stone), and *çiçek* (flower) (b). The term sürme (c), which is the dark dye or kohl used as a cosmetic to outline eyes, is extended in weaving to mean the outline of the top.

Göbek literally means "navel, umbilical cord, or belly" but it also means the central area of anything. The process of weaving a kilim design is described as "gathering the göbek." The weavers typically begin weaving a motif at its central point, the göbek. The uncompleted area around the göbek is called the *yedirme*, which literally means "to fill the stomach."[7]

In their conversations about the photographs of flatweavings, the yörük women revealed the importance they place on center-periphery structure. The focus of their evaluations was on the elements of design that separate and come together, on the colors that were woven inside and outside the top, and on the "mouth" of the loom, which, in this context, meant how well the piece was woven. For instance, the way they perceive a diamond motif is as a line, which separates and then comes back together again; a line forming an enclosure, creating an inside and an outside (d). The central core of their aesthetic might be summarized in the following way: "If design elements separate and come together and form a clearly defined center-periphery orientation; if color harmony is achieved by balancing the colors inside and outside a motif or design area; and if the mouth of the loom has been filled properly, then a kilim is . . . pretty."[8]

This study reveals that kilims, for these women,[9] function as mirrors of their roles as nurturers and life-givers, reflecting the central role women play in the tribal order. The mouth of the loom that they fill, after all, has produced over the ages the basic conditions required for life: the sheltering tent, clothing, bedding, storage bags, rugs, and kilims. Not only is the act of weaving one of their many nurturing functions, but it is also an activity that differs from all other tribal activities in that it allows the women to transcend their nurturing function to become the artistic voice of their people.

Like the culturally selected symmetries described in chapter 5, the sense of embodied experience these women operate on serves as the prism through which they see life, and, ultimately, as the mold by which they shape the central aspects of their daily life, including their weavings. As with the culturally determined symmetries, this yörük sense of embodiment is an unconscious but nevertheless profound force in the way that these rural women experience their world and the way in which they create their world of design. The kilim for these tribal people, as the fieldwork proves, shares the same basic structure as the other central cultural activities of their lives.

While much more anthropological work needs to be done by way of fleshing out this role, fieldwork like this demonstrates that kilims and other weavings are an important expression of tribal culture. It is the tribal woman herself and her world, not the "Goddess of Anatolia," that is the real subject of kilims.

The Kilim as a Form of Personal Expression

While a powerful, unconscious form of cultural expression seems to be one important element in the creation of a kilim, this does not preclude the possibility of conscious, personal expression.

Ethnographer Henry Glassie,[10] through his analysis of several contemporary flatweavings and his perceptive interactions with Sebire Aktaş, the woman who wove them, captures how an Anatolian weaver typically creates design and encodes meaning.

In 1966 Sebire became one of the hundreds of thousands of rural immigrants to Istanbul, residing at the time of Glassie's fieldwork with her family in a *gece condu* (squatters' settlement) in the city. Until early adulthood she was a typical village woman living in a remote village near Sivas in eastern Anatolia. Two of her weavings, completed when she was still a villager, were the main focus of this ethnographic study: cecim A dating from about 1961, when she was still living in her father's house, and cecim B, woven in 1964 in her husband's house.[11]

The second weaving, cecim B, demonstrates a hand that has become much freer and inventive as

Sebire's cecim B, with its expanded lexicon of motifs.

she expands her design vocabulary beyond the repetition of a small repertoire of traditional motifs into highly individual experiments that increasingly consist of motifs from the Turkish alphabet, kufic script, and kilim border designs as well as other sources. In cecim A, she used only 24 different motifs, while in cecim B she used 51 different motifs. The two cecims capture the evolution of a design as an Anatolian weaver grows in maturity, skill, and independence.

Her use of alphabetical letters as motifs is particularly interesting. In borrowing from the real world, as opposed to working with the abstract, and in substituting motifs of her own choosing instead of those from the traditional repertoire,

she behaves atypically for an Anatolian weaver. However, she remains firmly within her native tradition by treating these borrowings in a typically Anatolian manner. She has predictably severed the connection between her borrowed motifs and the real world models and abstracted and stylized these borrowings, turning them to her own design purposes and, in some cases, investing them with her own personal meanings. As seen in chapter 5, Anatolian weavers tend to translate borrowed foreign images into their own idiom.

Aside from a few motifs, Sebire is not being literate when she uses letters from the alphabet, but instead appropriates them to remake them for her own purposes. Letters inserted into the stripes of her cecim function chiefly as visual elements. She uses them as is; she reverses them; she turns them upside down; she tips them on their side; she presents them in fragmentary form; she mixes them with a large repertoire of motifs drawn from traditional textile designs. The repertoire of motifs from both cecims is found in the margin (e).

Not all of these alphabetical motifs have associational meanings but are part of inventive play; indeed, these alphabet motifs seem to function in the same way as much of the geometric vocabulary in Anatolian kilims does. However, there are also motifs that function mnemonically. For instance when asked for the meaning of a certain kufic script symbol (see #42 in e) in her weaving,[12] she revealed that it did not have a traditional meaning to her. The symbol reminded her of a particular household in her native village where she learned it.[13] While the motif had its origins in an ancient tradition, its personal meaning mattered for Sebire. When questioned about other motifs, she revealed through her answers that, to her, the significances of the motifs were not literal but associational. For her, the cecim she created functions as a document of memory, a hosting of symbolic reminders of family and friends, an abstract portrayal of social affinities developed during the creative process of weaving.[14]

This associational function becomes clearer when she discusses other motifs—letters in her repertoire that do function in a more literal way. "Z" (#19 in e) stands for Zeynep, her husband's younger sister, with whom she worked for three months to produce a carpet. Further elaborating, Sebire explains that "Z" represents the love she developed for Zeynep during that collaborative work. When asked about "S," the letter most repeated, she explains it stands for Sebire. Interestingly, what she did not explain is that the "S" form is also the çapraz (#24 in e), a talisman commonly found in Anatolian weavings as an ancient, traditional motif and generally believed to ward off evil. In Sebire's cecim, however, it is the personal meaning, not the traditional meaning, which is intended.

That she may also have had the traditional meaning in mind is suggested by the way she chooses to spell out her name (#53–60 in e). The "S," instead of being upright like the rest of her name, is presented on its side. Two more S shapes follow the spelling of her name, and they are on

their sides in the more typical çapraz (#59 and 60 in e) form. The repetition of "S" throughout cecim B may have functioned on several levels.

She spells out her name at the center of her cecim, symbolically setting herself in the middle of this context of friends and family, memories of the past and present, and the recalling of different places and pastimes. In design terms, she herself is the "medallion" around which this highly personal constellation of associations is grouped.

Thus, it would seem that while the Anatolian weaver works in traditional forms and draws freely from inherited motifs, she is not consciously communicating the larger cultural meaning. Indeed, it seems she is more likely to be oblivious of the ancient meanings and origins of the motifs she perpetuates. Instead it is on a highly personal, associational level that she actually communicates her conscious meaning. In a rural culture, which until recently was not literate, traditional weavings apparently functioned for Anatolian women as a diary of treasured memories recorded in wool. As seen in chapter 7, with the dowry weaving occasion in Susanoğlu, the weaver's subtext of associational meanings is traditionally supplemented by the contributions of weavers who are friends and relatives. In weavings in which collaboration is not involved, and in pieces that are not intended for commercial sale, the tribal weaver apparently has freedom to invest a weaving with personal meanings. Even if we attempted to discover the personal level of meaning invested in the old kilims, we are cut off from successfully doing so since the associational meanings died with the weavers and their families. It is only in exceptional cases, as with this contemporary ethnographic work with a living weaver, that such a hidden level of meaning ever surfaces for us.

Knowing that this level of meaning exists, regardless of whether we can interpret it, adds immeasurably to our understanding and appreciation of tribal kilims.

The Kilim as an Expression of Turkic Aesthetics

The relationship of the Anatolian tribal weaving tradition to the larger Ottoman culture, and to the Islamic art tradition itself, has long been a matter for debate. Recent ethnographical fieldwork suggests that Anatolian rural culture may, indeed, share an aeshetic with Ottoman culture.

The starting point in approaching the relationship of Anatolian tribal weaving to the more urban, court-oriented Ottoman arts is formulating the aesthetic that underlies Turkic arts and crafts. Despite the collapse of the Ottoman Empire, this aesthetic still lives on in the ateliers, workshops, and cottages of the modern Turkish Republic. An understanding of this aesthetic should provide insights into how the rural weaving population of Anatolia actually regards its own creative process.

An invaluable start on understanding this aesthetic can be found in Henry Glassie's *Turkish Traditional Art Today*.[15] Focusing on the still vital Turkish arts and crafts of ceramics, woodworking, metalworking, calligraphy, and weaving, Glassie has teased out from his interactions with artists and craftspeople the framework of a Turkish aesthetic. As he put it: "I went to [them] and asked them to teach me, telling me what art is."[16] While he is primarily dependent for articulation of these principles on urban craftsmen, artists, and dealers, he has also been able to elicit a great deal from rural weavers, making a credible case that women working in the rural weaving culture of Anatolia are part of a larger aesthetic descending from Ottoman and Selçuk times.[17]

Given the Turks' long interaction with the West and their close proximity to European culture, it is surprising how great cultural differences still are. In the West our practice is to divide art and craft according to the mediums employed. For instance, painted canvas and carved marble are classified as fine art and placed at the top of the arts hierarchy, while pottery and weaving are the products of craft and lower on the scale.

Another component of this distinction is utility. Fine art by our definition is not utilitarian—in a sense it must be "useless" to qualify. By contrast, craft is defined as being chiefly utilitarian, with decorative features. These categories of art and craft are, however, not based solely on the medium employed and its function, but also reflect all kinds of value-laden distinctions. When judged by Western standards, most art is automatically consigned to a level beneath our fine arts, being conveniently assigned to less prestigious categories such as "folk art" or "ethnographic art."

Thus, the Anatolian kilim from a Western perspective has the triple handicap of being a utilitarian craft item, a product of a non-Western tradition, and a rural product of nomads and peasants. Also involved in the Western judgment of art are matters of social class, ethnicity, education, formal training, and even imperialism. It is no accident that the West's belated enthusiasm for the kilim erupted out of the social ferment of the 1960s when a questioning of the high art traditions of the West stimulated an intense interest in the cultural artefacts of other world traditions previously dismissed or denigrated.

By contrast, in Turkish traditional culture (I stress traditional since the westernized segments of the Turkish population have adopted western art forms), very different kinds of distinctions are made since Turkish arts and crafts alike have always served a strongly utilitarian function. Like most cultures, the Ottoman world did not find its artistic expression in works that were purely aesthetic. Thus, the robust kilims of the nomads and villagers and the elegant textiles and ceramics of the court and urban traditions shared a common role in being chiefly utilitarian objects invested with artistry. It would appear that the palace, the rural cottage, and the tent, despite the obvious differences in their artistic traditions, share at bottom a common artistic ethos.

Sanat: The Turkish Concept of Art

Art in the Ottoman tradition finds its expression in any medium and can be the expression of any artist or artisan on any level. Thus, a work of art (*sanat* in Turkish) can be a ceramic bowl, a carved wooden Koran holder, a decorated dowry chest, a silk embroidery, or a kilim. A maker of art can be a middle-class calligrapher, a working-class dowry chest maker, or an illiterate rural weaver.[18] Whether something is art or not depends not on the medium or the social or educational level of its maker but on whether the artefact projects a particular kind of expression or attitude invested in it by its maker—that is, an expression that can be received and understood by its owner or appreciator.

Art, according to the aesthetic that has come down to the present in Turkey, enters an object as the result of the actions and attitudes of its creator or maker. The term for this expression in Turkish is *zevk*, a complicated term for which no one English word will suffice. While "taste" would be a dictionary choice, it is more complicated than that. Zevk is a matter of principled choice. There are always choices in ways to be and choices in the way one expresses oneself; it is the sum total of these choices

39
40
41
42

43
44
45
46
47
48

49
50
51
52

53
54
55
56
57
58
59
60
61
62
63
64
65
66
67

68
69

e.

that results in a way of being, zevk. Since there are many ways of being, there are many kinds of zevk. Presumably there are as many forms of zevk as there are different kinds of people, and there are many levels of consciousness about zevk as well.

Zevk, however, does not only reside within the creator and the artefact created. For an artefact to fully exist as sanat, it must be communicated and received. Zevk is, in its totality, both intention and response. Through its zevk "an artefact communicates feelings that jar the creator and patron in oneness of choice."[19]

Emek vs. Zevk

Turks, it might be said, tend to categorize works by actions, by the commitment of the creator. Not all works created are sanat, since not all works are invested with this kind of expression. Some works are simply made and sold; for these, Turks use the word *emek* when zevk is absent. While both sanat and emek are positive terms, emek is a more restrictive activity, involving labor done only for the purpose of livelihood. Lacking is the "dedication by the worker to the work itself, a fit into materials of the artist's being."[20]

A kilim in the Turkish understanding would be sanat if it is more than just work and, in particular, more than just work aimed at making a living. A kilim would be art if it functions as an expression of the weaver herself, if it is "alive with the signs of the weaver's presence," if there is a sense of the "freedom of the weaver," or if the kilim gives "the sense of the presence of another."[21] It is the view of some Turkish rug dealers that even a weaving produced in a cottage industry or factory context can be sanat if it is done with " . . . the willful compliance of the weaver, if she is free to be an active creator in the process."[22]

The conditions of the tribal weaver of the past were extremely conducive to the production of sanat since the women wove kilims in a noncommercial situation and were free to reinterpret and rework the designs of the past in their own way. The tribal weaver had the freedom to express herself through what she selected from the traditional repertoire, in how she recombined motifs and elements, and in how she infilled the traditional designs with a subtext of her own. Thus, she both accepted and altered traditional designs and incorporated them into highly personal artefacts intended for her dowry and certain ritual functions.

The weaver's work at the loom, as seen in chapters 1–4, definitely involved emek in the sense of labor and skill. She shares with her fellow artisans in urban areas the term *işçilik*—that is, craftsmanship, skill, and care, or technical mastery. The livelihood element of emek would not have applied to her since kilims in the older tribal world were not usually woven for commercial sale. Given that weaving was one of a tribal woman's only avenues for personal expression and one of her most pleasurable activities, and that the kilims she wove were not for sale, the tribal weaver before the twentieth century lived in an environment that was ideal for the emergence of zevk.

The işçilik demonstrated by the Anatolian weavers of the past is incontestable and the envy of professional weavers worldwide. Perhaps we are less inclined to recognize their weavings as sanat. But certainly the best of the ancient Anatolian tribal weaving production is, from the Turkish point of view, a combination of zevk and işçilik, terms that are not mutually exclusive. It is through will that the artistic spirit is revealed and it is also through will that technical mastery and the command over materials and processes are achieved.[23]

The Three Turkish Modes: Sade, Ciddi, and Canlı

Glassie has convincingly demonstrated that Turkish arts, whether the medium is wood, pottery, metal, glass, or wool, tend to cluster in three different modes. These modes are identified in Turkish as the *sade*, the *ciddi*, and the *canlı*.

A Turkish artisan sees in the sade mode a kind of plain style in which form is primary and function more utilitarian. A sade artefact exhibits the material of its making rather than obscuring it with elaborate ornamentation. While there can be decoration, it is minor and subordinate to form. In the kilim repertoire, the plain striped kilims used as workcloths in food processing areas or on kitchen floors or the special cloths employed in bread making are characteristically sade. Likewise, practical items such as saddlebags, storage bags, and animal trappings are usually in the sade mode.

An excellent example of this mode is the Cappadocian drying cloth (plate 1) used to dry strips of dough, which would then be stored for winter use. With its large, plain ivory field edged with finger-like motifs, the weaving is striking in the simplicity of both its design and palette. The minimal edges have a kind of "less is more" aesthetic, and the kilim derives its power from the huge expanse of negative space that is framed. The field of ivory weaving demonstrates the beauty of the wools and weaving technique rather than functioning as the canvas for an elaborate design. There is little to distract from the materials and process. Similarly a plain, undecorated earthenware jug, a wooden chest with little or no carving, and a copper ewer with no incised ornamentation are seen chiefly in terms of form, workmanship, and materials.

We can see the sade mode in other kinds of kilims, such as the classic Yüncüs of plates 2 and 3, and in the rhomboid and hexagonal Yüncü designs in plates 9, 10, and 11. With their large areas of negative space, minimal use of ornamentation, and simple palettes of red, blue, and white, they are decidedly sade in character. In the prayer kilim category, the Karapınar and Obruk kilims depicted in plates 57, 58, 61, 63, and 65 are also in the sade mode because of their simple architectural renderings of the mihrab, the minimal use of decorative ornament, and their subdued palettes.

The use of the sade mode also seems to derive from certain cultural influences. As we will see, designs that descend from the Selçuk period[24] and designs derived from Central Asian felt designs, for instance, also fit the requisites of the sade mode without necessarily being weavings intended for a utilitarian function.

The term sade can be applied to a kilim as a whole or to certain aspects of a kilim. For instance, the mihrabs of the Obruk (plate 61), Konya (plate 63), and Yahyalı prayer kilims (plate 65) are in the sade mode—that is, they emphasize form and material. Unlike the mihrabs of most Turkish prayer kilims they are bare of ornamentation. The effect of these unadorned mihrabs— in dark brown, salmon pink, and maroon—is to bring them into high relief and to call attention to the materials, the abrashed wools that depict the mihrab. In contrast, the Elmadağ prayer kilim (plate 62) is a kilim design that undoubtedly began as sade but which in this version has absorbed ornamentation and been transformed into another mode. Examples of this kilim design survive in which the mihrab consists of a plain field, the

A Bergama region striped drop cloth being used for food preparation.

Yüncü Yörük saddlebag (back side).

mihrab being minimally represented only by a simple triangular form. It would appear that over time the original sade rendition has been moved into another mode, the ciddi.[25]

In the ciddi, form tends to be covered by ornament. The heavy use of ornamentation is also typical of the canlı, the third mode. These two modes differ from the sade in their heavy use of ornament, but they differ from each other in character. The effect of ciddi is serious, while that of canlı is playful. In the ciddi mode a simple overall composition seems to be an insufficient display of mastery for the Anatolian weaver, who complicates the design by enfolding symmetrical composition into symmetrical composition, overlaying a simple overall design with secondary structural principles such as checkerboard patterns, diagonal designs, and banded designs.[26]

The transition from the sade classic Yüncü (plates 2 and 3) to the ciddi mode can be seen in the polychrome Yüncüs (plates 4, 5, 6, 7, and 8). As explained in chapter 9, the transition from plain trunks to trunks infilled with geometric motifs may be seen as a process of Anatolianization (whereby Central Asian motifs take on Anatolian characteristics). The result of this absorption of geometry was also to move the Yüncü design from the sade to the ciddi.

Thus, the classic Yüncü, with its plain, simple, overall design and somber palette becomes ciddi as the design is complicated by the layers of symmetrical geometry inserted into its central motifs, side borders, and banded designs of its skirt borders. The Konya kilim (plate 20) is an even more complicated ciddi version of what must have originally been a simple, banded design decorated with horizontal rows of hexagons. This design seems to have become more complicated over time with the addition of vertical banding created by rows of tiny triangular motifs alternating with vertical columns of stacked hexagons. Thus, a tension is created between the horizontal and the vertical orientations of the design. Further complication is introduced through color changes as, for instance, the different colorations of the vertically oriented hexagons (particularly those outlined in white) take the eye diagonally across the kilim. The tension is further complicated by the interplay of verticals, horizontals, and diagonals. Add to that the streams of geometric motifs in boxes running vertically down each side border and the bands of the

same motifs, but unboxed, running horizontally in the skirt border, and the ciddi results. Similar tours de force can be seen in the Konya main kilims in plates 48 and 49.

Canlı, the third mode, would translate as "alive with color." It is any brightly colored thing, something that is playful, less controlled, and more open to what might be called "accidence."[27] Canlı can be applied to a kilim, a ceramic bowl, a dowry chest, or even a child dancing in a garden. While the canlı artefact can be as ornamented as the ciddi, the design does not exhibit the same degree of control and order. Creating an exuberant celebration of color, the weaver in the canlı mode tends to overwhelm or loosen up the underlying order of the design. While the ciddi also uses color to great effect, its palettes tend to be a balance of bright and dark colors and are selected to reveal the structural order of the design. In the canlı mode, by contrast, there seems to be a celebration of color for its own sake.

An example of the canlı mode is the Konya Yörük kilim in plate 18, which is a riot of joyful colors like poppy red, vermilion, orange, deep crimson, purple red, deep aubergine, pale lilac, deep indigo, light blue, chartreuse, bottle green, yellow, apricot, brown, wheat, and ivory. This rainbow of fifteen bright and pastel hues overpowers any deep, dark, contrasting colors. Only after absorbing this explosion of color does one become aware of the overall design of a centered row of hexagons set in horizontal bands.

Similarly the Rashwan kilim in plate 19 is a celebration of lively, bright, pastel colors: ivory, wheat, rust, grape-purple, blue-green, blue, aubergine, brown, yellow, sand, apricot, and burnt orange. In this kilim, however, there seems to be an inclination to the ciddi but one ultimately becomes aware of the structural order of the design. In contrast, the Konya kilim in plate 25, with its dark aubergine background and its colors of ivory, dark and mid-blue, crimson, rust, dark and light green, brown, black, and pale orange, has a kind of sobriety and control. Its use of color is definitely subordinated to the requirements of the design.

In the prayer kilim category the very lively, exuberant Rashwan kilim in plate 66 is another example of the canlı mode with its twelve colors: ivory, brown, mid- and dark blues, mulberry, grape purple, rust, yellow, pale green, pale blue-green, and white. In addition to the luminous, flamboyant palette, its drawing has a looseness and freedom not usually found in Anatolian prayer kilims. The rambunctious spirit of the kilim suggests either a very young, perhaps inexperienced, girl at work or a very lively, energetic, ebullient personality chafing at the confines of this usually more ciddi design.

The antithesis to the canlı mode is the Karapınar prayer kilim (plate 57), which is a kilim in a decidedly sade mode. With its austere, simple, architectural mihrabs, a minimum of additional ornamentation, and a basic, five-color palette of crimson, mid-indigo blue, green, ivory, and blue-green, it creates a mood quite different from that of the canlı Rashwan prayer kilim.

A kilim that straddles both the sade and ciddi styles is the Konya prayer kilim (plate 61), which has an austere brown abrashed mihrab in the sade mode but is more ciddi in character overall. It moves into the ciddi mode in its main and minor borders, which are decorated with vertical rows of geometric motifs. These are divided by vertical crenellated lines, which, because of the length of the crenellations, set up a horizontal tension. The crenellations create a design element called parmaklı—that is, fingered or with fingers. The total effect of this design is one of order and control not playfulness. The sober palette of eight colors—aubergine, brown, green, olive, tan, terra cotta, ivory, and indigo—contributes to the serious mood. The palette contributes to the mood of sobriety because it eschews pastels, bright colors, and high contrasts in favor of dark, rich colors.

An example of the canlı that depends more on playfulness in its design than color is the Obruk kilim (plate 17). As a whole the design is in the ciddi mode. Its major structural principle is the banded design consisting of alternating wide bands in ivory and terra cotta framed by a main border of hooked geometric motifs with small skirt borders of the same motif in partial form. The ivory bands are decorated with large hourglass-shaped motifs, which give a vertical tension to the largely horizontal design. These motifs are surrounded with diamond-shaped and small cruciform geometric motifs. The terra-cotta bands are divided into narrower bands by horizontal ivory lines. In these narrower bands horizontal rows of geometric motifs are spaced evenly across the field. Centered in these bands are two hexagonal motifs.

It is the two hexagons that introduce the canlı mode. The Obruk kilim design as a whole is very much in the ciddi mode with its complicated design, its appearance of order and control, and its restrained, sober palette. In sharp contrast to this ordered whole, the central, hexagonal motifs disintegrate into chaotic, fragmented motifs. Thus, the Obruk kilim encapsulates a dramatic tension between order and seeming chaos in its design. In a sense, the highly ordered elements of the kilim seem to emerge from the original chaos of the hexagons.

Two prayer kilims that clearly demonstrate differences between the ciddi and the canlı modes are from Erzerum (plates 72 and 73). The formats of the kilims are basically similar, consisting of a mihrab decorated with a lamp or tree form, set into a central field, and framed by a series of borders. However, the Erzerum kilim of plate 72 is static and orderly; its palette is restrained and somber. As a result its simple, blue mihrab with the elegant, hanging mosque lamp stands out in high relief. The Erzerum in plate 73 is, by contrast, very dynamic, almost pulsing with life. Its palette is exuberant and lively, made particularly so by the high contrast created by the white cotton background of the main border decorated with aggressive, stylized carnations. This canlı main border competes strongly with the mihrab. Further, the mihrab itself is exuberantly covered with motifs as is the field into which it is set. The visual dominance of the mihrab is effectively deemphasized by the overall canlı character but, compensating for this weaker focus, the kilim has a joyful sense of liveliness and play.

In contrast, the Erzerum kilim has a main border in dark maroon decorated with motifs in subdued colors. In this kilim the main border serves as a foil to the simple blue mihrab within. Thus, in one version of the Erzerum prayer design a greater respect for form is shown and color plays a supporting role; in the other version there is a reveling in color and ornamentation which tends to deemphasize and, to a degree, overshadow the basic form.

Indeed, the degree to which the canlı stands out as the exception in prayer kilims suggests an understanding among the weavers that a certain formal, serious character is required for kilims associated with namaz, or ritual prayer. These same weavers also knew how to manipulate color and design to achieve the different effects required by the mode. Undoubtedly, the ritual or practical functions kilims were intended for determined which modes the weavers chose.

It is highly probable that the canlı mode came more into use in the past century as Anatolian tribal culture began to weaken and break down, and the ritual functions of kilims became less understood and appreciated. Additionally, the adoption of a much wider, livelier palette was made possible and, undoubtedly encouraged, by the introduction of synthetic dyes in the last century. The new color possibilities that packaged dyes offered may have pushed kilim design more in the direction of the canlı. At this stage in the evolution of the kilim, canlı begins to take on negative connotations.

As has already been suggested, factors other than intended use may also shape the choice of modes. While the sade, as we have seen, is more associated with the practical and the utilitarian, there may also be cultural forces at work. Prayer designs that seem to have their roots in Selçuk design (plates 57, 58, 61, 62, 63, and 65) are more in the sade mode, while prayer kilims that derive from the Ottoman tradition (plates 70, 71, 72, and 73) are more in the ciddi and, sometimes, canlı modes.

The austere, plain, abstract character of Selçuk art and the more colorful, decorative Ottoman tradition, with its lively floral motifs and compositions, seem to be two facets through which the three basic modes that define Turkish arts are reflected. It would not be too great a generalization to say that Selçuk art tends more towards the sade mode while the Ottoman tends to the ciddi and canlı. This hypothesis is corroborated by the fact that the weaving centers that surround the old Selçuk Turkish capital of Konya, such as Karapınar, Obruk and Aksaray, have produced the bulk of the prayer kilims in the sade mode. As seen in chapter 9, another powerful cultural factor that may influence modes of design is the influence of Central Asian felt designs on Anatolian kilims.

Classic Yüncü kilims owe their sade character to the simple, bold, minimally colored silhouette-like designs characteristic of Central Asian feltwork. Thus, the mode of a kilim design may be determined by the intended use of the textile or by influences flowing from other cultural and textile traditions, or a combination of these.

The three modes—the sade, the ciddi, and the canlı—and the interplay between them help to explain the incredible diversity of Anatolian kilim design. The terms used thus far in discussing kilims, such as the categories of seccade and main kilim, have done little to elucidate stylistic differences in kilim design. Further, not all stylistic differences have been satisfactorily explained by identifying provenance either. Thus, the recognition of these three modes provides a valuable way of sorting out the marked differences in design and character typically found in the Anatolian kilim repertoire. The degree to which these categories of mode are applicable to the kilim as well as the other Turkish arts demonstrates that the tribal weavers of Anatolia were part of the larger Ottoman culture and were, if only unconsciously, participating in a shared aesthetic.

It is the işçilik of its tribal weavers, demonstrated not only in their weaving but in the preparation of their materials, that has brought worldwide attention to the Anatolian kilim. And it is the zevk of these weavers that elevates the Anatolian kilims of the past from being mere decorative textiles, making them one of the glories of Near Eastern art.

Conclusion

Anatolia's kilims, as well as its other weavings, are complex artefacts that mirror basic cultural constructs in Anatolian tribal life. The kilims, enriched and developed through the contributions of its weavers over the centuries, serve as an important medium of personal expression; in their best examples, they achieve the level of sanat, absorbing much of their essential form and character from the Turkic aesthetics they share with Ottoman culture.

While it is true that we can never see or experience the kilims as their makers did, nor completely escape the preconceptions we have (which largely derive from our experience of Western art), we can give these superlative weavings the respect they deserve by seeing them for what they actually are, rather than imposing meanings and functions that obscure their essential, unique character.

Plates

It would be impossible, even if one were to include thousands of examples, to claim to capture a true sampling of the immense variety of Anatolian kilims. Therefore, the examples here included should not be regarded in this light. Even if it were possible to include many more examples and to work for such a representative sampling, the final selection would be as much a product of individual and national tastes as a true sampling. The selections of Turks, Germans, Americans, and Britons, for instance, would be very different. The kilims included here represent what I believe to be exceptional examples of kilims produced

by major Anatolian weaving groups. These examples are drawn from private American collections.

It should be kept in mind that these photographic plates are actually only an approximation of the weavings themselves. No matter how excellent the photography and printing process, it is ultimately only the designs and colors of the kilims that come through in photographic plates. A very important dimension of weaving is almost completely lost—what the French call *matière*, that is the visual and tactile qualities of the surface of the weaving. The kilim detail above attempts to illustrate some of the dimension that has been lost. The technical analyses at the end of the book, which provide pertinent information about each kilim, also help to fill in this dimension.

PLATE 1
5'10" × 8'2"

PLATE 2
4'9" × 6'6"

PLATE 3
5'2" × 8'

108

PLATE 4
5'9" × 8'11"

PLATE 6
5'8" × 8'10"

PLATE 7
6'10" × 11'4"

PLATE 8
5'10" × 11'

PLATE 9
2'10" × 11'4"

PLATE 14
5'8" × 11'8"

PLATE 15
5'5" × 11'6"

PLATE 17
4'1" × 7'2"

PLATE 19
5'3" × 9'0"

PLATE 21
5'3" × 13'5"

PLATE 26
4'3" × 5'8"

PLATE 27
3'10" × 5'4"

PLATE 28
3'2" × 5'3"

PLATE 29
7'4" × 8'10"

PLATE 30
4'7" × 10'

PLATE 31
5'4" × 7'10"

PLATE 34
3'8" × 4'5"

PLATE 35
3'6" × 5'

PLATE 36
3'9" × 5'10"

PLATE 40
5'7" × 10'6"

PLATE 42

5'6" × 13'1"

PLATE 45
4'10" × 13'3"

PLATE 46
5'6" × 12'4"

PLATE 47
6' × 13'

PLATE 48
5'5" × 13'10"

PLATE 51
6'1" × 12'9"

PLATE 53
4'4" × 10'8"

PLATE 54
4'6" × 15'

PLATE 56
4'7" × 13'9"

PLATE 58
3'6" × 5'11"

PLATE 59
3'6" × 5'

PLATE 60
3'3" × 4'11"

PLATE 61
4' × 5'6"

PLATE 63
3'5" × 5'5"

PLATE 64
3'7" × 5'4"

PLATE 65
4'5" × 6'2"

PLATE 66
2'5" × 4'9"

PLATE 69
4'4" × 5'

PLATE 72
4'10" × 5'7"

PLATE 73
4'8" × 6'2"

Technical Analysis

NOTES:

1. Unless otherwise indicated, all kilims woven in one piece in slit-weave tapestry
2. Measurements taken across middle points of sides and ends
3. Z = one Z-spun yarn thread; Z2 = two Z-spun yarn threads, unplied; Z2S = two Z-spun yarn threads, S-plied; Z3S = three Z-spun yarn threads, S-plied
4. If a descriptive category is omitted, it is not applicable

PLATE 1
Cappadocia
2 panels
1st half of 19th century
5'10" × 8'2" (178 × 249 cm.)
Warp: wool: ivory, Z2S, 8/in
Weft: wool: Z2S, 18–23/in.
Colors (2): ivory and blue
Ends: both: extra-weft line of blue

PLATE 2
Balıkesir
Northwestern Anatolia
1st half of 19th century
4'9" × 6'6" (148 × 177 cm.)
Warp: wool: ivory, ivory and brown Z2S, 12/in.
Weft: wool: Z2S, 24–33/in
Colors (3): deep indigo, abrashed madder red, ivory
Ends: top: 1¼/in.; bottom: ½/in. red & blue stripes, plain weave
Other: outlining; small extra-weft motifs

PLATE 3
Balıkesir (Yüncü Yörük)
Northwestern Anatolia
19th century
5'2" × 8' (161 × 250 cm.)
Warp: wool: ivory, Z2S, 15 /in.
Weft: wool: Z2S, 23–28/in.
Colors (5): midnight blue, madder red, light blue, ivory, terra cotta
Ends: both: 4/in. blue & red stripes, plain weave
Other: extra-weft motifs; outlining; tassels; eccentric wefting; twining

PLATE 4
Balıkesir (Yüncü Yörük)
Northwestern Anatolia
2nd half of 19th century
5'9" × 8'11" (179 × 278 cm.)
Warp: wool: ivory, Z2S, 12/in.
Weft: wool: 2Z, 25–35/in.
Colors (7): crimson, pale terra cotta, abrashed dark blue, mid-blue, blue-green, brown, ivory
Ends: both: 4/in. red plain weave
Other: outlining: wool and cotton; extra-weft motifs

PLATE 5
Yüncü Yörük or Karakeçeli
Northwestern Anatolia
1st half of 19th century
5'8" × 8'9" (173 × 267 cm.)
Warp: wool: ivory, Z2S, 15/in.
Weft: wool: Z2S, 23–34/in.
Colors (8): red, blue, melon, blue-green, white brown, dark and mid-blue, rust
Ends: top: red & blue stripes; bottom: red, blue, beige, aubergine stripes; both: plain weave
Other: outlining; extra-weft motifs

PLATE 6
Balıkesir (Yüncü Yörük)
Northwestern Anatolia
2nd half of 19th century
5'8" × 8'10" (173 × 269 cm.
Warp: wool: ivory, Z2S, 12/in.
Weft: wool: Z2S, 28–32/in.
Colors (7): red, dark & mid-blue, blue-green, ivory, yellow, rust
Ends: top & bottom: 2/in. red band, plain weave

PLATE 7
Balıkesir (Yüncü Yörük)
Northwestern Anatolia
Fragment
Circa 1800
6'10" × 11'4" (183 × 345 cm.)
Warp: wool: white, Z2S, 12/in
Weft: wool: Z2S, 20–24/in.
Colors: (5): dark blue, dark green, red, brown, ivory
Ends: top: green, red stripes; bottom: green band; both plain weave
Other: extra-weft motifs

PLATE 8
Balıkesir (Yüncü Yörük)
Northwestern Anatolia
1st half of 19th century
5'10" × 11' (178 × 335 cm.)
Warp: wool: ivory, Z2S 11/in.
Weft: wool: Z2S, 25–28/in.
Colors (9): red, dark & mid-blue, maroon, rust, yellow, green, dark brown, white
Ends: both: green and maroon stripes, plain weave
Other: outlining; extra-weft motifs

PLATE 9
Balıkesir (Yüncü Yörük)
Northwestern Anatolia
1st half of 19th century
2' 10" × 11'4" (88 × 354 cm.)
Warp: wool: ivory, Z2S, 11/in.
Weft: wool: Z2S, 21–24/in.
Colors (5): indigo blue, madder red, green-blue, yellow, ivory
Ends: both: 3/in. red, blue & white stripes, plain weave
Other: extra-weft motifs

PLATE 10
Balıkesir (Yüncü Yörük)
Northwestern Anatolia
1st half of 19th century
4'1" × 8'1" (127 × 252 cm.)
Warp: wool: ivory, Z2S, 15/in.
Weft: wool: Z and 2Z, 27–31/in.
Colors: (7): deep indigo, light blue, brown-red, aubergine, deep crimson, rose madder, ivory
Ends: both: 2/in. blue & aubergine stripes/ plain weave
Other: outlining; extra-weft motifs

PLATE 11
Balıkesir (Yüncü Yörük)
Northwestern Anatolia
2nd half of 19th century
5'5" × 6'9" (165 × 206 cm.)
Warp: wool: ivory, Z2S, 15/in.
Weft: wool: Z2S, 21–28/in.
Colors (4): blue, red, rust, white
Ends: both: 1/in. blue & red stripes, plain weave
Other: outlining; extra-weft motifs; bands in extra-weft

PLATE 12
Balıkesir (Yüncü Yörük)
Northwestern Anatolia
Late 18th century
3'2" × 4'8" (97 × 142 cm.)
Warp: wool: ivory Z2S, 13/in.
Weft: wool: Z2S, 29–38/in.
Colors (6): red, white, mid-blue, yellow, rust-orange, dark aubergine.
Ends: both: 4/in. varicolored narrow stripes, plain weave
Other: knotted motifs

PLATE 13
Cappadocia
Central Anatolia
Radiocarbon dated: 1438–1654
Estimated age: 18th century
4'8" × 10'1" (142 × 307 cm.)
Warp: wool: ivory 2ZS, 12/in.
Weft: wool: 2ZS, 23–30/in.
Colors (10): rust, mid-blue, terra cotta, rust, white, dark brown, green, aubergine, beige, melon yellow
Ends: both: 1/in. varicolored stripes, plain weave
Other: outlining; extra-weft motifs

PLATE 14
Malatya (Kurd)
Eastern Anatolia
19th century
2 panels
5'8" × 11'8" (177 x 364 cm.)
Warp: wool & goat hair: ivory, beige, & brown, Z2S, 17/in.
Weft: wool: Z2S, 26–40/in.
Colors: (9): indigo, rust, rose, madder, green, yellow, ivory, aubergine, deep brown
Ends: both: 2/in. red and blue bands, plain weave; remains of heavy square braids with triangular bases
Sides: 4 bundles of 2 thicker warps, overcast in a variety of colors
Other: alternate bands in supplementary weft (reverse soumak) technique using white cotton

PLATE 15
Malatya (Kurd)
Eastern Anatolia
19th century
2 panels
5'5" × 11'6" (169 x 359 cm.)
Warp: wool: ivory, Z2S, 13/in.
Weft: wool: Z2S, 27/in.; cotton, Z2S, 36/in.
Colors (12): midnight blue, mid- and light blue, rust, cochineal red, abrashed green, white, terra cotta, brown, deep aubergine, light yellow, mulberry
Other: outlining; extra-weft bands in supplementary weft (reverse soumak) technique

PLATE 16
Malatya (Kurd)
Eastern Anatolia
1st half of 19th century
4' × 8'10" (122 × 276 cm.)
Warp: wool: ivory and beige, Z2S, 9/in.
Weft: wool: Z, Z2S, 23–55/in.
Colors (11): deep and mid-indigo, green, yellow, deep crimson, rust, pink, deep aubergine, pale purple, ivory, brown
Ends: both: 1/ in. yellow and brown stripes, plain weave
Other: outlining; extra-weft motifs

PLATE 17
Konya (Obruk?)
South Central Anatolia
19th century
4'1 × 7'2" (127 × 224 cm.)
Warp: wool & goat hair: ivory & brown: Z2S, 13/in.
Weft: wool: 2Z, 28/in.
Colors:(9): ivory, terra cotta, deep brown, aubergine, rust, green, dark and mid-blue, camel
Ends: upper: 3/in. red, blue, aubergine stripes; warp tassels; lower: 2/in. red band; both: plain weave
Other: outlining; eccentric wefting

PLATE 18
Yörük
South Central Turkey
Mid-19th century
2 panels
5'1 " × 12'4" (159 × 385 cm.)
Warp: wool: ivory, Z2S, 13/in.
Weft: wool: Z2S, 20–32/in.
Colors (16): poppy red, vermil-

ion, orange, deep crimson, purple red, deep aubergine, pale lilac, deep indigo, light blue, chartreuse, bottle green, yellow, apricot, browns, wheat, ivory
Other: outlining; extra-weft motifs

PLATE 19
Rashwan (Kurd)
Southeast Anatolia
19th century
2 panels
5'3" × 9'0" (164 × 281 cm.)
Warp: wool: ivory and gray, Z2S, 11/in.
Weft: wool & cotton: 2Z & Z2S, 30–36/in.
Colors (12): ivory, wheat, rust, grape purple, blue-green, blue, aubergine, browns, yellow, sand, apricot, burnt orange
Ends: both: 1/inch bands in aubergine, brown, & crimson, plain weave

PLATE 20
Konya region
South Central Anatolia
Late 19th century
2 panels
5' × 11'6" (156 × 359 cm.)
Warp: wool: ivory, Z2S, 12/in.
Weft: wool: Z, Z2S, 28–56/in.
Colors (9): ivory, mid- and light blue, crimson, apricot, dark aubergine, light green, browns, yellow
Ends: both: 2/in. brown bands, plain weave

PLATE 21
Niğde
South Central Anatolia
2 panels
2nd half of 19th century
5'3" × 13'5" (160 × 409 cm.)
Warp: wool: ivory Z2S, 16/in.
Weft: wool & cotton: Z2S, 26–44/in.
Colors (7): mid-blue, green-blue, green, pinkish red, brown, beige, aubergine
Ends: both: aubergine & blue stripes, plain weave
Other: outlining

PLATE 22
Konya
South Central Anatolia
Early 19th century
4'5" × 13' (135 × 396 cm.)
Colors (16): poppy red, vermil-

Warp: wool: ivory, Z2S, 12/in.
Weft: wool & cotton: Z2S, 24–30/in.
Colors (7): red, mid-blue, yellow, aubergine, ivory, melon, white
Ends: both: 4/in. yellow bands, plain weave
Other: outlining; extra-weft motifs; cloth swatches

PLATE 23
Aydınlı
Western Anatolia
2 panels (fragment)
18th century
5' × 6'3" (152 × 191 cm.)
Warp: wool: ivory, 2ZS, 15/in.
Weft: wool: Z2S, 24–34/in.
Colors (9): maroon, ivory, pale blue, moss green, dark green, medium aubergine, dark brown, mustard, pink

PLATE 24
Aydınlı
Western Anatolia
2nd half of 19th century
4' × 5'9" (122 × 175 cm.)
Warp: wool: ivory Z2S, 10/in.
Weft: wool: Z2S 29–33/in.
Colors (6): rust, ivory, blue, green, dark brown, pale green
Ends: top: blue band; bottom: brown band; both: plain weave
Other: outlining

PLATE 25
Konya region
South central Anatolia
1st half of 19th century
2 panels
4'5 " × 10'7" (135 × 323 cm.)
Warp: wool: ivory, Z2S, 14/in.
Weft: wool: Z2S, 29–34/in.
Colors (11): ivory, aubergine, dark and mid-blue, crimson, rust, dark and light green, browns, black, pale orange
Ends: top: 2/in.; bottom 4/in., bands of varicolored stripes; both: plain weave
Other: outlining; extra-weft motifs

PLATE 26
West Anatolia
19th century
4'3 " × 5'8 " (133 × 177 cm.)
Warp: wool & goat hair: ivory & brown, Z2S, 13/in.
Weft: wool & cotton: Z2S, 36/in. & Z3S, 24/in.

Colors (11): aubergine, purple, black-brown, white cotton, wheat, yellow, green, terra cotta, burnt orange, deep indigo, mid-blue
Ends: top & bottom: stripes in wheat, terra cotta; both: plain weave
Other: outlining; rows of complementary weft; eccentric wefting

PLATE 27
Aydınlı
Western Anatolia
19th century
3'10" × 5'4" (120 × 166 cm.)
Warp: wool: ivory, Z2S, 11/in.
Weft: wool: Z and Z2S, 24–60/in.
Colors (10): poppy red, purple red, pink, apricot, yellow, aubergine, abrashed indigo, blue-green, ivory, black
Ends: top: ½/in. flat braiding, plaited warps with blue beads & teased tassels; bottom: ½/in. red band, plain weave, warps plaited and braided with teased tassels
Other: outlining; rows of symmetrical knotted pile in field; stripes of complementary weft

PLATE 28
West Anatolia
19th century
3'2 " × 5'3 " (100 × 164 cm.)
Warp: wool: ivory, Z2S, 13/in.
Weft: wool: Z2S, 27/in.; cotton and metallic thread details
Colors (11): deep indigo, blue-green, purple red, rust, pink, apricot, wheat, pale green, brown, aubergine, ivory
Ends: top & bottom: red and blue stripes, plain weave
Other: outlining; eccentric wefting

PLATE 29
Van (Kurd)
Eastern Anatolia
19th century
7'4" × 8'10" (229 × 276 cm.)
Warp: wool: ivory, Z2S, 11/in.
Weft: wool: Z2S, 26–30/in.
Ends: both: 1/in. rust red band, plain weave
Colors (10): rust, cochineal red, terra cotta, mid- and light indigo blue, blue-green, ivory, brown, black, apricot
Other: outlining; eccentric wefting

PLATE 30
Southeastern Anatolia
Mid-19th century
2 panels
4'7" × 10' (143 × 312 cm.)
Warp: wool: ivory, Z2S, 14/in.
Weft: wool: Z2S, 23–32/in.
Colors (12): cochineal, medium indigo, green-blue, melon, pink, terra cotta, chartreuse, brown, mulberry, rust, aubergine, black
Ends: both: varicolored stripes, plain weave
Other: outlining; details in metallic thread

PLATE 31
Helvacıköy
Western Anatolia
Late 19th century
2 panels
5'4" × 7'10" (166 × 244 cm.)
Warp: wool: ivory, Z2S, 16/in.
Weft: wool: Z2S, 35/in.
Colors (7): ivory, vermilion, red-brown, yellow, celadon, light blue, black
Ends: both: varicolored stripes, plain weave; knotted warp fringe
Other: extra-weft motifs

PLATE 32
Afyon
Western Anatolia
Circa 1800
4'7" × 7'2" (140 × 249 cm.)
Warp: wool: ivory, 11/in.
Weft: wool: Z2S, 22–26/in.
Colors (10): maroon, pale blue, pale green, rust, ivory, dark and light brown, aubergine, mustard yellow
Ends: both: blue & red stripes, plain weave
Other: extra-weft motifs

PLATE 33
Afyon
Western Anatolia
Mid-19th century
5'4" × 14' (163 × 427 cm.)
Warp: wool: brown and white, brown Z2S, 10/in.
Weft: wool: Z2S, 20–32/in.
Colors (7): red, salmon, mid-blue, pale green, dark brown, aubergine, white
Ends: top: 2/in. striped; bottom 2/in. red band; both: plain weave
Other: outlining; extra-weft motifs: wool & cotton

PLATE 34
Konya
South Central Anatolia
19th century
3'8" × 4'5" (114 × 138 cm.)
Warp: cotton: Z2S, 14/in
Weft: wool: Z, 50/in.; metallic thread details
Colors (10): silver, black, dark crimson, ivory, green, red-brown, burnt orange, blue, brown, aubergine, browns

PLATE 35
Konya
South Central Anatolia
19th century
3'6" × 5' (109 × 156 cm.)
Warp: cotton: undyed, Z2S, 16/in.
Weft: wool: Z2S, 30/in.; cotton: Z2S, 40/in.; metallic thread: 40/in.
Colors (11): white cotton, midnight blue, abrashed green, magenta, brick-red, pale terra cotta, cocoa brown, sepia, yellow, metallic gold
Ends: bottom: flat warp braid
Other: outlining, extra-weft motifs

PLATE 36
Malatya (Rashwan Kurd)
Eastern Anatolia
19th century
3'9" × 5'10" (117 × 182 cm.)
Warp: cotton: undyed, Z2S, 16/in.
Weft: wool: Z, Z2S; white cotton, Z2S, 28–50/in.
Colors (10): dark aubergine, white, midnight blue, mid-blue, deep crimson, rust, sandy yellow, apricot, browns
Ends: both: warp ends knotted & webbed

PLATE 37
Afyon (Yerli)
Western Anatolia
Late 19th century
3'4" × 5'7" (104 × 174 cm.)
Warp: white cotton: Z2S, 12/in.
Weft: wool: Z2S, 14/in.
Colors (9): ivory, pale and deep yellow, rust, terra cotta, dark brown, celadon green, light and dark indigo
Ends: both: twisted, knotted warps
Other: stripes of complementary wefting

PLATE 38
Afyon
Western Anatolia
19th century
3'10" × 6'3 " (120 × 195 cm.)
Warp: wool: ivory, Z2S, 15/in.
Weft: wool: Z2S, 21/in.
Colors (9): green, tomato red, ivory, red-brown, indigo, apricot, brown, dark aubergine, yellow
Ends: top: green band, plain weave; warp ends knotted and webbed; bottom: red and blue extra-weft stripes on 2/in. ivory band
Other: outlining; extra-weft motifs

PLATE 39
Aydınlı
Western Anatolia
1st half of 19th century
2 panels
5' × 11'11" (156 × 372 cm.)
Warp: wool: ivory, Z2S, 14/in.
Weft: wool: 2Z, 21/in.
Colors (9): ivory, light and dark indigo, brown, aubergine, sea green, crimson, apricot, brown-red
Ends: both: varicolored stripes, plain weave
Other: outlining; extra-weft motifs

PLATE 40
Aydınlı
Western Anatolia
19th century
2 panels
5'7" × 10'6" (174 × 328 cm.)
Warp: wool: ivory, Z2S, 11/in.
Weft: wool: Z2S, 28–38/in.
Colors (12): ivory, light and dark indigo, madder-red, terra cotta, apricot, olive, yellow, aubergine, green, browns, black
Ends: both 1/in. red and blue stripes, plain weave
Other: outlining, extra-weft motifs

PLATE 41
Konya
South Central Anatolia
1 panel of 2 (fragment)
18th century
2'7" × 11'9" (79 × 358 cm.)
Warp: wool: ivory, Z2S, 13/in.
Weft: wool: Z2S, 19–30/in.
Colors (9): crimson, chartreuse,

ivory, mid-blue, sienna, yellow, dark brown, mauve, pink
Other: outlining; extra-weft motifs

PLATE 42
Konya (Hotamış Türkmen)
South Central Anatolia
Mid-19th century
2 panels
5'6" × 13'1" (172 × 346 cm.)
Warp: wool: ivory, Z2, 13/in.
Weft: wool: Z and Z2S, 26–30/in.; cotton Z3S, 22/in.
Colors (14): dark, medium and light blue, green, chartreuse, madder red, ivory, white (cotton), abrashed terra cotta, aubergine, pale yellow, metallic threads, dark and light brown
Ends: both: varicolored stripes, plain weave
Other: outlining; extra-weft motifs; eccentric wefting

PLATE 43
Konya
South Central Anatolia
Circa 1800
3 panels, fragment
4' 9" × 13'1" (145 × 399 cm.)
Warp: wool: ivory, Z2S, 13/in.
Weft: wool: Z2S, 30/in.
Colors (9): indigo, mid-blue, light blue, green, pink, crimson, light orange, light brown, light aubergine

PLATE 44
Karapınar
South Central Anatolia
Late 19th century
5'3" × 13'4" (160 × 406 cm.)
Warp: wool: ivory, ivory & brown, Z2S, 10/in.
Weft: wool & white cotton: Z2S, 16–21/in.
Colors (8): mid-blue, pale green, white, rust-orange, aubergine, yellow, dark brown, light brown
Ends: top: ¼/in. aubergine band; bottom in. blue band; both: plain weave
Other: outlining

PLATE 45
Sivas
Eastern Anatolia
19th century
3 panels
4'10" × 13' 3"(151 × 351 cm.)

171

Warp: wool: ivory, Z2S, 13/in.
Weft: wool: Z, Z2S, 27–55/in., cotton, Z3S, 22/in.
Colors (9): ivory, browns, crimson, pale terra cotta, yellow, aubergine, light and dark indigo, light green
Ends: both: warps twisted and knotted
Other: outlining; extra-weft motifs

PLATE 46
Konya (Hotamış Türkmen)
South Central Anatolia
19th century
5'6" × 12'4" (172 × 385 cm.)
Warp: wool: ivory, Z2S, 12/in.
Weft: wool: Z2S, 23/in.
Colors (11): ivory, browns, rust, light and dark aubergine, mid- and dark indigo, bottle green, light blue-green, deep and pale yellow
Ends: both: 1/in. varicolored stripes, plain weave

PLATE 47
Konya (Hotamış Türkmen)
South Central Anatolia
Mid-19th century
6' × 13' (187 × 406 cm.)
Warp: wool: ivory, Z2S, 13/in.
Weft: wool: Z2S, 27/in.
Colors (9): deep and pale pink, browns, ivory, dark and light indigo, celadon, crimson, pale yellow
Ends: bottom: braided and knotted warps
Other: outlining; extra-weft motifs

PLATE 48
Central Anatolia
19th century
5'5" × 13'10" (169 × 438 cm.)
Warp: wool: ivory, Z2S, 14/in.
Weft: white cotton: 32/in.; wool, Z2S, 26/in.
Colors (12): ivory, white cotton, olive, rust, tomato red, light and dark indigo, blue-green, green, apricot, pale aubergine, yellow
Ends: varicolored stripes of plain weave
Other: outlining; extra-weft motifs; rows of complementary wefting

PLATE 49
Central Anatolia
19th century
5' 7" × 12'7" (174 × 366 cm.)
Warp: wool: ivory, Z2S, 12/in.
Weft: wool: Z2S, 30/in.; cotton, Z2S, Z3S, 20/in.
Colors (8): white, indigo, rust, burnt orange, deep green, olive, tan, browns
Ends: both: remnants of orange band, plain weave
Other: outlining; eccentric wefting; extra-weft motifs; rows of complementary wefting

PLATE 50
Kutahya (Karakeçeli)
Northwest Anatolia
Late 19th century
5'9" x 8'9" (179 × 273 cm.)
Warp: ivory and beige wool: 10/in.
Weft: wool: Z2S, 18/in.
Colors (8): deep crimson, ivory, midnight blue, blue-green, celadon, yellow, brown, black
Ends: both: 2/in. varicolored stripes, plain weave; plaited, braided warp ends
Other: complementary weft rows; extra-weft motifs

PLATE 51
Cappadocia
Central Anatolia
2 panels
6'1" × 12'9" (185 × 389 cm.)
Warp: wool: ivory, Z2S, 10/in.
Weft: wool: Z2S, 33–44/in.
Colors (9): red, blue, chartreuse, dark brown, fuchsia, rust, light and dark yellow, beige
Ends: both: varicolored bands with zig-zag supplementary weft line, plain weave
Other: outlining; extra-weft motifs

PLATE 52
Cappadocia
Central Anatolia
19th century
4'4" × 12'5" (132 × 378 cm.)
Warp: wool: ivory, Z2S, 11/in.
Weft: wool: Z2S, 36/34 in.
Ends: top: 3/in. varicolored stripes; bottom: 4½/in. varicolored stripes; both: plain weave
Other: outlining; extra-weft motifs

PLATE 53
Aydınlı
Taurus region
2nd half of 19th century
4'4" × 10'8" (132 × 325 cm.)
Warp: wool: brown, white & brown, white: Z2S, 10/in.
Weft: wool: Z2S, 23–28/in.
Colors (8): red, white, blue, pale aubergine, dark green, medium & dark brown, yellow
Other: top: red band; bottom red & blue stripes; both: plain weave

PLATE 54
Niğde/Konya (Hotamış Türkmen)
South Central Anatolia
2 panels
18th century
4'6" × 15' (137 × 457 cm.)
Warp: wool: ivory, 2ZS, 12/in.
Weft: wool: Z2S, 23–28/in.
Colors: (9) ivory, mid- and light blue, beige, cochineal red, terra cotta, dark and medium brown, aubergine
Ends: both ½/in red stripe, plain weave
Other: outlining

PLATE 55
Van (Kurd)
Eastern Anatolia
19th century
4'6" × 10'4" (137 × 322 cm.)
Warp: wool: brown, Z2S, 14/in.
Weft: wool: Z2S, 29/in.
Colors (8): ivory, midnight blue, brown, grape, burnt orange, red brown, dark blue-green, tan
Ends: both: bands of aubergine, plain weave; oblique interlacing warps

PLATE 56
Karapınar (Hotamış Türkmen)
South Central Anatolia
19th century
4'7" × 13'9" (140 × 429 cm.)
Warp: wool: ivory, Z2S, 13/in.
Weft: wool: Z, 30/in.
Colors (12): ivory, rust, black, brown, aubergine, deep celadon, olive, yellow green, rose, deep madder, dark and mid-indigo
Ends: both: 4/in. aubergine bands, plain weave

PLATE 57
Karapınar (Hotamış Türkmen)
South Central Anatolia
19th century
4'2" × 7'4" (127 × 229 cm.)
Warp: wool: ivory, Z2S, 9/in.
Weft: wool: Z2S, 24–32/in.
Colors (5): crimson, mid-indigo blue, green, ivory, blue-green
Other: outlining; extra-weft motifs; tassels

PLATE 58
Obruk region
South Central Anatolia
Mid-19th century
3'6" × 5'11" (109 × 185 cm.)
Warp: wool: ivory and beige, Z2S, 10/in.
Weft: wool: Z, Z2S, 27/in.
Colors (6): ivory, brown, madder red, aubergine, apricot, green
Other: outlining; eccentric wefting

PLATE 59
Reyhanlı
Southeastern Anatolia
19th century
3'6" × 5' (109 × 156 cm.)
Warp: wool & goat hair: ivory & gray, Z2S, 19/in.
Weft: wool: Z2S, 29/in.
Colors (10): white cotton, ivory, cochineal-grape, midnight blue, light blue, dark green, yellow, dark olive, gray-blue, black
Ends: top: 1½/in. band, warp ends knotted and webbed; bottom: 2/in. varicolored stripes; both: plain weave
Other: extra-weft-motifs

PLATE 60
Helvacıköy
Western Anatolia
Late 19th century
3'3" × 4'11 " (101 × 153 cm.)
Warp: wool: ivory, Z2S, 18/in.
Weft: wool: Z, 36/in.
Colors (8): vermilion, ivory, celadon, yellow, black, red-brown, light blue, aubergine
Ends: both: warps twisted and knotted
Other: complementary weft stripes; knotted pile tufts; extra-weft motifs

PLATE 61
Obruk
South Central Anatolia
Mid-19th century
4' × 5'6" (122 × 172 cm.)
Warp: wool: Z2S, 13/in.
Weft: wool: Z, 2Z, 30/in.
Colors (8): aubergine, brown, green, olive, tan, terra cotta, ivory, indigo
Other: outlining; eccentric wefting; extra-weft motifs

PLATE 62
Elmadağ
Western Anatolia
1st half of 19th century
3'11" × 4' 8" (120 × 143 cm.)
Warp: wool: ivory and brown, Z2S, 12/in.
Weft: wool: Z, 28–30/in.
Colors (9): red, maroon, green, blue, orange, yellow, brown, ivory, purple
Ends: top: maroon band; bottom: green & maroon stripes; both: plain weave
Other: outlining

PLATE 63
Konya
South Central Anatolia
19th century
3'5" × 5'5" (104 × 165 cm.)
Warp: wool: ivory, Z2S, 3/in.
Weft: wool: Z2S, 20–38/in.
Colors (7): salmon, light blue, dark blue, ivory, beige, medium brown, terra cotta
Ends: both: brown band, plain weave; knotted warps
Other: outlining; extra-weft motifs

PLATE 64
Aydınlı
Taurus region
Mid-19th century
3'7" × 5'4" (109 × 163 cm.)
Warp: wool: ivory, Z2S, 10/in.
Weft: wool: Z2S, 21–34/in.
Colors (6): red, blue, ivory, brown, aubergine, beige
Ends: top: red & white stripes, braided tassels; bottom: red & white stripes; both: plain weave
Other: outlining

PLATE 65
Yahyalı
Central Anatolia
Late 19th century
4'5" × 6'2" (138 × 192 cm.)
Warp: wool: ivory, Z2S, 14/in.
Weft: wool: Z2S, 24/in.
Colors (9): deep madder, indigo, ivory, pale aubergine, light green, black, apricot, yellow, pale purple
Ends: both: warps knotted and twisted together
Other: outlining

PLATE 66
Malatya (Rashwan Kurd)
Eastern Anatolia
19th century
2'5" x 4'9" (75 x 148 cm.)
Warp: wool & goat hair: ivory & gray, Z2S, 10/in.
Weft: wool: Z2S, 26/in., white cotton and metallic thread details
Colors (12): ivory, browns, slight, mid- and dark blues, mulberry, grape purple, rust, yellow, pale green, pale blue-green, wheat
Ends: knotted warps
Other: outlining; extra-weft motifs

PLATE 67
Nevşehir
Central Anatolia
19th century
2'11 " × 4'7" (91 × 143 cm.)
Warp: wool: ivory & brown, Z2S, 12/in.
Weft: wool: Z, 45/in.
Colors (9): tomato red, indigo, dark green, yellow, ivory, apricot, dark browns, aubergine, black
Ends: red & green stripes; bottom: beige, green, & red stripes; both: plain weave

PLATE 68
Malatya
Eastern Anatolia
19th century
3'8" × 4'6 (114 x 140 cm.)
Warp: wool: ivory, Z2S, 13/in.
Weft: wool: Z, & white cotton, 40/in.
Colors (9): pale green, grape purple, brown, aubergine, white cotton, sand, pale blue-green, deep crimson, indigo
Ends: both: red band, plain weave
Other: outlining; extra-weft motifs

PLATE 69
Erzerum-Bayburt
Northeastern Anatolia
19th century
4'4" x 5' (135 × 156 cm.)
Warp: wool: ivory, Z2S, 11/in.
Weft: wool: Z, 31/in.; white cotton, Z2S, 34/in.
Colors (10): deep crimson, brick-red, rose madder, dark blue-green, midnight blue, light blue, black, browns, ivory, yellow
Ends: both: knotted fringe
Other: outlining; extra-weft motifs

PLATE 70
Erzerum
Northeastern Anatolia
19th century
4'5" × 6'5" (138 × 164 cm.)
Warp: wool: brown, Z2S, 13/in.
Weft: wool: Z2S, 30/in. cotton, Z
Colors (10): white cotton, brown, red, orange, mustard, black, gray, dark blue, olive, aubergine
Ends: both: warp ends knotted
Other: date or inscription at top of spandrel

PLATE 71
Bayburt
Northeastern Anatolia
Dated 1259 AH (1843 AD)
4'6" × 5'11" (140 × 185 cm.)
Warp: wool: ivory, Z2S, 11/in.
Weft: wool: Z2S, 22/in.; metallic thread details
Colors (8): green, red, deep and pale yellow, browns, dark blue, mid-blue, red-brown

PLATE 72
Erzurum
Northeastern Anatolia
Dated 1292 AH (1875)
4'10" × 5'7" (151 × 174 cm.)
Warp: wool & goat hair?: brown, Z2S, 9/in.
Weft: wool: Z2S, 26/in.
Colors (10): dark blue, light blue, ivory, abrashed crimson, browns, faded purple, green, tan, yellow, deep red-brown
Ends: both: remnants of braided and plaited fringe
Other: outlining; eccentric wefting

PLATE 73
Erzurum
Northeastern Anatolia
2nd half of 19th century
4'8" × 6'2" (146 × 192 cm.)
Warp: wool: ivory, Z2S, 12/in.
Weft: wool: Z2S, white cotton, Z2S, 16/in.
Colors (7): deep rust, blue-green, deep indigo, mid- and light yellow, browns, apricot
Ends: top: brown band; bottom: varicolored stripes, braided meshwork; both: plain weave
Other: outlining

Notes

CHAPTER 1

1. E. J. W. Barber, *Prehistoric Textiles: The Development of Cloth in the Neolithic and Bronze Ages* (Princeton, NJ: Princeton University Press, 1991), 26.
2. Jon Thompson, *Oriental Carpets from the Tents, Cottages, and Workshops of Asia* (New York: E. P. Dutton, 1988), 51.
3. G. Geraint Jenkins, *From Fleece to Fabric: The Technological History of the Welsh Woolen Industry* (Wales: Gomer Press, 1987), 6.
4. Ibid., 6.
5. Thompson, 51.
6. Conversation with Marla Mallett, Atlanta, Georgia, June 1992.
7. Barber, 40.
8. Ibid., 263.
9. Ibid., 42–43.
10. Ibid., 41.
11. Ibid., 52–53.
12. Ibid., 65.
13. Ibid., 65–67.
14. Jenkins, 24.
15. E. H. Gombrich, *The Sense of Order: A Study in the Psychology of Decorative Art* (Ithaca, NY: Cornell University Press, 1984), 33.

CHAPTER 2

1. Paul Murshak, "Synthetic Dyes: A History: Part III." *Oriental Rug Review* 4(4), July 1984), 8.
2. Harald Böhmer, "Carpets from the Yuntdağ Region in Western Anatolia." *Oriental Carpet and Textile Studies*, 3(2), 178.
3. Cornelia Montgomery, "The Significance of Indigo Blue in Near Eastern Carpets and Textiles." *Oriental Carpet and Textile Studies*, 3(2), 227.
4. Ibid., 226.
5. Ibid., 230.
6. Ibid., 227.
7. Possibly there is a physiological explanation for the attraction to red: Long wave lengths, which appear as red, may cause a slight increase in heart rate; however the re-

search on this subject is still on the iffy side. Conversation with Professor Israel Abramov, Psychology Department, Brooklyn College, June 18, 1992.
8. Barber, 230.
9. Thompson, 59.
10. Ibid., 60.
11. Montgomery, 227.
12. Barber, 235–39.
13. Manfred Bieber, "The Kavacık Project: Contribution to the Conservation and Advancement of the Turkish Carpet Tradition in the Istanbul Region." *Oriental Carpet and Textile Studies*, 3(2), 175.
14. Jenkins, 12.
15. Walter B. Denny, "Anatolian Rugs: An Essay on Method." *Textile Museum Journal*, 3(4), December 1973, 18.
16. While some might object to the comparison with children, this writer regards such a comparison as a compliment, since it is precisely because of the preservation of certain child-like sensibilities that, in part, what we would regard as artistic sensibilities are formed.
17. Harald Böhmer, "The Revival of Natural Dyeing in Two Traditional Weaving Areas of Anatolia." *Oriental Rug Review*, 3(9), December 1983, 4.
18. Abramov, conversation, June 19, 1992.
19. Böhmer, "The Revival of Natural Dyeing," 4.
20. Ibid., 4.

CHAPTER 3

1. Barber, 99.
2. Ibid., 166.
3. This "history" of the evolution of the loom is speculative since the evolution took place outside recorded history.
4. Barber, 82–83.
5. Ibid., 91.
6. Anthony N. Landreau, "Kurdish Kilim Weaving in the

Van-Hakkari District of Eastern Turkey." *Textile Journal*, 3(4), 39.
7. There is a loom innovation common in most parts of the world (but not in Anatolia) where tapestry weaving is carried on that facilitates tapestry weaving whereby the loom is equipped with fixed heddle bars with rather long heddles which can be grasped in bunches to open the alternate shed in sections. Conversation with Marla Mallett, June 1992.
8. Anni Albers. *On Weaving*. (Middletown, CT: Wesleyan University Press, 1965), 67.
9. Ibid., 25–26.

CHAPTER 4

1. Barber, 203.
2. Marla Mallett, conversation, June 1992.
3. Albers, 38–39.
4. Ibid., 68.
5. Irene A. Bierman, "Medieval Flatweaves in the Urban Middle East." (In *Flatwoven Textiles*, Cathryn M. Cootner, Ed. Washington, DC: Textile Museum, 1981), 161.
6. Helmet Neuman, "Between Science & Passion." *Hali, the International Magazine of Carpets and Textiles* #92, May 1997, 76–85; Jürg Rageth, Ed., *Kilims and Carbon-14 Dating: A New Approach* (Basel, 1997).
7. Those most involved in promoting the new carbon-14 methodology are many of the same dealers and collectors who just a decade ago were enthusiastically embracing James Mellart's archaeological expertise to promote the so-called Goddess Theory, which in its most extreme version claimed an eight-thousand-year history for Anatolian kilims stretching back to Neolithic times (this is further elaborated later in the

book). Significantly at their 1997 symposium the Goddess Theory was no longer in evidence. Thus, the promotion of AMS carbon-14 dating for kilims is not the first time that scientific approaches have been appropriated to legitimize the Anatolian kilim as an ancient artefact. It is obvious that proving the great antiquity of certain extant kilims is a great factor in determining their value. Certainly, it is, therefore, to the benefit of dealers in and collectors of kilims to support any theory, no matter how tenuous, which demonstrates great antiquity.
8. Rageth, 79. In the words of one of its proponents, the methodology is problematic because the carbon-14 dates arrived at can only be interpreted allowing for an error factor of 100–200 years. In carbon dating artefacts that are over 2,000 years old such a margin of error would seem less significant; the same margin of error for dating artefacts that are at most around 350 years old makes the process virtually meaningless.
9. Jürg Rageth, Ed., *Kilims and Carbon-14 Dating*.

CHAPTER 5

1. Gombrich, 4–5.
2. Ibid., 7.
3. Dorothy K. Washburn and Donald W. Crowe, *Symmetries of Culture: Theory and Practice of Plane Pattern Analysis* (Seattle: University of Washington Press, 1988). While this valuable approach to the analysis of design has interesting applications to Near and Middle Eastern weaving, the authors do not make any direct application of its methodology to kilim and carpet design.
4. Ibid., 15–16.

175

5. Ibid., 12.
6. Ibid., 23.
7. Ibid., 43–50.
8. Ibid., 21.
9. Henry Glassie, *Turkish Traditional Arts Today* (Bloomington & Indianapolis: Indiana University Press, 1993), 802.
10. For examples of this process see plates 36, 47, 48, 49, and 50.
11. Glassie, 802.
12. Werner Brüggemann, "Carpets and Kilims: A Contribution to the Problem of the Origins and Designs in Kilims." *Oriental Carpet and Textile Studies, 3*(2), 76.
13. Barber, 132–33.
14. The remaining structural principles are discussed in chapter 8.
15. Conversation with Josephine Powell, Istanbul, Spring 1988.
16. Edmund O'Donovan, *The Merv Oasis: Travels and Adventures East Of the Caspian During the Years 1879–80–81*, 2 vols., (London, 1882), I: 413–414.

CHAPTER 6

1. Hilmi Dulkadır, "The Sarakeçeli Tribe and Their Flatweaves." *Oriental Carpet and Textile Studies, 3*(2),189.
2. Thompson, 51.
3. Belkis Balpınar, *The Goddess from Anatolia: IV Anatolian Kilims Past and Present* (Milan, Italy: Eskenazi, 1989), 9.
4. Barber, 292. She makes the valuable point that in rural societies worldwide and throughout the ages weaving was carried on as a social responsibility, not as a form of enforced labor.
5. Balpınar, 51.
6. Ibid., 51.
7. Ibid., 47.
8. Ibid., 8.
9. Ibid., 9.
10. Cathryn M. Cootner, Ed., *Anatolian Kilims: The Caroline and H McCoy Jones Collection* (London: Hali Publishing, 1990), 25.
11. Balpınar, 9.
12. Thompson, 58.

13. Cathryn M. Cootner, Ed., *Flatwoven Textiles. The Arthur D. Jenkins Collection, vol.1* (Washington, DC: Textile Museum, 1981), 152.
14. Thompson, 58.
15. Manfred Bieber, "A Contribution to the Conservation and Advancement of the Turkish Carpet Tradition in the Istanbul Region," *Oriental Carpet and Textile Studies 3*(2):170.
16. Professor Louise Hainline, Psychology Department, Brooklyn College, New York. Conversation, June 19, 1992.

CHAPTER 7

1. Gombrich, 243–44.
2. Denny, 14.
3. Albers, 68.
4. Ibid., 67.
5. Gombrich, 217.
6. Ibid., 222.
7. Ibid., 225.
8. Ibid., 218.
9. Yosuf Duru, "Flatwoven Rugs Made by Yörüks," (Istanbul, 1977), 63.
10. Balpınar, 5.
11. Belkis Balpınar, "Establishing the Cultural Context of a Group of Anatolian Cicim Rugs." *Hali, The International Magazine of Carpets and Textiles* 4(3) (1982), 265.
12. Belkis Balpınar, *Anatolian Kilims* (Milan: Eskenazi, 1984), 49.
13. Ibid., 45.
14. Balpınar, *The Goddess IV*, 46.
15. Ibid., 48.
16. Belkis Balpınar, "Establishing the Cultural Context of a Group. . .", 67.
17. Anita Landreau, "Weaving in Susanoğlu," essay in *Flowers of the Yayla: Yörük Weaving of the Toros Mountains*, Anthony N. Landreau and Ralph S. Yohe, Eds., (Washington, DC: Textile Museum, 1983), 83–94.
18. Ibid., 85–87.
19. Barber, 376.
20. Anita Landreau, 83.
21. Barber, 373.
22. Montgomery, 232.
23. Ibid., 229.
24. Gombrich, 223. He is discussing the conclusions of Franz Boas in *Primitive Art*.

25. Ibid., 226.
26. Ibid., 247.
27. Peter Alford Andrews, "Tent Screens to Kilims: Discussion of 'An Argument for the Origins of Anatolian Kilim Designs' by Josephine Powell," *Oriental Carpet and Textile Studies 3*(2): 61.
28. Barber, 292.
29. Balpınar, *Goddess IV*, 47.
30. Andrews, 63.
31. Josephine Powell, "An Argument for the Origins of Anatolian Kilim Designs," *Oriental Carpet and Textile Studies 3*(2): 51.
32. Ibid., 58.
33. Ibid., 58.
34. Ibid., 58.
35. Andrews, 62.
36. Peter Alford Andrews, "From Khurasan to Anatolia," *Oriental Carpet and Textile Studies, 3*(2): 46-49.
37. Barber, 375.
38. Powell, "A Reply to Dr. Andrews's Counter-Argument," *Oriental Carpet and Textile Studies, 3*(2): 69.
39. Gombrich, 233–34.
40. Powell, "A Reply to Dr. Andrews's," 69.
41. Belkis Balpınar and Udo Hirsch, *Flatweaves of the Vakıflar Museum Istanbul*, (Wesel, Germany: Uta Hülsey, 1982), 11.
42. Ibid., 12.
43. Ibid., 12.
44. Kubra Alieva, "The Syncretic Nature of the Ornamental System of Azerbaijan," *Oriental Carpet and Textile Studies, 3*(2): 158.
45. For further discussion, see Walter B. Denny, "Saff and Sejjadeh: Origins and Meanings of the Prayer Rug," *Oriental Carpet and Textile Studies, 3*(2): 93–103.
46. Balpınar, *Anatolian Kilims*, 49.
47. Ibid., 19.
48. Barber, 373–74.

CHAPTER 8

1. A case has been made by James Opie for the influence of Iranian weaving traditions in the Zagros mountains on Anatolian kilims. He argues that Zagros mountain weav-

ing traditions significantly influenced Anatolian kilim design, and these influences were transmitted to Turkic Anatolian weavers by way of the Kurds. It is becoming evident that a discussion of origins can no longer ignore the influences of such territories as the Caucasian and Zagros mountain regions, nor the influences of non-Turkic Anatolian populations such as the Kurds and Armenians.
2. Josephine Powell, "A Reply to Dr. Andrews's," 70, endnote 6.
3. Barber, 127.
4. Ibid., 28.
5. Ibid., 93.
6. Ibid., 99.
7. Ibid., 83.
8. Mallett, conversation, June 19, 1992.
9. Barber, 112.
10. Ibid., 202.
11. Ibid., 203. The reference is to S. I. Rudenko.
12. Ibid., 225.
13. Ibid., 133.
14. Ibid., 213.
15. This is a group of artefacts identified as Early Bronze Age, including a textile said to be woven in wool in "kilim technique" measuring approximately 2½' by 5½' with geometric lozenges arranged within the main field, and lozenges within stripes along the end border. This kilim was described as having been excavated during World War II in Dorak, northwestern Anatolia, and alleged to have disintegrated upon contact with the air. Mellaart does not claim to have seen it but to have based his "sketch" on an archaeologist's "sketch." When challenged to document his sketch and notes, Mellaart claims not to have been able to find the house of the unidentified Izmir woman where the artefacts were housed, the artefacts themselves, the archaeologist's original sketch, or any other substantiating

evidence. The episode, known as the Dorak Affair, has cast, doubt on Mellaart's credibility. The sources are Barber, *Prehistoric Textiles*, 170–71, and conversation with Mallett, June 1992.

16. Barber, 197–98.
17. Ibid., 202–203.
18. James Mellaart, *The Goddess of Anatolia II*, (Milan: Eskenazi, 1989), 44.
19. Mallett, conversation, June 22, 1992.
20. Ian Bennett, "The Mistress of All Life," *Hali, International Magazine of Fine Arts and Textiles* #50 (April 1990), 117.
21. Ibid., 118.
22. Murray Eiland, Jr., "The Goddess from Anatolia," *Oriental Rug Review 10*(6): 19–26.
23. Marla Mallett, "A Weaver's View of the Çatal Hüyük Controversy," *Oriental Rug Review 10*(6): 32–43.
24. Mary Voigt, "The Goddess from Anatolia: An Archaeological Perspective," *Oriental Rug Review 11*(2) (Dec/Jan 1991): 33–41.
25. Barber, 217.
26. Ibid., 11.
27. Mallett, conversation, June 1992.
28. Barber, 223.
29. Ibid., 21.
30. Ibid., 28.
31. Ibid., 99–100.
32. Mallett, "A Weaver's View," 32.
33. Ibid., 42.
34. Ibid., 36.
35. Ibid., 34–35.
36. Ibid., 41.
37. Mellaart, 20.
38. Voigt, 38–39.
39. Mallett, "A Weaver's View," 41.
40. Mellaart, 59–60.
41. Bennett, "A Mistress," 116.
42. Udo Hirsch, *The Goddess From Anatolia I* (Milan: Eskenazi, 1989).
43. Brüggemann, 71–83.
44. Gombrich, 223.
45. Balpınar, *The Goddess IV*, 43.
46. Ibid., 49–54.
47. Ibid., 50.
48. Mellaart, 58.
49. Ibid., 58.

50. Ibid., 59.
51. Brüggemann, 82.
52. Eiland, 19.
53. Brüggemann, 81.
54. The weavings entering Western rug markets from the Caucasian regions since the collapse of the USSR are beginning to cast light on the links between the Anatolian and Caucasian weaving regions.
55. Thompson, 155.
56. Ibid., 155.
57. Balpınar, *The Goddess IV*, 44.
58. Ibid., 44.
59. Andrews, "From Khurasan," 46–49.
60. Ibid., 50, end note 24.
61. Brüggemann, 76. Brüggemann's valuable term, "structural principle," refers to the overall organization of a design.
62. Yanni Petsopoulos, *Kilims: Flatwoven Tapestry Rugs* (New York: Rizzoli, 1979), 28–63. Brüggemann, 81.
64. For an interesting debate on the subject, see Josephine Powell, "An Argument for the Origins of Anatolian Kilim Designs," 51–60; Peter Alford Andrews, "Tent Screens to Kilims," 61–64; and Josephine Powell, "A Reply to Dr. Andrews's Counter-Argument," 65–70 in *Oriental Carpet and Textile Studies 3*(2).
65. For plates and diagrams of representative screens, see Josephine Powell, "An Argument," 54–58.
66. Ibid., 54–55.
67. Ibid., 58–59.
68. Andrews, "Tent Screens to Kilims," 62.
69. Powell, "A Reply," 66–67.
70. Barber, 221.

Chapter 9

1. I exclude the prayer kilim from the count since its design tradition mostly originates from Ottoman not Anatolian tribal sources. Thus the horn/hexagon combination is one of the important defining elements of what I have called Anatolia's "tribal eye."

2. For other examples of the classic style see: Belkis Balpınar, *Vakiflar*, Plates 43, 44; Guran Erbek, *Kilim Catalogue*, plates 18 & 19; Rainer Kressl, *Art as Tradition: Anatolia* (Prague, 1995), Plate 92; Petsopoulos, *Kilims: Masterpieces from Turkey* (Rizzoli, New York, 1991), Plate 21; Petsopoulos, *Kilims*, Plates 88, 89, and 92; Vok, *Anatolia*, Plate 57 (but this has only one tree).
3. The use of white in Central Asian feltwork of the quilted variety, interestingly enough, functions as a kind of white piping serving to mask where the cut-out motifs have been sewn together. It appears that what was originally introduced for largely practical purposes—to hide the connecting threads—became part of the Yüncü aesthetic. As a result, the white outlining of motifs was transferred to Yüncü kilims, where the original masking function was no longer necessary. Thus, white outlining, it would seem, became part of the traditional design of the Yüncü.
4. Türck, *Ullrich*, p. 109
5. Ibid., p. 109.
6. Ibid., p. 111.
7. Ibid., p. 96. The Selçuk army, it has been established, arrived without women; marriage with Greek and Armenian women was the rule. Almost the entire Selçuk ruling class was made up of half-castes—the children of mixed marriages brought up in the Islamic faith.
8. Ibid., pp. 111–112. Significantly, the migrating Türkmen tribes in the seventeenth century chose to keep their white felt tents.
9. Ibid., p. 111.
10. Ibid., p. 111. It has been established that around 1900 the Anatolian population within modern borders was around 11 million; 7 million of which were Turks. In an historical perspective, the Turkish population over an

800-year period increased from 5 percent to 60 percent of this total through immigration, conversion, and intermarriage. It is generally agreed that the proportion of immigrants over this period was 15–20 percent. Thus, conversion and intermarriage were major factors in the Turkification of Anatolia.
11. Türck, p. 110. An argument has been made for a Near Eastern origin for the Yüncü design of a trunk bracketed with horns. A fragment of Tulunid Egyptian fabric of the ninth or tenth centuries (in the David Collection in Copenhagen) gives an intriguing glimpse of a trunk-like form with hooked branches on a red field with four animals around it. The fragment is referred to as a "kilim" by proponents anxious to find ancient indigenous sources for Anatolian kilim design. However, a more accurate description is that it is a slit-weave tapestry fragment. The term kilim has a specific application that includes more than just the weaving technique employed. Referring to any weaving in slit-weave tapestry as a kilim makes the term meaningless, as in the "kilims" of pre-Columbian South America. Furthermore, the Tulunid textile is too ambiguous in its fragmented state and there is no evidence for any direct link between this Egyptian textile tradition and the weavings the Yüncü have produced. It would seem more likely that we are dealing only with a striking resemblance.
12. Türck, p. 100. Alevites typically have an elitist way of thinking, mixed with mysticism, a particular belief in the right way to God, and special ideas about social justice. They do not follow the commandments of Sunnite orthodoxy. While they accept Ali as the rightful successor to the Prophet, they

do not devote themselves to the Shia. They are viewed with suspicion and hostility by both the Sunni and Shiite branches of Islam.

13. Other examples can be found in Balpınar, *Vakiflar*, plate 45; Cootner, plate 24; Kreissl, *Art as Tradition: Anatolia*, plate 10; Petsopoulos, *Kilims*, plates 93 and 94; Petsopoulos, *Kilims: Masterpieces*, plates 18 and 19; and Rageth, *Kilim: Primitive Symbols*, plate 2.

14. A similar treatment is found in Balpınar, *Vakiflar*, plate 47. This Yüncü-like kilim is attributed to the Karakeçeli, near neighbors of the Yüncü, in the region of Balıkesir/Kutahya.)

15. For another example that resembles Yüncü kilims of this type, but which is attributed to the neighboring Karakeçeli, see Balpınar, op. cit., plate 47.

16. For examples, see, Balpınar, op. cit., plates 33, 34, 40, 41, 47, & 49; Cootner, *Anatolian Kilims*, plate 72; Kreissl, *Art as Tradition*, plates 41 & 45; Petsopoulos, *Kilims: Masterpieces*, plate 23. Tribes in areas as far afield as Karapınar and Akşehir in the Konya region (Balpınar, plates 33 & 34), the Aydınlı of Aydın, Manissa, and Fethiye (Balpınar, plate 35) and Antalya (Petsopoulos, *Kilims: Masterpieces*, plate 30) also exhibit kilims with similarities.

17. Ullrich Türck, p. 94. Conceivably this design also had its origins in Anatolia. In the second half of the fifteenth century unsuccessful Türkmen rebellions against the Ottomans led to the exodus of large numbers of Türkmen to Azerbaijan, where they merged into the confederation of the Shahsavan.

CHAPTER 10

1. In the hands of scholars and connoisseurs of this persuasion, the Anatolian kilim is reduced to being a convenient trampoline on which they vigorously exercise their Jungian fantasies.

2. Patricia Daugherty, "Through the Eyes of the Weavers: Aesthetics and Culture of Tribal Yürük Women of Turkey," *Oriental Carpet and Textile Studies*, 5, pt. 1. Danville, CA. 1999. pp. 161–66.

3. Ibid., p. 161.

4. Ibid., p. 163.

5. Even though this description may strike some as politically incorrect, remember that we are describing the actual practices and perceptions of an ancient, traditional culture.

6. Daugherty, p. 163.

7. Ibid., p. 163.

8. Ibid., p. 165.

9. Obviously, before conclusions can be reached about the Yörük generally or Anatolian nomads as a whole, much more fieldwork will have to be carried out amongst the scattered, surviving populations.

10. Henry Glassie, *Turkish Traditional Art Today*.

11. Cecims are loosely called kilims, but technically they are warp-faced flatweaves in vertically striped designs with infilled motifs formed by the substitution of supplementary warps. These technically difficult pieces are not usually done collaboratively, as tapestry and knotted weavings are. In Sebire's case, working solo seems to have allowed her much more individual expression, particularly in her cecim B.

12. Kufic is the name given to the early, bold, noncursive calligraphic script. This script, like Sebire's "Turkish alphabet," became a decorative element over time and did not function in a literal way.

13. Glassie, p. 218.

14. Ibid., p. 219.

15. Bloomington, IN: Indiana University, 1993.

16. Glassie, *Turkish Traditional Art Today*, p. 94.

17. While his observations drawn from contemporary weavers seem on the whole applicable to the tribal weavers who are the subject of this book, it should be kept in mind that he is interacting with contemporary weavers influenced by cottage industries that are very much a part of the modern Turkish economy, with women who have either physically left the rural world or who are on the way to mentally doing so. Unfortunately, for us his focus does not include the few tiny pockets of tribal weaving populations in which domestic weaving continues apart from the cottage industry.

18. For the outlines of the following discussion I am indebted to Glassie's *Turkish Traditional Arts Today*. However, his discussion does very little with the kilim, as his chief weaving focus is on knotted rugs and carpets.

19. Glassie, p. 95.

20. Ibid., p. 98.

21. Ibid., p. 99.

22. Ibid., p. 99.

23. Ibid., p. 108.

24. The Selçuk period refers to the first Turkish state in Anatolia that flourished from the eleventh to the fourteenth century. Its capital was the city of Konya in south-central Anatolia.

25. Since sade weavings usually lack the kind of decoration that would appeal to most Westerners they are minimally represented in collections and exhibitions and, consequently, in the plate section to this book.

26. Glassie, pp. 797–849.

27. Ibid., p. 849. "Accidence" is a French term that Glassie uses as a positive description of "happy accidents."

Glossary

A Key to Turkish Pronunciation

The modern Turkish alphabet, adopted by the Turks in the 1920s, replaced the former Arabic alphabet, which was used by the Turks since their conversion to Islam over 1,000 years ago. The new alphabet was designed to be phonetic and, in comparison with English, it is. Here is a key to Turkish pronunciation (where it differs from English). In all cases, Turkish pronunciation gives equal stress to syllables.

a: "ah" as in "father."

â: the cirumflex adds a glide to the vowel.

c: "dj" as in the English "J."

e: "eh" as in "bet."

g: hard g as in "get."

ğ: the "g" is silent or sounds like "y;" it lengthens the vowel that precedes it as in Bağdad (bahhh-dad).

i: pronounced "ee" as in "beet."

ı: this has no counterpart in English; it is somewhere between "pit" and "put."

o: as in "pot."

ö: makes it similar to an umlaut, as in "oeuvre" in French.

ş: "sh" as in "shirt."

u: "oo" as in "noon."

ü: the umlaut gives it a sound lacking in English, but like the French "tu."

v: a very liquid sound that often crosses with the English "w" (a consonant missing in Turkish); i.e., tuvalet is pronounced like "toilette."

abrash (also abrağ: ah-brahsh): dappled, mottled, or speckled. In weaving it designates the subtle gradations of color, which are usually an accident of the spinning and dyeing processes within the same color of dyed yarns. It is a valued defect in weavings, particularly those of nomadic and peasant origin because of the color nuances it produces.

ağhrepli (ah-reh-plee): an abstract motif that represents a scorpion and functions as a talisman to ward off the evil eye. See figure r on page 57.

ağzi (ah-zee): literally the mouth; in weaving it refers to the point where the shed is opened to receive the wefts.

ak kaz (ahk-kahz): literally the white goose; in weaving it refers to Central Asian abstract motifs that represent the white goose—a shamanist symbol of an auspicious bird. It is regarded as the shaman's familiar and a symbol of the reconciliation of opposites. See figures x and y on page 80.

alaçuval (ahla-choowal): A large brocaded storage bag for clothing and special items that is traditionally displayed in a row in the back of the tent or cottage. The preparation of these bags was the responsibility of the mother-in-law-to-be and has traditionally been part of the trousseau of a new bride.

Alindje Khan: A mythical Oghuz king in Mongolia believed to have fathered twin sons, Tatar and Mongol; Turks supposedly descend from the latter.

Anatolia (also Anadolu; ah-na-dough-loo): it is the great land mass bounded by the Black Sea to the north, the Mediterranean Sea to the South, the Aegean Sea to the West, and the Zagros Mountains to the east. However, the term is relative. For those who live in the more Westernized coastal areas of what we call Anatolia, it is the interior, or high plateau region, that is called Anatolia.

aniline dyes: synthetic dyes first produced commercially in the 1860s to facilitate uniformity in mass-produced yarns. Synthetics quickly replaced natural dyes, which had been in use for thousands of years.

asymmetrical knot (also Persian or Senneh knot): a pile-weaving technique in which the knot wraps around two warps, but only one of those warps is encircled entirely, hence the asymmetry. This technique is commonly used outside Anatolia. See figure o on page 36.

Atropos (Greek: the Unturnable or Inflexible): One of the three Fates in Greek mythology—three sisters believed to spin out man's destiny. Atropos cuts the thread that terminates human life.

axle of the universe: a vertical axis—usually represented as a tree, pillar, or post—that in the Central Asian shamanic view connected the upper, middle, and lower worlds.

Aydınlı Yörük (eye-duhn-luh yuh-rook): A major tribe of the Yörük with its center in the Aydın region south of Izmir in Western Turkey. Over the past century it has migrated further and further east and presently occupies a swath in the southern mountainous region of Anatolia extending from Aydın to Adana.

bab (Arabic: bahb): a gate or doorway.

bilateral symmetry: a form of mirror symmetry in which the size, shape, and relative position of parts are mirrored on the opposite side of an invisible vertical dividing line or axis. See figure a on page 41.

bilateral-horizontal symmetry (also double symmetry): a form of mirror symmetry in which both bilateral symmetry and horizontal symmetry are present. See figure c on page 41.

canlı (djahn-luh): playful, free; in weaving aesthetics it refers to a mode in which form and restraint give way to playfulness, improvisation, and a celebration of color.

çapraz (chah-prahz): an S-shaped weaving motif (see figure s on page 57) that acts as an amulet or talisman.

carding: a mode of arranging wool fibers by pulling them back and forth between a pair of paddle-like wooden implements that have rows of short spikes, in order to randomize them (rather than align them as in combing) and produce a fuzzy, soft yarn suitable for sweaters and socks.

Çatal Hüyük: a Neolithic site in the Konya region of Anatolia.

cecim (djheh-djeehm): a warp-faced weaving commonly woven in the eastern regions of Anatolia and beyond. A long narrow panel cut into segments is decorated with narrow vertical strips containing tiny motifs, the lengths of which are aligned and sewn together to create a wider fabric.

center-periphery structure: a mode of design derived from a sense of embodiment, in which motifs are seen as enclosed forms with an inside and an outside.

179

chunking: a psychological term denoting a way of memorizing a large body of material that would be difficult if not impossible to grasp mentally by breaking it into smaller units—i.e., memorizing a patch of starry sky by chunking it into constellations.

cicim (djidjim): an overlay-underlay brocaded flatweaving often used as a cover or for curtains and frequently woven in strips.

ciddi (djee-dee): a design mode in Turkish arts in which complexity of form and restraint in the use of color are characteristic.

combing: organizing wool fibers by drawing them through a wooden block set with large evenly spaced metal teeth in order to align them, thereby preparing them for the spinning of a yarn suitable for carpet weaving. See the photo on page 14.

çomçali (chom-cha-luh): literally, a ladle or large spoon; in weaving it refers to the motif that weavers in Khurasan refer to as *ak kaz*.

continuous weft: a weaving technique in which the weft runs continuously across a weaving from one selvedge to another. The opposite would be discontinuous weave, in which the weft goes back and forth between color areas.

core motifs: traditional motifs and designs that have survived from ancient traditions.

counter shed: the secondary shed on a loom formed by *heddles* as string loops, which are attached to a bar running above and perpendicular to the warps; the function of this bar is to facilitate the return of the weft back through the warps. See figure a on page 28.

developer solution: a chemical solution into which dyed yarns are dipped in order to alter or enhance color and fix the dye again.

discontinuous weft: a technique in which the weft runs back and forth in a designated color field, thus allowing for the introduction of multi-colored designs.

distaff: the knob-headed stick around which the *roving* is wound.

DOBAG Project: The acronym for the weaving cooperative founded in northwestern Turkey by Harald Böhmer to revive the use of natural dyes and return weavers to traditional designs. This project not only rejuvenated weaving in this region but has set off an Anatolian-wide return to traditional methods.

double interlocking-weft technique: a tapestry weaving technique whereby slits are obviated by having the wefts from laterally adjoining color fields interlock with each other at every pattern juncture. See figure k on page 33.

dove-tailing: a flatweaving technique whereby slits are obviated by having wefts from adjacent fields share the warp that forms the boundary between them. See figure l on page 33.

dowry kilim: woven by a young Anatolian girl for her dowry.

drop spindle: a handheld spinning utensil composed of a shaft and a whorl (flywheel). See figures a and b on page 16.

eccentric weft: a technique of tapestry weaving whereby the wefts are made to deviate from the horizontal of the weaving grid and allows the weaver to work in curvilinear designs.

elibelinde (el-ee-beh-lin-deh): literally "hands on hips"; anthropomorphic woven motifs consisting of a form that suggests a head and torso with arms akimbo (usually interpreted as female and, sometimes, goddess figures) that are used in Anatolia as well as other regions.

embodied experience: An anthropological term identifying a primary mode by which certain tribal groups organize their life experiences. In this case, Yörük women, whose primary function is to nurture, tend to conceptualize their world using the image of a container with a mouth as receptacle.

emek (eh-mehk): work that is done for the sole purpose of making a living, as opposed to work which is also a form of expression.

endogamous: a tribe, clan, or ethnic group that forbids intermarriage with other groups.

extra-weft motifs: motifs created by floating extra wefts on a ground fabric.

felts: wool fabrics made by a combination of pressure, heat, and motion whereby raw wool becomes a fabric without the technologies of spinning and weaving.

fermenting: a preparatory stage in which hanks of wool are soaked for a period ranging from three to ten months in a solution of wheat bran, sour dough, and mordant salts in order to make the wool more receptive to the dyes.

fleece: the pelt-like mass of intermeshed wool that is cut and then peeled off the sheep in a single piece by the shearer.

flying shuttle: a mechanization of the weaving process effected in 1732 whereby foot pedals control the shedding devices of the loom.

flywheel (also *whorl*): one of the two elements of the drop spindle, made of rock, metal, or wood, which is attached to the shaft.

funerary kilim: woven specifically for funerary use.

gece condu (geh-dje khon-doo): literally a house set up

overnight. The custom in Turkey is that if you can get your roof up overnight, before sunrise on unoccupied land, the land belongs to you. Hence the term can refer to squatters' settlements.

göbek (goh-behk): literally the bellybutton or belly; the center point of a design or medallion where the weaver begins.

Goddess theory: a now discredited theory in which it was claimed, based on very questionable sketches of supposed Neolithic frescoes, that Anatolian kilim design descended directly from ceremonies associated with the worship of a mother goddess in Neolithic times.

gökköl (goh-kuhl): a term sometimes used to describe an Anatolian weaving motif, which means "light blue arms," "celestial arms," or "arms of the sky," suggesting ancient religious significances.

göz: literally "eye"; in weaving, it is a motif which abstractly suggests an "eye" (Turkish: guhz) and is usually included to ward off the evil eye.

gul (gool): a carpet or kilim medallion usually of Turkmen origin.

hali (hah-luh): a knotted weaving; a rug or carpet

heddle: mechanical part of the loom, whereby the shed can be created by a single action facilitating the insertion of the weft into the warps.

horizontal ground loom: a primitive loom composed of two parallel logs spaced at a requisite distance and staked into the ground to provide the basic frame around which the warp threads are woven (see the photo on page 28).

horizontal symmetry: a form of mirror symmetry in which the size, shape, and relative position of parts are mirrored on the opposite side of a horizontal dividing line.

Hotamış Türkmen (hoh-tuh-muhsh turk-men): A large tribal group in the Konya region noted for its kilim weavings, The group originated in Central Asia and maintained its identity into recent times.

indigenous theory: A theory of weaving origins which would ascribe weaving innovations and design to indigenous Anatolian populations, as opposed to ascribing them to groups which migrated into the region—for instance, the Türkmen who entered Anatolia in the eleventh century.

indigofera tinctoria: a plant dye derived from the roots of indigo plants.

interlocking technique: a tapestry weave technique whereby slitting is obviated by having different colored wefts from adjoining fields interlock at the boundaries of their color areas.

iprik (ee-preek): a ewer; the metaphoric image represents life giving water; such symbolic representation is a feature of many prayer kilims (see figures ff and gg on page 66).

isçilik (ish-djee-leek): workmanship.

istar (iss-tahr): the loom.

Kabataş (kah-bah-tash): the black stone of the Kaba, around which Islamic pilgrims process during their pilgrimage at Mecca; an abstract, squarish motif.

Kavacik Project (Kha-vah-djuhk): a weaving project in the Istanbul region, which is part of the Turkish renaissance of old wool processing practices such as a return to natural dyes and handspun wool.

kışlık (kuhsh-look): a place where nomads winter.

Klōtho (Greek: the spinner): One of the mythical Three Fates, Klōtho eternally spun (on a drop spindle) man's destiny.

Koç boyunuzu (koach-boy-oo-noo-zoo): a ram's horn; a major horn-shaped motif often used to bracket hexagons and trunk-like forms as well as other motifs.

Konya (kone-yah): both a major Anatolian city and province in south central Turkey; it was once the capital of the Selçuk Empire and before that ancient Iconium.

kufic: an ancient Arabic script that has come to be purely decorative rather than literary.

Lachesis (Greek: Allotment): one of the mythical Three Fates, she decides the length of man's thread of life.

madder dye (*rubia tinctorum*): a common plant dye made from the roots of the madder plant, which are dried and ground into powder and put into the dye bath to produce red colors.

main kilim: large, long kilims (approximately 5' x 12') believed to have been woven for use as tent surrounds and to cover loaded camels during migrations and weddings. See the photos on pages 60 and 64.

matière (French: maht-ee-air): the visual and tactile qualities of a weaving.

medresseh (meh-dreh-seh): Muslim theological school.

mihrab (mee-rahb): an architectural term referring to the gate-like niche in the eastern wall of the mosque that serves to orient the prayers of the faithful to Mecca; in weaving it is the central feature of prayer designs. See figures u to ee on pages 64–65.

mnemonic: assisting or intending to assist memory; mnemonic motifs are inserted by weavers to trigger memories.

mordant: chemical or mineral substances used in the dye bath to help fix the dyes to the yarns.

muska (mooh-skah): an amulet or charm, intended to ward off the evil eye and bring good luck; particular motifs serve this purpose. See figure p on page 57.

namaz (nah-maz) Muslim ritual prayer.

nazarlık (nah-zah-look): an amulet or charm intended to ward off the evil eye and bring good luck; particular designs and artefacts such as beads, pieces of calico, and feathers serve this purpose (see figure q on page 57).

oak gall: a swelling of plant tissue caused by insect parasites that forms large lumps on oak trunks and limbs; this is used in dyeing to produce certain hues as well as for tannin in leather curing.

orthogonal: in flatweaving, a method of weaving that accepts the ninety degree orientation of warp and weft, (as opposed to using remedial techniques such as eccentric wefting) which necessitates designs that are rectilinear and usually geometric and abstract.

Ovis orientalis: the primitive, goat-like animal from which domesticated, wool-bearing sheep evolved.

parmaklı (pahr-mahk-luh): motifs with long finger-like extensions or crenellations.

Pazyryk: a region in the Altai of southern Siberia where a large cache of textiles dating from the late fifth and/or early fourth century B.C. were found preserved in ice. These artefacts cast important light on the evolution and origins of certain textiles.

ply: one of the strands in a yarn.

Qazak (also Kazak): a Central Asian Turkic people found in Kazakistan and neighboring regions; also a town in Azerbaijan famous for a particular rug design called a Kazak.

Qirgiz (also Kirghiz): a Central Asian Turkic people found in Kirghistan and neighboring regions.

ram's horn motif: see *koç boyunuzu*.

reciprocal design: instead of the customary figure/ground relationship , there are two fields of equal or fluctuating weight so that what is dominant and what is recessive is never resolved.

reed screen: a yurt or tent fixture that is run around the outside of the structure when the wool covering is raised for ventilation and as partitions between different areas. It is made of plant canes that have been twined together and elaborately decorated with designs formed by colored wool wrappings.

Reseda luteola: A yellow dye found in a great variety of plants; weld is one of the best examples.

roving: the soft bundle of wool fibers that have been aligned by combing in preparation for spinning (see photo on page 15).

sade (sah-deh): simple, pure, plain weaving with little or no ornamentation; with the focus is primarily on form and materials.

saf (sahf): the row of mihrabs found on multiple prayer pieces.

salat (sah-lat): the ritual prayer of Muslims.

sanat (also zanaat; sah-naht): art, skill, craft.

seccade (seh-djah-deh): a prayer-sized rug or kilim.

Selçuk (sehl-djoohk): the founders of the first Turkish empire in Anatolia (centered in Konya) during a period coinciding with the European Middle Ages.

slit-weave tapestry technique: a weaving technique characteristic of the Anatolian kilim in which the wefts of adjoining color fields, when meeting on the vertical, turn back on their own warps without sharing warps or interlocking with each other. This creates a slit in the fabric. See figure e on page 32.

S-spin: a yarn produced by spinning the wool in a counter-clockwise direction. This produces a yarn in which the trend of the spiral conforms when held in a vertical position to the slant of the central portion of the letter S. See figure c on page 16. This is a characteristic of yarns spun outside of Anatolia.

structural principle: the overall design of a kilim as opposed to its individual motifs. See figures z to gg on page 81.

sumuk (soo-muhk): a term in the Caucasus for a carpet that translates as "for the bones," hence this is a ritual carpet woven as a funerary textile.

supplementary weft-weave: a flatweaving in which the design is effected by brocading wefts onto the surface of the ground weave.

sürme (suhr-meh): the dark kohl outlining the eye; also refers to the outline of a motif.

symbolic potential: a term coined by E. H. Gombrich to designate images that possess an evocative power and attract meaning.

symmetrical knot (also Turkish or Ghiordes knot): this pile-weaving technique is formed by yarn ends wrapped in opposite directions around two warps, the yarn ends emerge together from between those warps. This is the primary knotting technique in Anatolia. See figure p on page 36.

teberrû (the-beh-roo): a gift, a votive offering.

Teke Province (Teh-keh): literally, goat province; it designates a region in southwestern Anatolia bounded by the Aegean and Mediterranean on two sides and high mountain chains on the north. In Greek, Roman, and Byzantine times it was known as Lycia.

Tioue Kioue (Chinese: tee-oo-kee-oo?): Thought to be the first historical reference to Turkic peoples, found in the Chinese Annals of A.D. 545. The term "Turk" may descend from this.

top (tope): ball or cannon; in weaving it refers to a motif or a constellation of motifs. See figure a on page 96.

transhumance: the seasonal movement of livestock between mountain and lowland pastures, which also involves the movement of the tribe.

Türkmen theory: A theory of weaving origins that credits the technologies and design traditions of what has descended to us as Middle Eastern weavings to the Türk-men tribes, which began to migrate into the region in the eleventh century.

vertical loom: a loom in which the frame is set upright, an arrangement better suited to indoor weaving.

warp: a yarn the weaver extends lengthwise on the loom; it can refer to a single yarn or the entire set of yarns. As the weaving proceeds, the warp becomes a major part of the superstructure of the weaving.

to warp: the process of tying the warp yarns to or looping them around the end beams of the loom. See photo on page 26.

warp-faced fabric: the warp yarns are so tightly jammed together that the wefts are hidden when they are inserted; thus, the warps carry the design. The warp-faced technique is used for fabrics that need to be especially strong.

warp-weighted loom: an upright loom in which the yarns hang down from a cross bar and are held taut by attached weights. See figure a on page 70.

weft: one pass of a yarn or combination of yarns through a shed; it can also refer to the aggregate of all the wefts that form the surface of a weft-faced weave. In kilims the weft is not just a structural element but also bears the design.

weft-faced fabric: when the weft yarns are so tightly packed that the warps are hidden.

wether: a male sheep castrated before maturity.

whorl: the weight attached to the shaft of a spindle.

woad (*isatis tinctoria*): a European herb related to the mustard family formerly grown for the blue dyestuff yielded by its leaves.

wool comb: used for processing wools in preparation for spinning. It consists of a wooden block or triangle with rows of evenly spaced spikes. See the photo on page 14.

yedirme (yeh-deer-meh): to feed, to cause to eat; in weaving it designates the area that remains to be woven.

yerli (yehr-lee): designates populations in Anatolia that identify themselves as indigenous, that is, predating the arrival of the Turkmen.

Yörük (or yürük) (yuh-rook or yoo-rook): someone who walks; the term is used both as a generic term for nomads, but it is also used to distinguish specific tribes and clans from Türkmen tribal groups.

zevk (zehvk): taste, style, pattern of committed personal choice.

Z-spun yarn: produced by spinning in a clockwise direction. The trend in the spiral or twisted element conforms when held in a vertical position to the slant of the central portion of the letter Z. Anatolian wools are generally Z-spun.

Acar (Balpınar), Belkis. *Kilim ve Düz Dokuma Yaygilar*. Istanbul: Akbank bir Kultur Hizmeti, 1975.

———. "The Rugs of the Yüncü Nomads." *Hali*, *11*(2), 1979.

———. "Yüncü Nomad Weaving in the Balıkesir Region of Western Turkey." In *Yörük, The Nomadic Weaving of the Middle East*, Anthony N. Landreau, Ed. Pittsburgh, 1978.

Albers, Anni. *On Weaving*. Middletown, CT: Wesleyan University Press, 1965.

Alleva, Kubra. "The Syncretic Nature of the Ornamental System of Azerbaijan." *Oriental Carpet and Textile Studies*, *3*(2), N. D.

Andrews, Peter. *Ethnic Groups in the Republic of Turkey*. Wiesbaden, Germany: Author, 1989.

Andrews, Peter Alford. "From Khurasan to Anatolia." *Oriental Carpet and Textile Studies*, *3*(2), N. D.

———. "Tent Screens to Kilims." *Oriental Carpet and Textile Studies*, *3*(2), N. D.

Balpınar, Belkis. "A Discussion on Central Asian Türkmen Influence on Anatolian Kilims." *Oriental Carpet and Textile Studies*, *3*(2), N. D.

Balpınar, Belkis , and Udo Hirsch. *Flatweaves of the Vakıflar Museum, Istanbul*. Wesel, Germany: Uta Hülsey, 1982.

———. *Anatolian Kilims*. Milan, Italy: Eskenazi, 1984.

———. "Classical Kilims." *Hali*, *6*(1), 1983.

———. "Establishing the Cultural Context of a Group of Anatolian Cicim Prayer Rugs." *Hali*, *4*(3), 1982.

Barber, E. J. W. *Prehistoric Textiles: The Development of Cloth in the Neolithic and Bronze Ages*. Princeton, NJ: Princeton University Press, 1991.

———. *Women's Work: The First 20,000 Years*. New York: Norton, 1994.

Batki, John. *Traditional Anatolian Kilims*. Bronxville, NY: Sarah Lawrence College Gallery, N. D.

Bennett, Ian. "The Mistress of All Life." *Hali*, #50, April 1990.

Bieber, Manfred. "The Kavacık Project: Contribution to the Conservation and Advancement of the Turkish Carpet Tradition in the Istanbul Region." *Oriental Carpet and Textile Studies*, *3*(2), N. D.

Bierman, Irene A. "Medieval Flatweaves in the Urban Middle East." In *Flatwoven Textiles*, Cathryn M. Cootner, Ed. Washington, DC: Textile Museum, 1981.

Black, David and Clive Loveless. *The Undiscovered Kilim*. London: Author, 1977.

Böhmer, Harald. "Migration of Central Asian Carpet and Flatweave Designs to Anatolia." In *Oriental Carpet & Textile Studies*, *5*, Pt. I, Murray L. Eiland Jr. & Robert Pinner, Eds. Danville, CA: International Conference on Oriental Carpets, 1997.

———. "Carpets from the Yuntdäg Region in Western Anatolia." *Oriental Carpet and Textile Studies*, *3*(2), N. D.

———. "The Revival of Natural Dyeing in Two Traditional Weaving Areas of Anatolia." *Oriental Rug Review*, *3*(9), December 1983.

Brüggemann, Werner. "Carpets and Kilims: A Contribution to the Problem of the Origins and Designs in Kilims." *Oriental Carpet and Textile Studies*, *3*(2), N. D.

Brüggemann, Werner and Harald Böhmer. *Rugs of the Peasants and Nomads of Anatolia*. Munich: Kunst und Antiquitäten, 1983.

Camman, Schyler V. R. "Symbolic Meanings In Oriental Rug Patterns, Part I." *Textile Museum Journal*, *3*(3), 1972.

Cassin, Jack. *Image, Idol, Symbols of Ancient Anatolian Kelims*. 2 Vols. Italy: Author, 1989.

Cootner, Cathryn M. *Anatolian Kilims. The Caroline and H McCoy Jones Collection*. London: Hali Publishing, 1990.

Cootner, Cathryn M., Ed. *Flatwoven Textiles. The Arthur D. Jenkins Collection, vol. 1*. Washington, DC: Textile Museum, 1981.

Daugherty, Patricia. "Through the Eyes of the Weavers: Aesthetics and Culture of Tribal Yuruk Women of Turkey." *Oriental Carpet & Textile Studies*, *15*, Pt. I, Murray L. Eiland Jr. & Robert Pinner, Eds. Danville, CA: International Conference on Oriental Carpets, 1997.

Daugherty, Patricia. "Anatolian Kilims Past and Present." *Oriental Rug Review*, *10*(6), August/September 1990.

Daumas, Henri. "A Fundamental Symbol in the Pattern of Many Anatolian Kilims." *Oriental Carpet and Textile Studies*, *3*(2), N. D.

Davies, Peter. *The Tribal Eye: Antique Kilims of Anatolia*. New York: Rizzoli, 1993.

Denny, Walter B. "Links Between Anatolian Kilim Designs and Older Traditions." *Hali*, *2*, 1979.

———. "Saff and Sejjadeh: Origins and Meaning of the Prayer Rug." *Oriental Carpet and Textile Studies*, *3*(2), N. D.

———. "Anatolian Rugs: An Essay on Method." *Textile Museum Journal*, *3*(4), 1973.

Dickie, James. "The Iconography of the Prayer Rug." *Oriental Art*, *18*(1), 1972.

Dulkadır, Hilme. "The Sarakeçeli Tribe and Their Flatweaves." *Oriental Carpet and Textile Studies*, *3*(2), N. D.

Dupaigne, Bernard. "Le Grand Art Décoratif des Turkmenes." *La Revue du Musée de l'Homme*, pp. 3–79.

Durul, Yusuf. *Yörük Kilimleri: Niğde Yöresi*. Istanbul, Turkey: Apa Offset Printers, 1977.

Eiland, Murray. Jr. "The Goddess From Anatolia." *Oriental Rug Review*, *10*(6), August/September 1990.

Emery, Irene. *The Primary Structure of Fabrics*. Washington, DC: Textile Museum, 1980.

Erbek, Guran. *Kilim Catalogue No. 1*. Istanbul, Turkey: Selçuk A.S., 1990.

Faegre, Torvald. *Tents: Architecture of the Nomads*. Garden City, NY: Anchor Press/Doubleday, 1979.

Glassie, Henry. *Turkish Traditional Art Today*. Bloomington & Indianapolis: Indiana University Press & Ministry of Culture of the Turkish Republic, 1993.

Gombrich, E. H. *The Sense of Order: A Study in the Psychology of Decorative Art*. Ithaca, NY: Cornell University Press, 1984.

Hull, Alastair and Jose Luczyc-Wyhowska. *Kilim, the Complete Guide*. London: Thames & Hudson, Ltd., 1993.

Jenkins, G. Geraint. *From Fleece to Fabric: The Technological History of the Welsh Woolen Industry*. Wales: Gomer Press, 1987.

Justin, Valerie Sharaf. *Flatwoven Rugs of the World: Kilims, Soumak, and Brocading*. New York: Van Nostrand Reinhold Company, 1980.

Koll, H., Ed. *Kultkelim: Ausgewählte Anatolische Flachgewebe*. Aachen, Germany: Author, 1999.

Kreissl, Rainer. *Art as Tradition: Anatolia*. Munich: Hirmer Verlag, 1995.

Landreau, Anita. "Weaving in Susanoğlu." In *Flowers of the Yayla: Yörük Weaving of the Toros Mountains*, Anthony N. Landreau and Ralph S. Yohe, Eds. Washington, DC: Textile Museum, 1969.

Landreau, Anthony N. and W. R. Pickering. *From the Bosphorus to Samarkand: Flatwoven Rugs*. Washington, DC: Textile Museum, 1969.

Landreau, Anthony N. and W. R.
Pickering, Eds. *Yörük. The
Nomadic Weaving Tradition of
the Middle East*. Pittsburgh,
PA: Chas. M. Henry, 1978.
Landreau, Anthony N., W. R.
Pickering, and Ralph S. Yohe.
"The Yörük Weavers of the
Toros Mountains" *Hali*, 3(3),
1981.
————. "Kurdish Kilim Weav-
ing in the Van Hakkari Dis-
trict of Eastern Turkey." *Tex-
tile Journal*, 3(4), 1973.
Landreau, Anthony N., W. R.
Pickering, Ralph S. Yohe,
Anita Landreau, and Daniel
Bates. *Flowers of the Yayla:
Yörük Weaving of the Toros
Mountains*. Washington, DC:
Textile Museum, 1983.
Mallett, Marla. *Woven Structures: A
Guide to Oriental Rug & Textile
Analyses*. Atlanta, GA: Author,
1998.
————. "A Weaver's View of the
Çatal Hüyük Controversy."
Oriental Rug Review, 10(6),
1990.
Mellaart, James, Udo Hirsch,
and Belkis Balpinar. *The God-
dess From Anatolia, 4 vols*.
Milan, Italy: Eskenazi, 1989.

Montgomery, Cornelia. "The
Significance of Indigo Blue in
Near Eastern Carpets and
Textiles." *Oriental Carpet and
Textile Studies*, 3(2), N. D.
Murshak, Paul. "Synthetic Dyes:
A History, Part III." *Oriental
Rug Review*, 4(5), July 1984.
Neuman, Helmet. "Between Sci-
ence & Passion." *Hali*, #92,
pp. 76–85, May 1997.
Opie, James. "The Animal Head
Design in Lori/Bakhtiari
Weavings." *Hali*, 5(4), 1983.
————. "Fragments of an
Ancient Puzzle, Parts I and
II." *Hali*, issues 53 and 54,
1990.
————. "Did Anatolian Kilims
Descend from Iranian Tribal
Tradition?" *Oriental Rug
Review*, 10(5), June/July
1990.
————. *Tribal Rugs: Nomadic and
Village Weavings from the Near
East and Central Asia*. Port-
land, OR: Tolstoy Press,
1992.
Petsopoulos, Yanni. *Kilims: Flat-
woven Tapestry Rugs*. New
York: Rizzoli, 1979.
————. *Kilims: Masterpieces from
Turkey*. New York: Rizzoli,
1991.

Powell, Josephine. "A Reply to
Dr. Andrews' Counter-Argu-
ment." *Oriental Carpet and
Textile Studies*, 3(2), N. D.
————. "An Argument for the
Origins of Anatolian Design
Kilims." *Oriental Carpet and
Textile Studies*, 3(2), N. D.
Rageth, Jürg, Ed. *Anatolian Kil-
ims & Radio-Carbon Dating: A
New Approach*. Basel, Switzer-
land: Second Symposium on
Anatolian Kilims, 1997.
————. *Kilim: Primitive Symbols
of Mythology, 2nd ed*. Rome:
Edizioni d'Arte, 1986.
Reinhard, Ursula. "Uber Kelim
Typen den Afcharen in Zen-
tral-Anatolian." *Hali*, 3(2),
1980.
————. "Turkic Nomad Weav-
ings in the Doshmealtı
(Antalya) Area of Southern
Turkey." In *Yörük*, A. N. Lan-
dreau, Ed. Pittsburgh, PA:
Chas. M. Henry, 1978.
Thompson, Jon. *Oriental Carpets
from the Tents, Cottages, and
Workshops of Asia*. New York:
E. P. Dutton, 1988.
Türck, Ulrich. *Kilims from Anato-
lia: An Exhibition*. West Falen,
Germany: Essen, 1995.

Voigt, Mary. "The Goddess from
Anatolia: An Archaeological
Perspective." *Oriental Rug
Review*, 11(2), December/
January 1991.
Washburn, Dorothy K., and
Donald W. Crowe. *Symmetries
of Culture: Theory and Practice
of Plane Pattern Analysis*. Seat-
tle: University of Washington
Press, 1988.
Wertime, John T. "A Guide to
Flatwoven Structure." In
*Flatwoven Textiles: The Arthur D.
Jenkins Collection, vol. I*. Wash-
ington, DC: Textile
Museum, 1981.

Photography & Illustration Credits

Note: Photos without captions in the text are described below.

Line drawings by John Batki, Syracuse, N.Y.

Kilim photography (Plates, frontispiece photos, and detail photos) by Christopher Burke, Quesada/Burke Studios (identified as QBS below)

Ethnographic photographs from the Josephine Powell Archives, Istanbul, Turkey (identified as JPA); the Ethnographic Museum, Budapest, Hungary (identified as EMB); and Peter Davies (identified as PD)

THE PHOTOS:

Frontispiece: JPA: #2386-35A: Anatolian woman spinning with a drop spindle, village of Kuzyaka, Erzincan Province, 1980.

p. 8: left JPA#2203A; right: JPA#2364-5

p. 9: JPA#2250-35

p. 10. top: JPA#230-3; bottom: JPA#2001-10

p. 12. JPA#2095-24A, 2095-20A, 20954-16A: sheep-shearing in the village of Yukarı Çavus, Çanakkale Province, 1977. JPA#2236-11A: A Saçıkara nomad sheep-shearing en route to winter pasturage near Sarız, Kayseri Province.

p. 13. JPA#2235-11

p. 14. JPA#255529

p. 15. JPA#2247-9

p. 16. courtesy of Peter Hoffmeister, Dörfles-Esbach, Germany.

p. 17. JPA#2260-16A

p. 18. QBS: details of plates 43 & 44

p. 22. top: JPA#2231(412-8); bottom: JPA#2556-7

p. 23: QBS: details of plates 14, 15, & 22.

p. 26. JPA#2003-21: adjusting the tensions on a large rug loom, village of Taşkale, Karaman Province.

p. 28. JPA#2230-9

p. 29. left: JPA#2277A; right: JPA#22776-37

p. 30. JPA#2250-35: inserting the weft-threads, Takmak village, Uşak Province, 1979.

p. 31: QBS: detail of plate 13

p. 32: JPA#2277-A: weaving with discontinuous wefts, Takmak village, Uşak Province, 1979.

p. 34: JPA#2217-19A

p. 38: QBS: detail of plate 11

p. 46: JPA#2001-16: two women beginning to weave a rag rug, Konya Province, 1976.

p. 48: JPA#2370-6

p. 52: QBS: details of plates 46, 28, 8, 25, 19, 36, 33, & 19

p. 60: EMB#80497

p. 61: JPA#2235(424-15)

p. 62: top: JPA#2232-24; bottom: JPA#2387-35

p. 64: EMB#81483

p. 65: JPA#2258-13A

p. 84: QBS: Kirghiz felt, Kirghizstan, 19th century

p. 88: PD.

p. 93: QBS.

p. 94: QBS: Anatolian kilim (Cappadocia), detail, 18th century

p. 97: cecim B by Sebire Aktaş, courtesy of Henry Glassie.

p. 101: PD.

p. 101: PD.

Plates 1–73: QBS

Index

Acknowledgments

In the summer of 1961, when I nervously haggled for my first kilim in the old rug bazaar of Kayseri, Turkey, I never dreamed that it would lead to the strange act of writing a book on this unknown and unappreciated artefact. But thus are we all led into strange paths by seemingly insignificant events. Even stranger to me is that in the barely four decades since, a sufficient body of research on kilims has been amassed, making the writing of such a book possible. Indeed I can still recall traveling in 1976 to the Textile Museum in Washington, D.C. intending to spend two or three days researching kilims, and discovering to my astonishment that after working in the library for forty-five minutes I had exhausted the topic.

Thanks to the patient efforts of hundreds of ethnographers, anthropologists, rug scholars, and connoisseurs a considerable body of research now exists. Obviously I am indebted to everyone in the field who worked to establish this new field of inquiry.

Researching and writing a book is a rather solitary activity, but there comes a time when the endeavor suddenly opens up into a conversation with others who have specialized expertise. My text has benefited immeasurably from the expertise and sympathy of experts from a number of disciplines who have read the manuscript and volunteered their comments and corrections, often exploring topics in conversations with me. In the kilim/carpet studies world this includes Dr. Murray Eiland, Jr., Professor Anthony Landreau, Marla Mallett, W. Russell Pickering, Josephine Powell, and the late Ralph Yohe. I am particularly grateful to Marla Mallett for saving me from errors in discussing the technicalities of the weaving process. In the field of anthropology, a field I am not expert in, I have gained immeasurably from the insights and suggestions of Mark Scherzer. And, in the fields of color psychology and psychology, I have received valuable advice from professors Israel Abramov and Louise Hainline. I am also deeply grateful to Whitney Ellsworth for patiently steering me through the publishing process. I thank John Batki for his excellent line drawings and Quesada-Burke Photography for their fine transparencies. And I appreciate very much the labors of editor Nancy Green and her assistant Christine Habermaas in working through the revision and expansion of the first edition.

And, finally, I would like to acknowledge those who generously allowed their kilims to be included in this book and subsidized the costs of photography. The lenders include:

The Anadolu Collection, New York City: plates 2, 4, 10, 14, 18, 19, 20, 25, 27, 28, 31, 34, 36, 40, 42, 45, 46, 47, 49, 50, 55, 56, 58, 60, 65, 66, 69, 70, 71, 72, 73.

Anonymous Lender, London, U. K.: plates 35, 48, 67, 68.

Anonymous Lender, New York City: plate 30.

Anonymous Lender, Middlesex, New York: plate 59.

Anne Ellsworth, New York City: plate 26.

Alex & Vicki Levi, New York City: plate 57.

Dr. Malkah Notman, Brookline, MA: plate 37.

Gerry Podany, Los Angeles, CA: plates 62 and 67.

Quesada/Burke, New York: plate 39.

Mark Scherzer, New York City: plate 17.

SK Collection, Greenwich, CT: plates 1, 3, 6, 8, 9, 11, 15, 16, 21, 24, 29, 32, 38, 51, 53, 61, 64.

Marilyn & Marshall Wolf Collection: plates 11, 13, 22, 23, 41, 43, frontispiece on pages 84 and 94.

Victor Teicher, Westport, CT: plate 5.

Turkana Collection, New York City: plates 7, 33, 44, 52, 54, 63.